N408701711172
11/88

# MY DAYS WITH GANDHI

# MY DAYS WITH GANDHI

Nirmal Kumar Bose

Sangam Books

Sangam Books Ltd.,
57, London Fruit Exchange, Brushfield Street,
London E1 6EP.

By arrangement with
Orient Longman Limited,
5-9-41/1 Bashir Bagh, Hyderabad-500029, India.

© 1974 Orient Longman Limited

*Published by*
Sangam Books Ltd. 1987

ISBN 0 86131 801 3

*Printed in India by*
Taj Press
3024, Gali Ahiran
B.G. Road Delhi 110 006.

# PREFACE

MANY years ago, I planned to write four books on Gandhi. The first was to be a book of collections from his English writings which would serve as an epitome of his thoughts on various subjects; the second was to give an outline of his economic and political ideas, while tracing their evolution; the third, on his personality and on the actual manner of his execution of ideas into practice, and the fourth, a critical account of the various satyagraha movements which have occurred, from time to time, on the Indian soil.

The first two books have already been published, while the third is now being placed before the public. I do not know if the fourth project will ever materialize, although such a study, undertaken in the manner in which the General Staff of an Army examines critically the effect of new arms or of new tactics on the course of campaigns, seems to me to be most essential for an understanding of the potentialities of satyagraha in which unarmed, common people try to establish their will through non-violence instead of violence. It is necessary to examine how the new technique works in relation to conflicts centering round social, economic or political disabilities; and how also it works under the leadership of a genius like Gandhi or independent of it. Such an undertaking would necessitate extensive travels across the whole of India, and a freedom from haste and from care which can hardly be afforded under the present limitations of my duties in the University.

In any case, even if the contemplated series closes down with the present volume, I do hope, the three books will collectively serve to present a more or less integrated picture of Gandhi as a man and of his ideas.

Many may not perhaps agree with the analysis presented here or on the emphasis laid upon different aspects of Gandhi's life or thoughts, but my humble submission is that I have spared no pains in order to make the study as objective as possible.

## PREFACE

The publication of this book has a curious history; and it is with a great deal of hesitation that I have finally decided to relate the story in brief. My manuscript was finished in 1950, two years after Gandhiji's assassination. Then it was submitted to the Navajivan Publishing House for publication. The Managing Trustee referred the book for criticism to the late Shri Kishorilal Mashruwala. In course of a lengthy review, the latter said, 'The publication of this speculative psycho-analysis of Bapu and some of his associates can be justified if it will (provided based on accepted facts) help the cause of the nation or humanity in any way.... Then the analysis and its publication must contribute something positive to advance his work and influence, or to correct the persons concerned. Otherwise it is an idle speculation which does not lead anybody anywhere. Bapu cannot be corrected of his errors if any, as he is no longer alive. His associates cannot benefit by the publication. They might resent it. No two men's cases being alike, the world too cannot profit by N. Babu's dissection of Bapu. Of course, it might encourage similar speculative writers to discuss these matters for centuries to come, and fiction writers to produce caricatures of Bapu and his associates.'

The Managing Trustee in forwarding the above criticism added, 'I am of opinion that you be better advised to leave out of the book Bapu's experiments in sex or Brahmacharya and reconstitute the book to say about Bapu's great work in Noakhali.'

When the Navajivan Publishing House could not thus publish the book in its existing from, I applied for permission to print it on my own account; as I held that an account of Gandhiji's personality could not be left out of the story of the most important phase of his political career. The reply came, 'Your letter of 6th June 1951 asking for permission from the Navajivan to include some of their copyright material in your projected book. The question would have been a simple one, but for the views we hold regarding the use of the material. Holding these views as we do, I find it impossible to allow the publication of that material.'

At about the same time, personal requests were received by me from very high quarters in the country to desist from any public treatment of such a controversial matter, particularly when, as one letter said, 'there are so many people who might be only too eager to exploit for their base personal ends what they care so little to understand.'

I have waited for nearly three years, during which the manuscript was submitted to numerous friends and publishers for their considered opinion. Some expressed the fear that the book may give rise to misunderstanding; while others held that it gave a more or less understandable explanation about some of the views and actions of Gandhiji.

I have thought long and reverently over the whole question, and have ultimately come to the conclusion that the possibility of misunderstanding alone should not deter one from expressing a view which one believes to be true or near-truth. It is natural that the explanation that I have tried to present does not cover all aspects of Gandhiji's great character. By drawing particular attention to one aspect, it may even have done injustice to the wholeness of that character. But, I believe, a view of the Himalayas from one particular point of view does not lose merit just because it does not show the whole mountain from all possible angles at the same point of time. Perhaps that is never possible. And that has been the reason why I have ventured to print the book on my own responsibility in spite of grave risks of one kind or another. My only strength has been the appreciation and encouragement of friends who have seen nothing wrong in the book and have done their best in helping me to communicate this particular study of Gandhiji to the reading public. To them, my gratefulness goes forth in an abundant measure.

37A Bosepara Lane
Calcutta-3
22nd January 1953                    Nirmal Kumar Bose

## CONTENTS

|       | Preface by the Author | iii |
|-------|----------------------|-----|
|       | Introduction | 1 |
| I.    | THE FIRST INTERVIEW | 8 |
| II.   | AT DELANG IN ORISSA | 13 |
| III.  | THE INTERVIEW AT SODPUR IN 1945 | 17 |
| IV.   | CONGRESS WORKERS' MEETING IN SODPUR, JANUARY 1946 | 23 |
| V.    | GANDHIJI'S ARRIVAL IN SODPUR IN OCTOBER 1946 | 28 |
| VI.   | HAPPENINGS IN BIHAR | 35 |
| VII.  | ON THE WAY TO NOAKHALI | 39 |
| VIII. | KAZIRKHIL | 43 |
| IX.   | CIRCUMSPECTION AND A CALL FOR COURAGE | 49 |
| X.    | THE DAILY ROUND | 69 |
| XI.   | DAYS FULL OF DARKNESS | 80 |
| XII.  | THE DARKNESS DEEPENS | 95 |
| XIII. | A FRIEND'S PARTING | 114 |
| XIV.  | THE PILGRIMAGE | 120 |
| XV.   | INTERNAL STRAIN | 133 |
| XVI.  | THE FIRST FORTNIGHT IN BIHAR | 139 |
| XVII. | TILL WE MEET AGAIN | 147 |
| XVIII.| AN EXCURSION IN PSYCHOLOGY | 163 |
| XIX.  | DARK CLOUDS OVER BENGAL | 179 |
| XX.   | DARKER CLOUDS OVER INDIA | 185 |
| XXI.  | ON A VISIT TO BENGAL'S CAPITAL | 192 |
| XXII. | CRISIS IN NON-VIOLENCE | 207 |
| XXIII.| BENGAL CALLING AGAIN | 220 |
| XXIV. | BUILDING UP FREE INDIA | 228 |
| XXV.  | THE FAST | 235 |
| XXVI. | MARTYRDOM | 249 |
| Appendix A. | Condition of Noakhali in May 1947 | 254 |
| Appendix B. | "Congress Position" by M. K. Gandhi | 264 |
| Appendix C. | "Last Will and Testament" of Mahatma Gandhi | 266 |
| Index |  | 269 |

INTRODUCTION

THE book deals with the last phase of Mahatma Gandhi's life which began with his journey from Delhi to Bengal in October 1946 and ended with his martyrdom in January 1948. In many respects, this period stands out as the most critical, and certainly the most dramatic, phase of Gandhi's great and eventful life.

It was during this period that two climaxes were reached simultaneously in his life; one in the personal. spiritual sphere, and the other in the sphere of his public and political relations. Although the two might seem to be unrelated, there was an underlying bond between the two. Indeed, Gandhi himself held that neither man's life nor his mind was capable of division into water-tight compartments; all parts acted and reacted upon one another.

Gandhi realized even while he was quite young that, in order to become a fitter instrument of human service, the sensual aspects of his being had to be brought under full restraint. There happened to be some accidents of personal history which also accentuated his desire for self-repression; but the demands of the ideal which he served naturally called for the same kind of sacrifice, so that service itself might be shorn of the taint of self.

In his endeavour to subordinate the lower elements of human nature, in order to follow more fully the discipline known as *brahmacharya*, Gandhi adopted a curious mental attitude which, though rare, is one of the established modes of the subordination of sex among spiritual aspirants in India. It was by *becoming* a woman that he tried to circumvent one of the most powerful and disturbing elements which belong to our biological existence. In his own case, the identification did not, however, reach the same measure of intensity which was in evidence in the case of the saint Shree Ramakrishna; but the feminine attitude developed as an important trait in his character ever since he began his practice of *brahmacharya*. And, as the identification was never complete, the desire to examine how far it had advanced at any point of time, remained a permanent necessity with him.

Gandhi felt more at home in dealing with the special problems which belong to womankind. He apotheosized womanhood; so much so that he finally came to the conclusion that progress in civilization consisted in the introduction into it of a larger measure of the love and self-sacrifice which woman, the mother of man, best represented in her own person. Women on their part drew readily near him, for they instinctively recognized in him one of their own kind. Their intimate association helped to strengthen those elements of non-violence of which he held them to be natural representatives; while such occasions were also utilized by him for examining how far his own identification had become complete.

This spiritual necessity of association with women and of constant self-examination by means of a technique reminiscent of the Tantras was, however, not appreciated by some of Gandhi's closest associates; and one of the painful climaxes which belong to the period under review lay in the fact that he was deprived of the inner companionship of some who had been a help and support to him in the past. This was so in spite of the fact that the non-co-operation of the latter was of a limited character. Yet, the separation seemed to have exercised a profound influence upon the sensitive soul of Gandhi. In a communication sent to some members of the Navajivan Trust, an organization specifically constructed for the propagation of his own ideas, he went so far as to say that, if the Trust could 'conscientiously take his help in the conduct of the Navajivan papers, then he would resume the task of editing them' from Noakhali. Otherwise, he would refrain, but would not misunderstand those who saw differently from him. It was an extraordinary offer of self-effacement, coming as it did from a man who held a unique position of leadership in the country.

About two months after this event, there developed another tragedy in the larger sphere of Gandhi's relations with the leaders of the Indian National Congress, in which he responded in approximately the same manner as he had done in the case described above. Gandhi was opposed to the division of India into predominantly Hindu and Muslim territories on the ground that this was going to be no solution of the communal problem. In his own way, he plodded on trying to create, in his little corner of work in Noakhali and Bihar, a condition of social justice and religious toleration to form the basis of political unity. Without this, he held, the non-violence of the Hindus was not likely to have any appeal to the fanatically inflamed and ignorant mass of Muslim peasants. And without such unity, the chances of the final liberation of India through a last act of satyagraha would suffer from uncertainty of success. But the communal riots broke out in such quick succession in different portions of India and with such mounting debasement of the popular character, that they threatened to undo all the work of decades past. The need of a quick remedy was so urgently felt by the leaders of the Indian National Congress that they lost both the faith and the strength to work out Gandhi's long-term programme. They confessed with great humility that they did not see how non-violence was going to lead the country out of the present impasse. Therefore, when the plan of agreed partition, coupled with the promise of ready transference of power, was offered to India by Lord Mountbatten, they saw in it an opportunity of escaping from the present intolerable position. The unending violence of mob rule could, at least, be subordinated by the organized violence of the State, in spite of the fact that the country was going to be divided into two. In this, the national leaders were both sincere and wise from their own point of view.*

But they were evidently mistaken in imagining that the war of independence had come to an end, for they failed to recognize in the riots and the proposal of division itself the

---

* On the 15th of January 1948, Gandhi himself justified Vallabhai Patel by saying, 'When power descended on him, he saw that he could no longer successfully apply the method of non-violence which he used to wield with signal success. I have made the discovery that what I and the people with me termed non-violence was not the genuine article but a weak copy known as passive resistance. Naturally, passive resistance can avail nothing to a ruler.'

last phase of the rear-guard action of British Power in retreat. Moreover, the act of choosing between two violences definitely implied that the path of organized non-violence was now forsaken, and there was nothing left to distinguish India from other nations of the world, who were themselves almost overwhelmed by the problem of national defence through modern armaments.

It is not unnatural, therefore, that Gandhi was overcome by an intense feeling of loneliness. When the Working Committee of the Indian National Congress decided, apparently against his advice, to accept the British offer, he suppressed himself so completely that, at the momentous session of the All-India Congress Committee called to ratify that Resolution, he advised the House not to divide itself, but stand by the Working Committee in its present decision; while he gave credit to the existing leadership for 'all the achievements of the Congress hitherto,' although in point of fact many of them happened to be no more than Gandhi's own creation. Perhaps his feeling was that the Congress, in its present form, could no longer serve as an instrument of organized non-violence which dared to bring about lasting peace in the world; and therefore he wanted to leave the organization undivided and strong so that it could, at least, be of some service to those who were launching upon a new career of administration in India.

An eventuality like this had arisen previously in 1940, when the Indian National Congress had made a provisional offer of helping Great Britain in the prosecution of the war. On that occasion, Gandhi had asked the Congress to declare unequivocally that it proposed to eschew the use of armaments in order to protect its just rights, and thus lay the foundation of lasting peace in the whole world. President Abul Kalam Azad had said on the occasion, 'We had not the courage to declare that we shall organize a State in this country without an armed force. If we did it would be wrong on our part. Mahatma Gandhi has to give the message of non-violence to the world and, therefore, it is his duty to propagate it; but we have to consider our position as the representatives of the Indian Nation meeting in the Indian National Congress. The Indian National Congress is a political organization pleaded to win the political independence of the country. It is not an institution for organizing world peace.' On another occasion early in 1942, when the same question cropped up again, Gandhi said, 'Non-violence has brought us nearer to Swaraj as never before. We dare not exchange it even for Swaraj, for Swaraj thus got will be no true Swaraj. The question is *not* what we will do after Swaraj. It is whether under given conditions we can give up non-violence to win Swaraj. Again, do you expect to win real Independence by abandoning non-violence? Independence for me means the Independence of the humblest and poorest among us. It cannot be obtained by joining the war.'

It is likely, in the opinion of the present writer, that the failure of faith in collective non-violence in the face of the Hindu-Muslim riots in 1946 was not the solitary cause of Gandhi's feeling of loneliness, although that might have been the principal cause. The subtle pain of the non-co-operation of those who had been entrusted with the propagation of his ideas was responsible, to a certain extent, in aggravating that feeling of loneliness.

That apart, shortly after the partition of India, it became gradually evident that Gandhi was not quite satisfied with the working of the Congress Government in Free India; and occasionally he gave public expression to the feeling in his after-prayer speeches. On the 26th of January 1948, he said, 'This day, 26th January, is Independence Day. This observance was quite appropriate when we were fighting for Independence we had not seen or handled. Now! We have handled it and seem to be disillusioned. At least, I am, even if you are not. What are we celebrating today? Surely not our disillusionment. We are entitled to celebrate the hope that the worst is over and that we are on the road to showing the lowliest of the villager that it means his freedom from serfdom and that he is the salt of the Indian earth. Let us not defer the hope and make the heart sick.' On another occasion he said, with a tinge of sorrow, that there was a time when India listened to him. Today he was a back number. He was told that he had no place in the new order, where they wanted machines, navy, air force and what not. He could never be a party to that. If they could have the courage to say that they would retain freedom with the help of the same force with which they had won it, he was their man. His physical incapacity and his depression would vanish in a moment.

Five months of unhampered Congress rule was, in the opinion of Gandhi, obviously enough for the Congress to establish its *bona fides* in respect of its desire to bring about full economic liberation for the masses; but he had not found the results very encouraging. The turning point seemed to have been reached on Independence Day, the 26th of January, when we suddenly find him awakened to a new sense of personal responsibility. On the following day, he wrote an article entitled 'Congress Position', in which he said, 'The Congress has won political freedom, but it has yet to win economic freedom, social and moral freedom. These freedoms are harder than the political, if only because they are constructive, less exciting and not spectacular.' In another letter of instruction written three days after, he said, 'Though split into two, India having attained political independence through means devised by the Indian National Congress, the Congress in its present shape or form, i.e. as a propaganda vehicle and parliamentary machine, has outlined its use. It has still to attain social, moral and economic independence in terms of the seven hundred thousand villages as distinguished from its towns.'*

The use of the term 'seven hundred thousand villages' carried a very special significance. It meant that Gandhi refused to draw a line of demarcation between the two parts of the country which 'had been split into two'. He wanted economic and social liberation for the entire land which he had served all his life, irrespective of whether it now formed two States or one. This was the task to which he wanted to dedicate himself anew; and, for this purpose, he also suggested radical changes in the Congress constitution so that it could be forged into an instrument for the final liberation through non-violent means. But the Fates had

* See Appendix for last two articles written by Gandhi.

apparently willed otherwise in so far as his active participation in the present task was concerned.

All that India could actually bestow upon Mahatma Gandhi during the days when he battled valiantly against his own sense of frustration, and was on the point of winning back his erstwhile strength, was nothing more than personal adoration and love, but shorn of the desire to experiment with the ideas and methods which alone gave a significance to his life. Politically, he had become virtually isolated through our new-found love for State power; and this isolation was unfortunately sometimes also accompanied by popular misunderstanding. And when the misunderstanding became acute, India did the worst that it could do, and we assassinated the Master. But the tragedy was that just when we thought that we had become victorious by putting an end to his life, that life came back, through the very martyrdom, into the full glory of its social significance. Our supreme blow brought about our own utter defeat.

This is the story which is related in the following pages: the tragedy of a great soul, how it hungered for the company of men and kept itself tied to their common joys and sorrows, of his daily ministration on behalf of love and mutual understanding between warring human communities, of his intense effort to discover a new way of winning freedom through which even the lowliest could vindicate their will in a just cause, of his great solitude on the deprivation of organizational support, and finally of his emergence into greater power through martyrdom when the body was shed and he became the embodiment of an Idea.

Perhaps some parts of this introduction will remain obscure; the fault is, however, mine, for I love to write in a language which is not my own. But I hope that when the reader goes through the story of the greatest phase of Gandhi's great life, as it expressed itself during the last year of his existence on earth, much of what I have tried to say but which has remained unsaid will reveal itself clearly before his mind's eye.

## I. THE FIRST INTERVIEW

WHEN I come to think of it, it appears strange that the two friends who were instrumental in introducing me to Gandhi are both now languishing in gaol, while the third who brought me into closer contact with him later on, has herself left the fold of politics and gone back to what was her primary interest in life, *viz.* Art.

In 1934, Khan Abdul Ghaffar Khan of the North-West Frontier Province was in gaol when his son Khan Abdul Ghani Khan returned from the United States after training in sugar manufacture. Ghani did not know where to go to, for the house of the Khans at Utmanzai had been taken possession of by the British Government. So he sought refuge at Santiniketan in Bengal where he was enrolled as a student under Principal Nandalal Bose in the Kalabhavan or Art School and lived under the guardianship of my friend Prof. K. R. Kripalani. It was in Kripalani's hostel that I often used to meet Ghani; and, later on, when the senior Khan Sahib came to Bolpur in the last week of August 1934, in order to meet his son, I had a chance of coming into close contact with this celebrated leader of the Pathans.

The Congress session was to take place about two months after in Bombay. Abdul Ghaffar Khan extended to Kripalani an invitation to be his guest on the occasion. I accompanied the latter to Bombay and then left for a few weeks in photographing temples in the south of the province. Then I joined Kripalani again and together we proceeded to Wardha on the 8th of November 1934. The Khan family had already left for Wardha in company with Gandhiji.\* We reached the place on the 9th of November 1934, and were accommodated as guests in Jamnalal Bajaj's house, which is not very far from the railway station.

That same day Khan Sahib had an appointment with Gandhiji in the afternoon; and he very kindly asked me to

---

\* '*Ji*' is a suffix which takes the place of 'Mr.' in Hindusthani. It is more respectful and intimate than the latter.

come with him to meet Mahatmaji, with whom I had never had the opportunity of coming into personal contact before. While at Santiniketan Khan Sahib had an occasion to visit a small school in the untouchables' quarters at Bolpur where I used to live; and while introducing me he said that I was a Congress worker engaged in constructive work among the untouchable castes.

It was about half-past four when we were ushered into a room at the top of the Mahila Ashram or Womens' Institute in Wardha, where Gandhiji had taken up his residence ever since his abandonment of Sabarmati Ashram. Sevagram had not yet come into being, and he occupied a clean and spacious room with a broad terrace in front in the upper storey of a brick-built building.

When we entered the room, we found Gandhiji seated behind a small desk near the southern end, close to a door which opened into a terrace. A spotlessly clean white sheet of handspun and handwoven khadi was spread over a durrie which covered almost the whole of the floor. The small desk in front had some paper and writing materials neatly arranged upon it. There did not seem to be many men about. Pyarelal, his secretary, was there, and a few women workers were also in attendance. What impressed me at the first glance was the perfect cleanliness and the almost ascetic simplicity of the furnishings of the room.

The time of interview had been fixed outside the usual hours reserved for that purpose. When all of us had seated ourselves in a semi-circle, Gandhiji opened the conversation. It appeared that there had arisen some difference between Ghani and his father. Abdul Ghaffar Khan had recently started a political journal in the Pushtu language, which was his mother tongue. He was naturally anxious to enlist Ghani's active support in the new enterprise; for his son had already earned a reputation as a good writer in Pushtu, and educated men were very rare in the Frontier. While stating his case, the elder Khan Sahib said that he did not expect his son to serve as a soldier, but why should he not employ such talents as he had in the service of his uneducated countrymen? Ghani was, however, reluctant and frankly confessed that he had no interest in politics and preferred to work in a factory, be independent, and spend his spare time in the pursuit of Art.

Gandhiji sat listening in silence, and when the two had finished, he turned to Kripalani and asked him what opinion Ghani's Principal held about him. Kripalani reported that the former had a favourable opinion about his talents but Ghani was never serious in his work but flirted with it. Gandhiji broke into a merry laughter and said, 'Ha! Ha! see that he does not flirt with anything else.' I never imagined Gandhiji could joke in this manner; but when he did, all of us joined in the laughter and the serious atmosphere of the room was appreciably dispelled.

Gandhiji now turned towards Abdul Ghaffar Khan and spoke in a more serious vein. He was of opinion that when God had endowed Ghani with talents in Art, we had no right to harness him to any other purpose. All we could do was to help him in his own growth, and therefore if Ghani promised to spend some time every year in Santiniketan, he would gladly find work for him in a factory. Kripalani now added that the Principal had also said that Ghani had a special talent for sculpture, and as he personally knew nothing of carving, Ghani could more profitably seek instruction elsewhere. Gandhiji, however, broke in and said, 'No, no. Nandalal knows the poetry of sculpture, and Ghani must imbibe it from him.'

Abdul Ghaffar Khan sat listening in silence and when Gandhiji pronounced his final judgement he took it with calmness, like the good soldier that he ever has been. What, however, appeared surprising to me was the tenderness with which Gandhiji treated the case of an artist in distress. In the midst of the political tension through which the country was passing in 1934, he had perhaps the right to call even an artist to soldier's duty; for had he not once written to the poet Rabindranath Tagore many years ago that a poet should lay down his lyre when the house is in flames and associate himself in work with the famishing millions of his countrymen?

When Ghani's case was thus over, Gandhiji turned to me and asked me to 'say something about myself'. It was an embarrassing question, but I succeeded in briefly recounting my antecedents. Then he said that Khan Sahib had informed him how I wanted to discuss a few questions with him. I then handed over to him four questions which had been brought in writing. He went through them carefully, and as none of the questions was of a private nature, asked me if he could discuss them in the present company. Of course, there was no ground for objection, and so he started his discourse. The report of the interview was subsequently corrected by him and then published in *The Modern Review* of October 1935. It was subsequently reprinted with some notes in the second edition of my *Studies in Gandhism*.

That same evening, we went out for a walk with Gandhiji. In spite of the fact that he was slightly bent by age, and put on loose sandals on his feet, Gandhiji could walk very fast indeed. We accompanied him across the dark-coloured, bare fields for over a mile when he turned back home. But as he did so, we noticed that he picked up a few pieces of stone which lay strewn in the midst of the fields. Khan Sahib and others did the same, and, on the latter's advice, I also picked up as big a block as I could comfortably carry. When we reached the Mahila Ashram, every one of us deposited his load on a heap which had already grown to a respectable size at a certain point in the garden.

The fact was, the Ashram was a little way off from the main metalled road, and one had to walk along a sticky, muddy path in the rains to reach it. Some engineer had been called, but his estimate had been too high for the Ashram. So Gandhiji had proceeded in his own direct manner to deal with the problem of road-building. He had promised to collect all necessary road-metal in the course of a few months and this, he expected, would reduce the cost of the road to a considerable extent. Thus, every morning and evening's walk was meant not only for keeping the inmates of the Ashram fit, but it was also to add to the 'wealth' of the establishment in a very different way.

In Gandhiji's opinion, there seemed to be no problem, however great, in whose solution the smallest individual could not contribute his mite. Indeed, he had the genius of discovering individual solutions in the most ingenious ways. His idea was, if we could multiply the number of dutiful individuals by many, that would lead to the solution of a problem, however massive it might appear at first sight to be.

## II. AT DELANG IN ORISSA

THIS was my first interview with Gandhiji and naturally I felt very grateful to the friends who had made the visit to Wardha possible. Several years passed by and there was no further occasion to come in contact with him except through letters which were also few and far between. One of these letters, however, may perhaps be quoted here as it illustrates Gandhiji's attitude towards others in a very characteristic manner. In February 1935, I had written two articles in the *Congress Socialist*, entitled 'Is Gandhi a nationalist?' The opinion had been expressed that he was after all, more of an internationalist, and more intimately tied to the poor peoples' cause to be a 'nationalist', in the usual sense of the term. But for the sake of India's freedom, there had come about an alliance between the radical Gandhiji and the nationalist forces; and the prediction was made that as Gandhiji became more and more radical in action, the nationalist forces would tend to drop away from his company.

Copies of these two articles were despatched to Gandhiji, who wrote back from Wardha on the 11th of March 1935:

Dear Nirmal Babu\*,

I have your note as also two numbers of 'Congress Socialist' containing your articles which you will be glad to know I had already seen, Masani having brought them to my notice and given me the two copies.

'I should not say that any of the articles contains an exposition of Varnashram or Non-violence, but in so far as you have touched upon either, I can say that you have given a fairly correct representation of the two doctrines as I have known them. As to the rest of the articles, whilst you have made an endeavour to be fair to me, there are several things in them on which I do not agree that they are accurate. I

---

\* '*Babu*' is the usual substitute for 'Mr.' in the case of Hindus in Bengal and 'Sahib' for Mussulmans.

don't think they correctly set forth the true state of things. This is, however, of no importance. It is enough that you have made your best endeavour to examine my position in an impartial spirit.

Yours sincerely,<br>
M. K. Gandhi.'

The reader will pardon me if, by way of digression, I speak for a moment about myself; for I am constrained to do so in the interest of the matter which follows immediately after.

My primary interest in life has always been Science. But political conflicts have also drawn me in, now and then, even when there was no compulsion in it, as in the case of satyagraha. But having been in the thick of it, I often observed that the interest of many workers in satyagraha was not very deep. They were more interested in dealing hard blows on the imperial system which had brought our country to the verge of ruin than in the conversion of the British opponent. There were perhaps few in Bengal who subscribed to the revolutionary import of Gandhiji's political method or of his decentralized economic system; and therefore that cause was losing by default. Men felt enthusiastic when the battle raged full and strong; but when it came to preparation or to a reconstruction of India's rural economy through revolutionary constructive activity, the latter fizzled down into dead routine which knew no expansion. On account of these observations, I had gradually drawn myself away in 1935 from either political or constructive activity and devoted myself to the propagation of the ideas for which Gandhiji seemed to stand.

Besides thus doing what little I could, I had also decided to meet the members of the Gandhi Seva Sangh in order to induce that organization to take up work in the intellectual sphere as part of their normal duties. The Sangh was formed of a band of the best workers from all over India, devoted entirely to Gandhiji's Constructive Programme; and there seemed to be no reason why they should not extend their activities into the ideological field.

With this end in view I made contacts with several

members of the Sangh in Bengal but things did not prove helpful enough. An unexpected opportunity presented itself through the good offices of Satish Chandra Dasgupta in the year 1938. In that year, during the months of January and February, I was on tour in the province of Orissa in connection with some archæological work. The annual gathering of the Gandhi Seva Sangh was to take place at a small village named Delang in the district of Puri. At the suggestion of Satish Babu the Secretary extended an invitation to me to visit the Conference; Satish Babu had already advised me to form personal contact with members of the Sangh and discuss my plans with them.

The Conference at Delang was held in the fourth week of March 1938. Numerous workers flocked to the village from all parts of India; and through the courtesy of Gopabandhu Chaudhuri, who was the Chairman of the Reception Committee, I was permitted to approach the members of the Sangh and discuss my projects with them. Kishorlal Mashruwala, J. B. Kripalani, Haribhau Upadhyay and others welcomed the idea; but everyone said, it would not be possible for the Sangh to undertake propaganda work officially, as Gandhiji himself was not in favour of such activity. He would rather welcome the activities of the members to speak for themselves; this, however, did not prevent individual members from undertaking propaganda work on their own responsibility. A few members of the Sangh looked on ideological re-armament as an unnecessary task; for, as one of them openly remarked, he had no faith in intellect or intellectuals.

As it was thus not possible for the Sangh to undertake intellectual work officially, I addressed a letter to the President conveying my suggestions in a practical form. My earnest request was that the Executive Committee should apply their mind to the letter before throwing out the proposal. It should be pointed out that I had no *locus standi* in the Sangh; I was only a visitor, and had thus no right of hearing except what might be extended through the courtesy of the members.

The proposals laid down in my letter dated Delang, the 27th of March 1938, were as follows:—

(1) Collection of Gandhiji's writings in some central place.

(2) Issue of booklets containing a critical edition of Gandhiji's writings on specific questions; each booklet being devoted to one particular topic like 'Zamindars and Tenants', 'Khadi', 'Hindu-Muslim relations', and so on.

(3) Translation of these booklets by members of the Sangh into provincial languages and publication in the form of vernacular booklets. If such publication did not prove economically feasible, then arrangements were to be made with some prominent periodical to publish the translation as a series of articles.

The letter was handed over to the Secretary, and a few hours afterwards Gopabandhu Chaudhuri conveyed to me the happy news that the letter had reached the hands of Gandhiji himself and he had approved of the general idea. There was consequently going to be an official resolution to that effect. A short while after, in the open session, I was delighted to find that a sub-committee was going to be set up for the purpose of popularizing the ideas which formed the basis of the Gandhi Seva Sangh, as well as for the exchange of experiences between members of the Sangh, scattered all over India. The sub-committee, as far as I remember, was formed of Kaka Kalelkar and Dada Dharmadhikari. This body, soon after, started the Hindustani periodical entitled *Sarvodaya*, of which complimentary copies were sent to me for a long while afterwards.

My object in attending the Conference was thus partly fulfilled. Although there was no occasion for me to meet Gandhiji in person at Delang, yet a close acquaintance with experienced workers devoted to non-violence, and drawn from all parts of India, was itself of inestimable value. Those precious interviews had, however, reinforced me in the belief that primacy should be given to Ideas before one could carry out even Action satisfactorily, otherwise action tended to degenerate into dead routine. It gave me one more justification for shunning political, or even constructive organization, in favour of service in the field of intellect, towards which I felt drawn both by inclination and by training.

## III. THE INTERVIEW AT SODPUR IN 1945

JUST as the Khan family had introduced me to Gandhiji, so they had also been instrumental in introducing me to a celebrated musician in Bombay, named Khurshed A. D. Naoroji. She was grand-daughter of the late Dadabhai Naoroji and had spent many years of her life in Paris in quest of Art. Khurshed was an artist by temperament and training, but had felt some void in her life which she proceeded to fill by serving in the cause for which Gandhi stood. She had once been sent to the North-West Frontier, among Pathan tribesmen across the border in order to plead with them on behalf of peace. It had been a brave and hazardous adventure for a lone woman; but she had come back triumphant, perhaps not so much objectively as subjectively. She had returned to Gandhiji confirmed in the belief that non-violence did succeed in opening the gates of understanding even in the hardest of hearts, through the shock of surprise, if only the non-violence was militant and brave enough.

It was about the middle of May 1942, that Khurshed came to Bengal on a very special mission. Netaji Subhas Chandra Bose was then broadcasting from some station in Europe to the people of India. Rangoon had fallen, and the air-port of Chittagong had been bombed by Japanese raiders. Khurshed proceeded to Chittagong in order to find out how the people would react in case the British withdrew and Netaji arrived with the Japanese forces. After her return from Chittagong she came into contact with various political parties in Calcutta in order to find out how they would react, in case Gandhi launched a movement for implementing the Congress's demand to the British for quitting India.

During this mission of Khurshed we became friends; so that when three years afterwards, I came back home from detention one of the first letters which welcomed me 'back to the larger prison' was from her pen. The sufferings of Bengal during the Quit-India Movement of 1942 had indeed been very severe. Midnapore had been subjected to brutal repression, which had however failed to break the strength of the *Jatiya Sarkar* (National Government) even in 1944. In the famine again, more than three and perhaps as many of five millions of men, women and children had lost their lives; although the official estimate put it down at a very low figure (1·5 million). Gandhi was anxious to visit Bengal personally, as well as some other parts of India. He was due towards the end of the year, and Khurshed wrote a letter to me from Bombay on 3-10-1945, in which she said:

'I have sent your letter (of the 26th) on to Gandhiji. I hope you will see as much of him as you can. If he asks you to stay with him for a short time, do so.'

This was followed by a letter from Rajkumari Amrit Kaur, dated, Poona 5-10-1945:

'Khurshedbehn has sent your letter to her to Gandhiji. He wishes me to write and tell you that you must certainly come and see him on his arrival in Calcutta which will be D. V. in the first week in November.'

Khurshed wrote again to me from Delhi on the 15th of October 1945, where she was serving under the I. N. A. Defence Committee, appointed by the All-India Congress Committee:

'Bapu* will be coming soon to Bengal and I trust you will be able to move about with him. I am very anxious that you should be with him for some time at least.'

Gandhiji actually arrived in Calcutta on the 2nd of December 1945. He put up as usual at the Khadi Pratisthan in Sodpur, which is about 10 miles from the city. Some of us were already there, as Satish Dasgupta uniformly drew upon our services as volunteers to cope with the additional work which Gandhiji's visit meant for his institution.

Soon after Gandhiji had arrived and had his rest, there was a meeting of the Rashtrabhasa Parishad (Institute of National Language) in his room. When this was over and he was taking rest, a friend of mine approached him for an autograph. The autograph was to be on a book entitled

---

* *'Bapu'* literally means 'father'. It was applied affectionately by many to Gandhiji.

*Selections from Gandhi* which I had compiled in 1934. Gandhiji asked my friend if he knew me; and, when he learnt that I was already there, he immediately sent for me. I came, and, without further ado, he told me how Khurshed had asked him to recruit me within the fold. But, in return, I asked Gandhiji, what sort of work he proposed to assign to me. 'Why? There is so much of sweeper's work at Sevagram!' I said, it was no use trying to frighten me that way but asked seriously what he proposed to do with me. For, as I told him, I was made for reading and writing; and, if I was in Sevagram, his own workers would feel, here was a man who did nothing but pore over books, while I would feel, here were men who did nothing but spin. So why should he tempt me to return the compliment in this fashion? Gandhiji laughed heartily, but then said that I should take a little time to think and see him again on the following day.

Thus on the 3rd of December 1945, I reached Sodpur once more, and handed over the following letter to Gandhiji:

Bapuji,

I am grateful you have asked me to be with you and to be one of you. Khurshed has perhaps placed my case in better light than it should.

Let me therefore place my own case before you. By profession and inclination, I am a scientist; and many years of my life have been spent in fundamental scientific research. That is my first love.

But beyond that, I recognize my social debts and social obligations. There, it is your writings which have opened up a new life for me. Ever since 1921, I have tried to do what little I can in the way of national service. But since 1932, I have specially taken up the task of reading all your writings carefully, and explaining your teachings through books and articles in English and Bengali. This in itself is a fairly heavy task and I devote all possible time to it, for it gives me a sense of social fulfilment.

But for this work, I require a kind of detachment which would not be possible in the midst of the heavy round of activities as at Wardha.

I would also pray that you will let me be, for the present, in Calcutta, so that the revised manuscript of *Studies in Gandhism* and *Selections from Gandhi* may be got ready by the time you leave Bengal.

Yours affectionately,<br>N. K. B.

To this he replied as follows:

Sodpur, 3-12-45.

Dear Nirmal Babu,

Your sweet letter. You will do exactly as you please.

In order to interpret my writings, you should be for some time in Wardha when it is fairly cool.

Yours,<br>Bapu.

I learnt later on from Pyarelal that a copy of this letter had been immediately posted to Khurshed Naoroji. The former also told me how Gandhiji wished to speak to me once more on the following afternoon. The interview was to take place during meal-time shortly before he left for the prayer meeting in the evening.

So, on the 4th of December 1945, I had my second interview with Gandhiji in the southern verandah of the room which he occupied at Sodpur. The interview began at 4-15 and lasted till 4-50 p.m.

As Pyarelal was busy elsewhere, a brief report of the interview was prepared by me and handed over to him for record. It is published below in its original form, with certain verbal alterations.

*Gandhiji*: You not only make a collection of my writings but also try to interpret them. For this, it is necessary that one should actually see me at work and not merely gather from my writings. If you remain with me and also travel with me, you may observe many things which will help you to understand me better.

I shall give you an example. In Midnapore, my food was once served in the house of the Raja of Narajole in a gold plate. Although it was against my principle to use a gold plate, yet for fear of creating a scene, I quietly took my meals. Similarly, once while I was travelling a fellow passenger saw me eating grapes. He was under the impression that I took only six-pice worth of food every day. So he criticized me for not living up to my ideal of complete identification with the poor. I thanked him and told him that he should advertise my weakness. Indeed, ideal and practice often departed from one another.

It is thus necessary for a man who wishes to understand an idea, to know also how it actually works out in practice.

Swami—, who was in South Africa, once complained to me that personally I was all right but the people round me were false. In reply I told him that I could not be better than those with whom I worked. We were collectively trying to put into practice a common ideal and if we turned to be no better than what we were, then the fault lay in its presentation. For that, no one could be held responsible except myself.

So you must not only observe me at work, but also see the institutions and men through whom I am working. See them when I am there and also when I am away, and try to find out how the ideal actually works out in practice.

I often ask myself, will these go to pieces when I am no longer there?

Romain Rolland did not meet me before he wrote my life, but such men are rare.

*N*.: But, Gandhiji, Rolland missed the creative side of your revolution, your Constructive Programme for building up a new life. He put undue emphasis on the destructive aspect of satyagraha. Of course, he was right in his estimation of the courage and heroism which went to make a satyagrahi.

*Gandhiji*: Yes, you are partly right. That is why Rolland wanted to come to India in order to see things for himself. But that was not to be.

So you see why I am anxious that anyone who really wants to understand an ideal, should also observe how it actually works out in life.

What struck me most during the interview was the detachment with which Gandhiji spoke about his own life, his aspirations as well as his achievements; and that with someone of whom he knew almost nothing.

The interview thus became one of the most treasured experiences of my life. It is astonishing how he said that, a man is best represented, not by the highest flights of thought which he reaches at rare moments, but by the actual measure of the ideals which he is able to weave into the texture of his daily life.

## IV. CONGRESS WORKERS' MEETING IN SODPUR, JANUARY 1946

GANDHIJI left Sodpur on the 18th of December for Santiniketan. From there he proceeded to the district of Midnapore, returning once again to Sodpur on the 5th where a political workers' meeting was to be held on the 5th and 6th of January 1946. More than seven hundred Congress workers and journalists gathered together from different parts of Bengal, and the questions which they wanted to discuss were of a widely varied nature. Satish Dasgupta entrusted me with the task of going through the numerous questions and putting them into shape before submission to Gandhiji. An authorized report of the proceedings was drawn up by Pyarelal and was published in the Calcutta papers on the 12th of January 1946.

Among the various questions discussed, there was one dealing with the theory of trusteeship in which I was specially interested.

Q. In many parts of Bengal, the cultivators are Muslims and the proprietors Hindus. Recently in some places, the Muslim tillers have refused to till the land under Hindu owners. What should the Hindu owners do under the circumstances?

A. Gandhiji replying said that the views he was going to express were strictly his own. As they all knew he was not even a four-anna* Congress member and therefore he could not speak as a Congressman. He spoke only in his personal capacity as a satyagrahi.

Although the question had been posed in a communal setting, the real cleavage as he saw it was not communal but economic. In Bengal the cultivators might be Muslim and the proprietors Hindu, but in Andhra both the cultivators and proprietors were Hindus and yet the same conflict was in evidence in some parts. His views, continued

---

* The annual subscription of the Indian National Congress was four annas or one-fourth of a rupee in those days.

Gandhiji, on the ownership of land were well known. The only rightful owner of the land was he who tilled it.

The present proprietors were morally entitled to hold land only if they became trustees for it. If the cultivators of the fields of a proprietor, who had become a trustee, refused to till the land for him, he would not sue them or seek otherwise to coerce them. He would leave them alone and try to earn his livelihood independently by his honest industry. If he has been discharging his function as trustee honestly, they would come to him before long in contrition and seek his guidance and help. For, he would use his privilege, not to fill his pockets by the exploitation of the labourers, but teach the latter co-operation and organization so as to increase their produce and generally ameliorate their condition. This would mean that the proprietor must himself become a cultivator 'par excellence'.

A proprietor who regarded his property merely as a means of satisfying his lusts was not its owner, but its slave. The proprietors of land in Bengal had, therefore, only to adopt his ideal of trusteeship and their troubles would end.

When Gandhiji had gone thus far, I took up a small piece of paper and sent him some more questions on the dais.

*Q.* Would the trustee's property be passed on to his children by inheritance?

*A.* A proprietor who holds his property as a trust will not pass it on to his children by inheritance unless the latter in their turn become trustees and make good their claim as such. If they are not prepared for it, he should create a trustee of his property.

It is demoralizing for an able-bodied young man to live like a parasite on unearned income. A father should inculcate in his children the appreciation of the dignity of labour and teach them to earn their bread by their honest industry.

But this did not seem to be satisfactory to me; for, private ownership was hardly touched by the kind of trusteeship which Gandhiji described that afternoon. As early as 1931 and 1934, Gandhiji had spoken about confiscation of property without compensation if it came into conflict with the best interests of the nation. He had also expressly stated in 1937, that, personally, he did not believe in inheritance. And I, therefore, asked myself why should he not be equally unequivocal in the present meeting.

So on the 7th of January 1946, I addressed a long and perhaps pedantic letter to him on the subject. Gandhiji read it with interest but remarked that there was some confusion in my mind; and if he got the opportunity in future, he would clarify the points raised in the letter. That opportunity actually came in February 1947 in the district of Noakhali, when he went back very nearly to a logically radical position. But, in the meanwhile, the letter which I addressed to him is reproduced below:

Bapuji,

Your answer yesterday regarding the inheritance of a trustee's property did not satisfy me, and I have a quarrel with you on that score.

I am attaching along with this letter your former writings on the subject; the relevant portions being marked in red on pages 3, 9, 25, 26 etc. Let me now argue my case.

You said yesterday that if cultivators or workmen refused to work under a proprietor, he should, on no account, force them to work but would depend on his own strength and God for his food. You also said that within a short time, the cultivators would return to him and beg him for his services. Now, this presumes that the man was not a mere proprietor, but had talents of which the peasants stood in need. Perhaps he had expert knowledge or some organizing ability which helped the peasants to raise better crops or earn more from their labours through his help than otherwise. For such service, the talented man has every moral right to ask for wages, or a commission, as you say. This is perfectly natural, as it is also natural for him to train his own son in such a manner that the latter may develop his talents in turn and employ them in the service of society.

But after having given his son the necessary training, why did you say yesterday, that you would not mind if the trustee handed over the property to the son? There is no harm in a man having faith in his son. But, if as you have said elsewhere, 'the only heir of a trustee is the public,' why should not the property pass on to the community on the death of the man?

There is also a point of law involved in the matter of transfer. If the rich man of today has really become a trustee after inner conversion, then, for him morally, the 'ownership' has already passed on to the community. He can no longer retain the right of disposal over that property on his death, unless the community specifically invests him with that authority. But even if the community takes the latter course, then he should choose the best man for the purpose rather than think of providing for his son in the first instance.

Personally, I believe, the property ought to belong to the State; or better still, to some voluntary organization like a village commune or a municipality, or an organization like the All-India Spinners' Association which is communally owned and run, not for profit but for public welfare alone.

In the future society of your dreams, talented persons will be allowed to earn more than less talented ones; nobody can have any quarrel over natural inequalities between man and man. The man who has earned more may even be allowed to spend more on himself than others, but within limits. But that would create very little disturbance in a society in which no man suffers from want of work and in which equality is the goal. But the right of transfer of unused portions of wealth should, under no circumstances, be left to the will of a private person. For it is this which lies at the root of the organization of capitalism. Capitalism has some good points in its favour, and so have numerous rich men individually. But today, social organization has reached a point when many of the good things which a rich man used to do, can be done much more efficiently by public institutions, based not on force but on voluntary association. That prevents many of the evils of capitalism. Thus, the good of society need not be left any longer to the caprices of those in whose hands money accumulates, not always on account of their personal ability but through the accident of birth. At the same time, such organizations tend to develop the initiative and public sense of a very large number of men and women, if they are worked in the right spirit. That in itself is a very desirable thing.

And, in order to create the organizations referred to above, one of the requisites is that the present law of inheritance should be substantially modified, if not done away with altogether, so that money may be found for financing the numerous democratic institutions referred to above. Of course, this can be done in progressive stages, as new institutions gradually take the place of old ones now run under private enterprise. The present method of inheritance will be a misfit in the non-violent society of your conception.

Will you not allow me to share with you the assurance that the final extinction of private property, in the sense outlined above, is the natural corollary of non-violence and of the theory of trusteeship? Of course, the new order has to be brought into being by conversion of the privileged classes of today, either by their own effort, or by means of the non-violent non-co-operation of those on whom they depend for the making and retention of wealth; that much is absolutely common ground. But I am asking you just now only about the logical implication of non-violence and not how much of it can be immediately brought into practice.

Yours affectionately,<br>N. K. B.

## V. GANDHIJI'S ARRIVAL IN SODPUR IN OCTOBER 1946

It is now past history how the Muslim League consistently demanded that the Congress should recognize its exclusive right to represent the Muslims of India, who formed a completely separate nation from the Hindus. Through the long train of tortuous negotiations between the Congress and the League, or between M. A. Jinnah and Gandhiji, this point was however never conceded to by those who believed in nationalism; logically it could never be done. The farthest limit of concession was reached in the proposed formula of C. Rajagopalachari;* but even this had been found entirely unsatisfactory by Jinnah. According to him, the sovereignty which the Formula promised was no more than in name; there were so many limiting clauses that, unless the Muslim League was assured that the Formula was open to modification, it was no use placing it before the League for consideration at all.

---

\* *The Rajaji Formula* (*July 8, 1944*).

Basis for terms of settlement between the Indian National Congress and the All-India Muslim League to which Gandhiji and Mr. Jinnah agree and which they will endeavour respectively to get the Congress and the League to approve:

(1) Subject to the terms set out below as regards the Constitution for Free India, the Muslim League endorses the Indian demand for Independence and will co-operate with the Congress in the formation of a Provisional Interim Government for the transitional period.

(2) After the termination of the War, a commission shall be appointed for demarcating contiguous districts in the North-West and East of India, wherein the Muslim population is in absolute majority. In the areas thus demarcated, a plebiscite of all the inhabitants held on the basis of adult suffrage or other practicable franchise shall ultimately decide the issue of separation from Hindustan. If the majority decide in favour of forming a sovereign State separate from Hindustan such decision shall be given effect to, without prejudice to the right of districts on the border to choose to join either State.

(3) It will be open to all parties to advocate their points of view before the plebiscite is held.

(4) In the event of separation, mutual agreements shall be entered

When negotiations thus failed, i.e. when the nationalists of India refused to accept the two-nation theory, the League decided to launch something which went by the title of 'Direct Action'.* The 16th of August 1946 was set apart for the proposed action. It was declared as a public holiday by the League Government of Bengal; and on that day, communal riots broke out on an unprecedented scale in the city of Calcutta. The offensive began from the side of Muslim mobs; but, within a few hours, the Hindus, who rightly or wrongly felt that the Government was entirely apathetic or had abdicated in favour of the rowdy elements, also struck back. The resistance stiffened in the course of the next three days; and, in the meanwhile, Calcutta saw the murder of several thousand men, women and children. The worst part of it was that people did not engage in open combat, it was the defenceless minority within each quarter of the town which was actually done brutally to death. Sensitive people lost their sensitiveness and became brutalized in the atmosphere of insecurity which prevailed on account of the virtual collapse of civilized government.

The mutual slaughter continued for some weeks, then the virulence abated, but the distrust and repugnance which had come into being in course of the brutalities, poisoned the roots of human relationship. And men began to air the view openly that Hindus and Muslims were so different from one another that it was not possible for them to live side by side.

Strategically, the Muslim League had thus gained a political point, they had virtually forced the general public into a position unacceptable to the leaders of the Indian National Congress. Although the Battle of Calcutta might not have proved decisive, enthusiastic followers of the two-

---

into for safeguarding Defence and Commerce and Communications and for other essential purposes.

(5) Any transfer of population shall only be on an absolutely voluntary basis.

(6) These terms shall be binding only in case of transfer by British of full power and responsibility for the Government of India.

* For a full account see Gopal Das Khosla: *Stern Reckoning*. Bhawnani and Sons, New Delhi.

nation theory felt that the war had to be carried on further and a decisive victory gained at some other advantageous point in Bengal.

Noakhali is a district in Bengal in which the population is 18% Hindu and 82% Muslim. The landed proprietors are mostly Hindu and collectively they own about three-fourths of the land. Noakhali is also a renowned centre of orthodox Islam. It is the district which sends out most of the Muslim divines and priests to the rest of Bengal; and these divines had consistently propagated the political ideas of the League. All through the League Government in Bengal, for about ten years, Noakhali had also been the seat of peasant discontent. The revision of Tenancy Laws as well as the new arrangements made for the repayment of peasants' debts initiated by the League Government had considerably weakened the economic strength of the propertied classes of Bengal; and many of the landholders had been compelled to migrate to the towns, where they now invested their capital in banking, insurance or trade instead of investing it any further in land or unprotected usury.

This was the economic position of the district. Geographically, it is one of the estuarian districts, where communication for a large part of the year is by means of waterways. And in October 1946, when most of the land was still under water, enthusiastic Muslim leaders of the district struck a heavy blow upon local Hindu inhabitants. The actual onslaught began on the night of the 10th, during the celebration of the Lakshmi Puja, when the Goddess of Prosperity is worshipped by the Hindu people. The outside world was however kept completely in the dark about the events for over a week, for the Government succeeded in blacking out all news. The first news however leaked through to the Press on the 17th of October; and almost simultaneously, Satish Chandra Dasgupta received a telegram from Gandhiji in Delhi, instructing him to send a batch of volunteers into the interior of Noakhali in order to find out what the actual state of affairs was.

There was a small group meeting in the office of the Khadi Pratisthan in College Square, Calcutta on the 18th, where we learnt that a band of volunteers had already left

## ARRIVAL IN SODPUR

in the morning and more were to proceed on the following day. Satish Babu also told us that Gandhiji was due in Sodpur within a very short time; and personally for the next few days, I was entrusted with the task of reading up all papers in order to prepare what might be termed a case against the Government of Bengal in connection with the Hindu-Muslim disturbances.

Gandhiji reached Sodpur at 5-30 p.m. on the 29th of October 1946.

The Governor of the Province at that time was Sir Frederick Burrows and H. S. Suhrawardy was the Chief Minister. It was a League Ministry which was in charge of the Government of Bengal.

Soon after Gandhiji had reached Sodpur, streams of people began to interview him and acquaint him with local conditions. Prafulla Chandra Ghosh, Annada Chaudhuri, Surendra Mohan Ghosh, Kiran Sankar Roy were all there. Satin Sen of Barisal had also come with a constructive proposal; he intended to gather together such men from all political parties as believed in non-violence, and who would risk facing the angry Hindu and Muslim mobs all over Calcutta. His idea was that such people should tour the riot-affected parts of the city, and by tactful propaganda, counteract the ugly feeling of communalism which had reared its head and which well-nigh threatened to break out in the form of riots in other parts of the province as well.

Gandhiji heard everyone in detail; he wanted to gather the actual facts before committing himself to any particular line of action. On the 30th of October 1946, there was an invitation from the Governor, whom he saw on the same day.* And while he was returning past one of the predominantly Muslim quarters of Calcutta an iron ring was hurled at his car, which fortunately did not hurt anybody but flew past between the passengers seated within. The riots indeed had once more broken out in Calcutta by about the 26th; and this mild attack on Gandhiji's car was no more than what had almost become the rule of the day. It was not directed, in any case, against Gandhiji in person.

\* The authorized report is given in the *Harijan*, 10-11-1946, p. 394.

My work in Sodpur continued as before. In the meanwhile, I had to interview some refugees from Noakhali in various camps in Calcutta and gather from eye-witnesses as much information as possible regarding the actual events in connection with the riots. Summaries of statements were placed before Gandhiji by Satish Babu almost every day. On the 4th of November 1946, there was an additional duty assigned to me. The morning papers had to be read out to Gandhiji. Pyarelal, Sushila Nayyar, Kanu Gandhi and many others had come in company with Gandhiji. But as they did not know Bengali, and most of the other Bengali volunteers had already left for Noakhali, a part of the work naturally fell to my lot. There was never any personal talk between Gandhiji and myself during these days, all was purely official and business-like. But I did not fail to notice one thing. Gandhiji looked worried, he was reserved, and sometimes he was not in the best of moods.

Several weeks afterwards, when we were together in Noakhali in the lonely camp of Srirampur, he told me the story of his meeting with Governor Burrows. Sir Frederick had asked for a personal interview with him, because he had been told that Gandhiji was an admirer of the well known Labour leader, George Lansbury, while Sir Frederick happened to be a close friend of his. Gandhiji accepted the personal invitation; but after the usual cordialities, the Governor asked him what he could do in order to restore peace in Bengal. Gandhiji had promptly replied that the British Governor could do nothing. He could only quit in terms of the British Government's proposal as early as possible. If anything had to be done, it could only be done through the Chief Minister who was the elected representative of the people. The Governor remarked that no one else had, so far, said the same thing to him. Gandhiji's reply was, that this was however constitutionally the only right position.

Major General Roy Bucher, who was then Chief of the Eastern Command of the Army in India, also met Gandhiji at Government House. To his offer of military aid, Gandhiji's reply had been, if the Chief Minister needed such service he would undoubtedly call for it; but then the military would have to function completely under the civil administration. There could be no question of the abdication of a popular government in favour of the military.

H. S. Suhrawardy, the head of the League Government in Bengal, saw Gandhiji on several occasions, and pleaded with him to delay his visit to Noakhali until conditions had become more settled there. He also said, there was considerable exaggeration in the reports. But Gandhiji wanted to reach the scene as early as possible and see things for himself before deciding upon any particular course of action. He was clear however with regard to one thing, the popularly elected Ministry held the primary responsibility of restoration of peace; and he was never tired of impressing this upon members of the Government who came to pay him a visit. They had to be effective and even-handed in their administration of justice.

The Congress in Bengal, as well as those who believed in Gandhiji's ideas, had however failed in the communal riots. The challenge of communalism which threatened to sweep aside the sense of nationalism, was there in an intense form before them. They did not, or perhaps could not, think of any plan of non-violent action which might prove effective. There was a prevailing feeling of helplessness before the magnitude of the forces of evil which were stalking the land; and perhaps all this left Gandhiji in a lonely, and, may be, also in a slightly disturbed frame of mind.

Hitherto, I had never come close enough to Gandhiji. All the past interviews had been, more or less, drawing room affairs; so that the vision of him, as a man living his life from day to day had been beyond my purview in the past. But the events of 1946 gave me an opportunity of coming closer to him, and to those who kept him company. On the 4th of November 1946, one of Gandhiji's secretaries was away on some business in Calcutta. The prayer meeting was held in the afternoon, and as an authorized report had to be immediately handed over to the Press, Satish Babu asked me to prepare it. I did so, and, as usual, submitted it to Gandhiji for correction. He listened to my reading and suggested some alterations.

Next day, i.e. on the 5th of November 1946, Gandhiji had asked Satish Babu to entrust me with the task of reporting. But owing to some preoccupation of mine, Satish Babu had not been able to communicate the order to me in time. Sushila Nayyar was in Sodpur that evening; and naturally, I did not prepare the report of my own accord. Towards evening, somebody spotted me in the crowd and told me how anxiously Satish Babu was looking for me. I hastened to his room, and then together we proceeded to Gandhiji's room. Gandhiji did not, at first, notice me, as I was standing on the door-step while Satish Babu was just inside the room. To my very great surprise, he broke into a temper and rebuked the latter for the kind of volunteer he had posted for special duties. The high voice went on for perhaps more than a couple of minutes, when Gandhiji suddenly noticed my presence. He told me, that now that I had heard everything I should go back to my duties without fail.

Somehow, it was a rather painful experience for me, for no one had actually assigned that task to me. The work had been undertaken on the previous evening only because of the absence of a secretary. But anyway, I met Sushila Nayyar immediately after and found her actually engaged in the preparation of the controversial report. I asked her, if I was still expected to do anything about it. She went for instructions to Gandhiji, and I believe, the matter was dropped there.

## VI. HAPPENINGS IN BIHAR

WHILE Gandhiji was still in Sodpur, news reached that riots had broken out in a most virulent form in Bihar. There the sufferers were Muslims, and the Government was in the hands of the Congress Party. A report in the *Morning News,* an organ of the Muslim League, stated that the number of persons killed was of the order of hundreds of thousands. In the official report published in February 1947 by the Bihar Provincial Muslim League, it was stated that the orgy of violence actually started on 25th of October 1946, which was celebrated as the Noakhali Day. There were killings in Chapra on that date, but the height was reached in the first week of November 1946, by which time about fifty thousand Muslims had been done to death. This was later found to be an exaggeration, the actual number of people killed having been in the neighbourhood of 7,000.

Jawaharlal Nehru, Abdur Rab Nishtar and other members of the Central Government rushed to Bihar from Delhi, and, in order to secure correct information, Gandhiji sent a wire through the Chief Minister of Bengal to Jawaharlal to the following effect:

'*Morning News* reports butchery by Hindus of Muslim passengers. Muslims fleeing from mob fury and Premier countenancing. Wire particulars.'

Jawaharlal sent the following reply:

'Report in *Morning News* grossly exaggerated and vague. Government here doing its utmost, but situation tense and grave in many places. Am staying on here with Nishtar. Vallabhai and Liaquat Ali going on to Delhi.'

There is one little thing to which the attention of the reader should be drawn in this connection, if it is only to illustrate how cautious Gandhiji was in the verification of every item of significant news. On the 6th of November 1946, under his instruction, I addressed the following letter to Sardar Vallabhai Patel:

Dear Sardarji,

Mahatma Gandhi wishes to draw your attention to the following news published in the *Hindusthan Standard* of 5-11-1946: "Allahabad, November 3rd.—'We warned the Viceroy that if Bengal outrages were not stopped, Bihar might start trouble which might be followed by the whole of India and the situation then would get entirely out of control. So far as Bihar is concerned, our fears materialised.'

"Thus observed Sardar Vallabhai Patel, Home Member, Interim Government, to some persons who met him and other members of the Interim Government, at Bamrauli Aerodrome *en route* to Calcutta."

The reply came:

'I have given no such interview or information to anybody at Allahabad or Bamrauli Aerodrome *en route* to Calcutta; nor have I seen the report in the Press. This is an absolutely false report, and I do not know how it happened to appear in that paper.'

In the post-prayer speech at Sodpur on the 4th of November 1946, Gandhiji referred to the telegram exchanged between him and Jawaharlal and went on to say,

'The Congress belongs to the people, the Muslim League belongs to our Muslim brothers and sisters. If Congressmen fail to protect Mussulmans where the Congress is in power, then what is the use of the Congress Premier? Similarly, if in a League Province, the League Premier cannot afford protection to the Hindus, then why is the League Premier there at all? If either of them have to take the aid of the military in order to protect the Muslim or Hindu minority in their respective provinces, then it only means that none of them actually exercises any control over the general population when a moment of crisis comes. If that is so, it only means that both of us are inviting the British to retain their sovereignty over India. This is a matter over which each one of us should ponder deeply.'*

On the 6th of November 1946, Gandhiji issued an appeal to Bihar, in which he said,

\* *Harijan*, 17-11-1946, p. 402.

'...I must confess that although I have been in Calcutta for over a week, I do not know the magnitude of the Bengal tragedy. Though Bihar calls me, I must not interrupt my programme for Noakhali. And is counter-communalism any answer to the communalism of which Congressmen have accused the Muslim League? Is it Nationalism to seek barbarously to crush the fourteen per cent of the Muslims in Bihar?

'...The misdeeds of Bihari Hindus may justify Qaid-e-Azam* Jinnah's taunt that the Congress is a Hindu organization in spite of its boast that it has in its ranks a few Sikhs, Muslims, Christians, Parsis and others. Bihari Hindus are in honour bound to regard to minority Muslims as their brethren requiring protection, equal with the vast majority of Hindus.

'I regard myself as a part of you. Your affection has compelled that loyalty in me. And since I claim to have better appreciation than you seem to have shown of what Bihari Hindus should do, I cannot rest till I have done some measure of penance.

'Predominantly for reasons of health, I had put myself on the lowest diet possible soon after my reaching Calcutta. The diet now continues as a penance after the knowledge of the Bihar tragedy. The low diet will become a fast unto death, if the erring Biharis have not turned over a new leaf....'**

With regard to the fast, Pyarelal reported, later on, that Gandhiji had written to Jawaharlal in a letter dated the 5th of November:

'The news from Bihar has shaken me. My own duty seems to me to be clear.... If even half of what one hears is true, it shows that Bihar has forgotten humanity. To blame it all on the *goondas* (rowdies) would be untruth. Although I have striven hard to avert a fast, I can do so no longer.... My inner voice tells me, "You may not live to be a witness to this senseless slaughter. If people refuse to

---
\* Qaid-e-Azam, 'the great leader', a title given fondly by the Mussulmans to Jinnah.
\*\* *Harijan*, 10-11-1946, p. 392.

see what is clear as daylight and pay no heed to what you say, does it not mean that your day is over?" The logic of the argument is driving me irresistibly towards a fast.... In any event you will go on with your work without a moment's thought about my possible death and leave me in God's good care. No worry allowed.'*

---

* *Harijan*, 17-11-1946, p. 403.

## VII. ON THE WAY TO NOAKHALI

AND thus, with a heavy heart, under the restricted diet which he had already imposed upon himself by way of penance, Gandhiji left Sodpur for Noakhali on the 6th of November 1946. The Government of Bengal had provided a special train fitted with a microphone for Gandhiji and his party. The train left Sodpur Station at about eleven in the morning.

The train reached Kushtia at about twelve. There was an immense crowd at the station, and as Gandhiji stepped on to the open door to speak over the microphone, the crowd quickly settled down to silence. Satish Babu had been straining himself too much for the last few weeks. It was usual for him to translate Gandhiji's Hindustani speeches into Bengali. But as he felt slightly indisposed and had a hoarse voice, the work was done by me. We reached Goalundo at about three in the afternoon. The Government had kept ready a special steamer, the *S.S. Kiwi*, for carrying the party 80 miles down the river to Chandpur, where he was to entrain for Chaumuhani in the district of Noakhali. The translation at Goalundo was undertaken once more by Satish Babu as he felt better by that time.

Portions of the speeches delivered in Kushtia and Goalundo are given below. It should be pointed out that the official reports were actually drawn up by Sushila Nayyar.

*Kushtia Station: 12·20 a.m., 6-11-1946.*

Gandhiji addressed a fairly large gathering at the railway station at Kushtia. He said that when he first heard about happenings in Noakhali, he felt that his place was no longer in Delhi but in the former place. His relation with Bengal dated back to a distant past. Those were great days when Deshbandhu Das was alive, and he toured Bengal in his company. In those days, there was brotherhood between Hindus and Mussulmans, and both shared equally in the Khilafat and Non-co-operation Movements. Then, large numbers of Mussulmans were also members of the Congress.

Gandhiji then said that he was merely a servant of God. Today, Bengal had touched his heart deeply, and his duty was to wipe away the tears of his suffering sisters. His body was in God's hands, and it was for Him to decide how the body was going to be used for service.

He had met the Chief Minister of Bengal and many other Mussulman friends, each one of whom had assured him that he did not want this ugly war to continue. The Government had made special arrangements so that he might move about freely and see things for himself. He would be able to say what his duty was only when the truth became clear to him.

He confessed that he had perhaps served Bihar more than Bengal. His heart was sick at the thought that the Hindus of Bihar had given way to madness. This madness must be shed before people could live in peace. It was futile to think that peace could be established only when one's antagonist was overwhelmed by superior violence. With all her armaments, Europe is no nearer peace in spite of her experience of two devastating wars. Gandhiji ended by saying that nation must learn to live with nation as a brother lives with his brother before peace can hold its sway over the world.

*Goalundo Ghat, 3 p.m., 6-11-1946:*

Addressing a gathering on the river bank at Goalundo from the deck of the steamer, Gandhiji told the audience that he had come to Bengal not for one day or one week but for as long as his services were needed in the province. He would like to travel from village to village as far as his body would permit. His intention was to visit every village, if possible, which had suffered from the riots.

Gandhiji warned the audience against believing that he had come to set one community against another. As a boy, he had among his friends, Parsis and Mussulmans. He had gone to South Africa in order to serve a client who was also a Mussulman. His intimacy with the Ali brothers in the days of the Khilafat Movement was well known. That did not mean, one was to sacrifice a principle for the sake of unity. 'Let us pray', he said, 'that the Hindus and Mussulmans of Bengal should become one in heart. But to be of one heart does not mean that all of them should be converted to a common religion.'

His object in coming to Noakhali was to ask the Hindus never to run away from their homes even if they happened to be in a microscopic minority. They should try to live with the Mussulmans where they were. Both had been nourished by the same corn which grew in the fields and both had quenched their thirst with water from the same river. Even if their brother came to slay them, they should refuse to run away, but make every effort to live with him in peace, without sacrificing honour.

As the steamer left the port of Goalundo at half past three, and I got ready my reports of the speeches, there was a call from Gandhiji's cabin. He was alone, and after he had heard my report, he handed over to me another which had been prepared by Sushila Nayyar, for comparison. Gandhiji said, as I was a professor, I should correct Sushila's report where necessary. On going through the other report, I returned it to him with the remark, 'Dr. Nayyar's report is more correct; mine contains a little of my own thoughts as well.' Gandhiji said, 'Yes, I have had the same feeling about your report.'

Chandpur was reached in the evening, when deputations of Muslim Leaguers as well as of Congressmen came to see Gandhiji. There were separate meetings on board the ship, of which reports were published by Pyarelal.* We left Chandpur by train at about ten on the following morning. Huge crowds of men and women came to see Gandhiji at almost every station, but at Laksam Junction, he had to address the meeting because many of the people were actually evacuees from the riot-stricken villages.** Chaumuhani was reached after one, when Gandhiji was taken to the house of Jogendranath Majumdar, where his headquarters had been fixed for the time being. The camp of the Congress workers was near by; and numerous volunteers belonging to the Khadi Pratisthan, the Bengal Provincial Congress Committee, the Abhoy Ashram and the Revolu-

* *Harijan*, 24-11-1946, p. 431 and 1-12-1946, p. 424.
** *Harijan*, 24-11-1946. p. 409.

tionary Socialist Party of India were also there, working in unison.

Gandhiji's speech on the 7th was rendered into Bengali at the prayer meeting by Satish Babu. Sushila Nayyar and Pyarelal were to be with Gandhiji all the time, while the volunteers who had already been working there for the last few days could draw up necessary reports and the like. So, I felt, my presence was no longer necessary. And after having consulted Satish Babu and his wife, I decided to leave for Calcutta on the following day. There was no definite work assigned to me, nor had Gandhiji decided upon any particular course of action. Relief operations were already in good hands. So, although, Satish Babu wanted me to be with him for any emergency, Mrs. Dasgupta agreed that there was immediately nothing for me to do and I might as well leave. In case of necessity, I could immediately be sent for from Calcutta.

Thus, on the 8th of November 1946, I left Chaumuhani by the afternoon train for Calcutta. Two days were spent on the way in Rajbari, so that Calcutta was actually reached on the 11th, and I went back to my duties in the University on the 12th of November 1946.

There was one interesting episode which should be related here before the present chapter is brought to a close. Rumour had it that when the riots started in Noakhali, the Muslim Superintendent of Police played some part in encouraging the rowdies by his complete inactivity. Some even went so far as to say that his co-operation was not always passive but active at times. Shortly before Gandhiji left for the prayer meeting on the 7th, E. F. McInerny, the District Magistrate, came to pay him a visit. As both emerged from the room, they found Abdullah Sahib, the Superintendent of Police, seated upon a bench near by. Abdullah Sahib stood up and the Magistrate introduced him to Gandhiji, who said with a laugh, 'Aha, so you are the Superintendent of Police. People say that you are a wicked person. Is that really so?'

Abdullah Sahib naturally felt very embarrassed at the question; but Gandhiji said to him, 'Now come along with me.' And so all of them proceeded to the prayer ground which was about a hundred yards away.

## VIII. KAZIRKHIL

GANDHIJI stayed in Chaumuhani from the 7th to the 9th of November 1946, when he moved on to a village named Dattapara. In the meanwhile, he had begun to visit the affected villages in company with government officials for evidence of the wanton destruction of life and property to which the country had been subjected. Non-official arrangements were immediately undertaken in order to ascertain the number of persons killed and houses burnt or property destroyed; and it transpired that the number of persons who had lost their lives was in the neighbourhood of three hundred, while more than ten thousand families had been left homeless. The loss to property actually ran to several crores of rupees. One of the Press representatives who was with us, had been in Singapore during and after its fall at the hands of the Japanese. His opinion was that the damage to property which had resulted from man's hands here was more frightful in appearance and certainly more extensive than anything he had witnessed in Singapore.

But, in spite of the magnitude of material damage, Gandhiji was more concerned about the political implications of the riots. Later on, he told me one day that he knew, in any war brutalities were bound to take place; war was a brutal thing. He was therefore not so much concerned about the actual casualties or the extent of material damage, but in discovering the political intentions working behind the move and the way of combating them successfully.

In the meanwhile, he wrote a letter on the 12th of November 1946 from Dattapara, and a messenger delivered it to me by hand in Calcutta on the 14th. The letter ran:

12-11-46.

Dear Nirmal,

You went away suddenly without seeing me. I was under the impression that you were with Satish Babu and therefore me to the end. Hemprabha Devi says you would come if I needed you. I do need you for any work that may be assigned to you by me directly or through Satish Babu. If you are agreeable, please come without delay.

Yours,<br>Bapu.

The train for Noakhali was on the following morning, and I reached Chaumuhani in the afternoon of the 16th. Gandhiji had already left Dattapara for another place named Kazirkhil on the 14th; and so, on the 17th, I reported myself at Kazirkhil to Satish Chandra Dasgupta. Amritlal Thakkar was also there, and when I went to pay my respects to him he congratulated me on my very good luck. But I was yet unaware as to what this meant.

Then on the following morning (18th), I presented myself to Gandhiji in his room. It was Monday, and hence his day of silence. When he saw me, he wrote out in pencil on two thin sheets of paper:

'I want you if you can and will to be with me wherever I go and stay while I am in Bengal. The idea is that I should be alone only with you as my companion and interpreter. This you should do only if you can sever your connection with the University and would care to risk death, starvation etc. Satish Babu knows all about my design. You will know from him.

'Secondly, I want you to collect from *Dawn, Azad, Morning News* and *Star of India* all the telling extracts from Qaid-e-Azam's and other League leaders' writings and speeches and put them in chronological order giving under each extract dates and origin.

'These two you can do simultaneously.'

After having read the note, I replied, 'The University releases me for your service as long as you are in Bengal. As for the rest, all I can say is that I shall try to fulfil your conditions; more than that I can hardly say.'

Next morning, on the 19th, Gandhiji interrogated me on my position in the University, what salary I drew, if I was married or had any dependents, if the University would grant me leave, and so on. I told him, there was nothing to prevent me from joining him on this score. But, my position was, I did not see any reason for severing my connection with the University; I could take leave without pay for an indefinite period, and some leave with pay was already due to me which I could avail myself of for the time being. Gandhiji did not insist upon my resignation from the University. But there was a more serious difficulty about which I needed a little time to think.

It transpired that Gandhiji's idea was to leave behind him all his old companions, each of whom was to be placed in charge of a rural centre. And he was to go forth alone to live among the Muslim peasants in order to win their heart and induce them to make it possible for the evacuees to return home and live in safety and honour. But as it was physically impossible for Gandhiji to live all by himself, he wanted to take one Bengali-speaking volunteer with him. As all the other volunteers had already taken up posts, and I was the only one who was still free, the choice had naturally fallen upon me. There was another worker, named Parasuram, a Tamil Brahmin from Malabar, who had been serving Gandhiji for the last two years as a stenographer. Gandhiji also wanted Parasuram to be with him.

This was the position. I asked Parasuram if he knew how to conduct the morning and evening services. He said, he had never done so but would not mind learning. Next morning, therefore, I sent the following letter to Gandhiji through the hand of one who was in attendance upon him at the time.

Kazirkhil, 20-11-1946.
Bapu,

Now that you have asked me to be with you, it is necessary that I should place my limitations before you so that I may not cause you any disappointment in future.

Personally, I have never prayed; but, in private life, I frequently try to relate my day's little work to the things which I hold dear in life. If anything comes in the way, I try to weed it out by conscious effort; but that is hardly prayer on any account.

So, when I try to join the early morning and evening prayers, I enjoy the two minutes' silence, and keep silent for the rest of the while. The community prayer has, so far, not touched my emotion; but I sometimes like keeping company with my friends when they pray and feel great things in the depth of their soul. That companionship may be physical, but I like it all the same.

If I am therefore alone with you in Srirampur, some arrangement has to be made for the community prayer, for I would be useless for that purpose. This I should place before you for full consideration.

Yours obediently,<br>Nirmal.

This was handed over to Gandhiji early in the morning, and it was on the same day that he was to leave for Srirampur on what has been picturesquely described by Pyarelal as 'A Venture in Faith.'* Gandhiji read the letter, called me and said in Hindustani, that he found nothing objectionable in it; for people like me had previously lived with him. In community prayers, there would naturally be people who held such views. And he also told me that he would have further talk on this subject if there was an opportunity in future.

And so we left the house of Kashi Pundit in Kazirkhil at 11-37 a.m. on the 20th and took a boat for Srirampur, which was about four miles away. There were two boats. In one of them, a bed had been prepared for Gandhiji. Satish Babu and others were with him, while I boarded the second one in which boxes and sundry other articles had been loaded. It took us more than two and a half hours to cover the distance of four miles, for the canal was choked tight in many places with water hyacinth and the boat had to be punted all along. We reached the landing place at about two, from where the camp was only a furlong away.

In course of the journey, Gandhiji drafted a statement, which was handed over for despatch to Satish Babu. It is reproduced below in full:

'I find myself in the midst of exaggeration and falsity. I am unable to discover the truth. There is terrible mutual

---

* *Harijan*, 24-11-1946, p. 412.

distrust. Oldest friendships have snapped. Truth and *Ahimsa* by which I swear and which have to my knowledge sustained me for sixty years, seem to fail to show the attributes I ascribed to them.

'To test them or better, to test myself, I am going to a village called Srirampur, cutting myself away from those who have been with me all these years, and who have made life easy for me. I am taking Prof. Nirmal Kumar Bose as my Bengali teacher and interpreter and Shri Parasuram, who has been my most devoted, selfless and silent stenographer.

'The other workers, whom I have brought with me will distribute themselves in other villages of Noakhali to do the work of peace, if it is at all possible, between the two communities. They are, unfortunately, all non-Bengalis except little Abha. They will, therefore, be accompanied by one Bengali worker each as teacher and interpreter, even like Prof. N. K. Bose will be to me.

'Distribution work and selection work will be done by Shri Satish Chandra Dasgupta of the Khadi Pratisthan. My ideal is to live in a local Muslim League family, but I see that I must not wait for that happy day. I must meanwhile establish such contacts with the Muslims as I can in their own villages. They should guarantee at the cost of their lives, if need be, the safety of the returning Hindu refugees. I am sorry to have to confess that without some such thing it seems to me difficult to induce them to return to their villages.

'From all accounts received by me, life is not as yet smooth and safe for the minority community in the villages. They, therefore, prefer to live as exiles from their own homes, crops, plantations and surroundings, and live on inadequate and ill-balanced doles.

'Many friends from outside Bengal have written to me to allow them to come for peace work, but I have strongly dissuaded them from coming. I would love to let them come if and when I see light through this impenetrable darkness.

'In the meantime, both Pyarelal and I have decided to suspend all other activities in the shape of correspondence, including the heavy work of the *Harijan* and the allied weeklies. I have asked Shri Kishorlal, Shri Kakasaheb, Shri Vinaba and Shri Narahari Parikh to edit the weeklies jointly and severally. Pyarelal and I may, if our work permits, send stray contributions from our respective villages. Correspondence will be attended to from Sevagram.

'How long this suspense will last, is more than I can say. This much, however, I can. I do not propose to leave East Bengal till I am satisfied that mutual trust has been established between the two communities and the two have resumed the even tenor of their life in their villages. Without this there is neither Pakistan nor Hindustan—only slavery awaits India, torn asunder by mutual strife and engrossed in barbarity.

'No one need at present be disturbed about my low diet. On receipt of the following wire from Dr. Rajendra Prasad:

> Letter received. Have already wired quiet. There have been no incidents for a week now. Situation satisfactory. Most earnestly desire resumption of normal diet. Myself going Delhi 19th.,

I resumed goat's milk from yesterday and propose to revert to normal diet as early as the system permits. The fututre is in God's keeping.'

## IX. CIRCUMSPECTION AND A CALL FOR COURAGE

THUS life began in the village of Srirampur. Ever since Gandhiji had returned to the shores of India in 1915, I do not think there was ever a period when he was physically so alone. All his tried workers who had spent the best part of their lives in making things easier for him, or in the execution of his ideas, had been sent away; and to me it appeared that Gandhiji was bent upon putting up with as much inconvenience as possible, if thereby he could somehow gain access into the hearts of the Muslim peasantry of Noakhali. Indeed, in a private letter to one of his relatives, dated 5-12-1946, Gandhiji wrote with reference to Abha Gandhi who had been, for the past few years, responsible for looking after his physical comforts, 'She was extremely sorry to leave me. But duty lay that way. So I have kept her away from me. I must own that I was getting accustomed to her service almost as a matter of habit. But a habit of taking service from a particular individual is inconsistent with hard austerity.'*

An interesting conversation took place between Gandhiji and myself shortly after we arrived at the village, and he had taken a little amount of rest. He called me as I was arranging things and asked me if I did not at all believe in God. I confessed that the problem whether God existed or not, or what was the primal cause of the Universe, had never seriously come into my life. I did not concern myself with the question of such ultimates.

'Don't you believe in anything?' he asked.

I said, 'Yes, as a scientist, I do believe in truth. For, in the laboratory or in our scientific investigations, we undoubtedly try to discover the truth by observation and experiment. Unless we believe that there is something worth striving for, why should we engage in the chase at all?

---

* *Harijan*, 5-1-1947, p. 476.

Truth may be like a carrot dangling before a donkey's nose, but it is there all the same.'

Gandhiji said, 'That will do'; and from that day onwards, never for once did he ask me any further question on the subject, nor try to interfere with my belief in any way whatsoever.

The house where we had put up consisted of a few detached huts made of wooden frames, with walls as well as thatches of galvanized iron sheets. The floor was mud, and the custom here is to besmear it every morning with a paste of cow-dung which cakes over and leaves the floor hard and clean. Gandhiji occupied a spacious hut in the centre of a courtyard, surrounded on all sides by thick groves of areca and coco-nut. There were other huts near by, only one having been completely destroyed and burnt during the disturbances. Several large tanks also existed within the compound of the house. The inmates belonged to one of the most ancient and respectable families of Noakhali; indeed, they were descended from one of the twelve feudal chiefs who had successfully defined the Muslim conquerors centuries ago and set up independent principalities in Bengal.

During the disturbances, most of the inmates had taken refuge elsewhere; but when Gandhiji came and settled down in their home, they began to return in small numbers. Suspicion and a feeling of insecurity had gone too deep during the disturbances to be eradicated at one stroke even if it were under the magic spell of Gandhiji's presence. The courage to face reality and to build up life anew had to be instilled through infinite patience, and naturally it required some considerable time and a change of attitude on the part of the Mussulmans.

From now onwards, I propose to present the reader with my personal diary as it was kept from day to day. The prayer meetings were held at various places, of which duly authorized reports were wired every day through the Press representatives who had their own establishment within the same compound. The interested reader will find the prayer reports published in the *Harijan* from the issue of the 5th of January 1947 onwards.

## CIRCUMSPECTION AND A CALL FOR COURAGE

*Srirampur, Wednesday, 20-11-1946:*

Anukul Chakraverty, whose entire homestead had been burnt, was one of the first to greet Gandhiji in Srirampur. The latter enquired of him, how many Hindus still lived in the village. He wished to visit the Muslim inhabitants of the village one by one in their own homes. Ismail Khondkar, a Muslim farmer who lives near by, welcomed him and said, it was Khuda's will which had brought such an evil day upon the land. Gandhiji corrected him by saying that it was true, circumstances could only be changed through the grace of God, but then every one had to perform his duty. God could only work through men. He had personally come to this village in order to perform his portion of duty.

Maulvi Waliullah Kari, another resident of the village, came a short while afterwards. To him, Gandhiji said in addition that his purpose was to bring sweetness where bitterness prevailed among men, in so far as lay within his power.

Swami Bodhananda of the Pravartak Sangha Relief Centre at Ramganj then saw Gandhiji. The latter enquired about Motilal Roy's health, who is the founder of the Sangha; particularly, if his eyesight had improved now, for he remembered that it was failing some time ago.

The prayer meeting was held at five in an open space within the compound. About a thousand people attended. While the meeting was in progress, Minister Shamsuddin Ahmed arrived there with Abdul Hakim, M.L.A. of Lakshmipur, Fazlur Rahman, M.L.A. of Begumganj, Hamiduddin, M.L.A. of Pabna, who is a Parliamentary Secretary, along with some local Muslim gentlemen. The Minister spoke for about half an hour after Gandhiji. He described the Government's attitude towards the miscreants and towards the riot-affected people and exhorted the Muslim inhabitants to invite their neighbours back home.

When the prayer was over, the ministerial party had a private interview in Gandhiji's room where the Government's proposal for forming peace committees was discussed. Manoranjan Chaudhuri, a resident of the district and an important official of the Hindu Mahasabha, was present near by. He was also invited to join the discussion. But his opinion was that, unless the Government rounded up the bad characters first, the peace committees would fail to inspire confidence.

During the debate between Manoranjan Babu and the ministerial party, angry words were exchanged. Gandhiji intervened and said, 'I have heard all that has been said with some amount of pain.' He advised Manoranjan Babu not to insist on making the suggested arrest a condition precedent to the formation of the peace committees. The appeal for peace from the Minister had a ring of truth about it, and it would be wise to place trust in it. Let the peace committees be formed, and then they might be entrusted with the task of naming the miscreants, when the proper authorities could be relied upon to bring them to book.

Manoranjan Babu had no objection to playing the game according to Gandhiji's advice. It was then decided that the Minister should meet local Hindu and Muslim leaders at 3 p.m. on the 22nd, when a common plan of action would be chalked out and intensive propaganda initiated by both official and non-official agencies.

The Government's present proposal is that there should be an equal number of Hindu and Muslim representatives on the peace committees, with a Government official as chairman. The Muslim members are to be nominated by the Hindus.

During the evening walk, when I was alone with him, Gandhiji enquired about the local economic situation. I told him how the Hindus were financially the stronger community. In course of the Second World War, the Muslim peasant had earned some money, while a new Muslim middle-class had also come into being under the patronage of the Muslim League Government. The latter were trying to step into the shoes of the Hindu middle-class. It was not a simple case of an exploited class trying to do away completely with exploitation. One middle-class was trying to oust another, through an alliance with the exploited on the score of religious and cultural unity. If the Hindus were to live here, the fundamental economic relation had to be set right. Gandhiji agreed, but said that, under the circumstances existing in Noakhali, this was not the problem to which we should address ourselves; it would create divisions as in Bihar.

What did he refer to in Bihar? Is it his intention to keep the various classes united at the present moment? His intention of liquidating all class interests through non-violent non-co-operation and substituting the primacy of mass interest has been made abundantly clear and has never been clouded either in his vision or expression.

*Srirampur, Thursday, 21-11-1946:*

Gandhiji had promised to visit Maulvi Waliullah Kari's house at 7-30 in the morning during his usual walk. But as it started drizzling, he took his constitutional walk within the room, and I hastened to the Maulvi Sahib's house to inform him that Gandhiji was not coming.

The only important interview which took place today was with a batch of Hindu political workers of the district. The party consisted of Manoranjan Chaudhuri, Naliniranjan Mitra, Pratul Chaudhuri, Anukul Chakraverty and a few others. The following is my original report of the meeting, but it was never corrected by Gandhiji.

The gentlemen had come to discuss certain demands which had to be satisfied before the peace committees could, in their opinion, function effectively. Gandhiji listened carefully to Manoranjan Babu who was the spokesman of the party and then said, \*'Your proposal that these demands should be satisfied before the peace committees can be formed, virtually means a summary rejection of the peace offer. This will only succeed in embittering feelings still further. The Government offer should be accepted on grounds of expediency. I do not however plead for peace at any price, certainly not at the price of honour. Let us act on the square, and let us put them in the wrong. It was exactly in this way that Indians were able to gain the silent sympathy of a large number of Europeans in South Africa. If, after a fair trial, the committees are found unworkable, you can come out with your honour in tact. That sense of honour will give you a courage which no man can beat.'

\* Not revised by Gandhiji.

Speaking about the plan of posting two workers (one Hindu and another Muslim, nominated by the Muslim League) in each village, Gandhiji said, 'If I succeed cent per cent in my own plan, then conditions will improve. But of this, there does not seem to be any prospect at the present moment. Yet, as a man of hope, I continue to hope against hope. In the present case, I confess through bitter experience that there is no sign of change of heart, but certainly there has been a change of plan. Considerations of expediency demand that the proposal should therefore be accepted.' He also added that hitherto our non-violence had been non-violence of the weak; but now that we had to apply it against a section of our own countrymen instead of against the British, it had to be non-violence of the strong.

The demands were now examined one by one. In place of the demand that certain Muslim officers should be replaced by Hindu officers, Gandhiji remarked that it was unreasonable and a *communal* demand. 'While putting forward such a proposal, you should ask yourself if the Muslims of Bihar can reasonably make a similar demand. In my opinion, the present demand is absurd and I would personally never countenance it. You can, of course, substitute in its place, "impartial officers in place of biased ones"; that would be fair.'

Then there was a demand for the removal of the Superintendent of Police. Gandhiji was also against it. In his opinion, the guilt lay elsewhere. The Chief Minister's wishes might have been carried out by this officer, for he could not obviously act on his own initiative. Someone remarked that Abdullah Sahib was a man without conscience. Gandhiji immediately replied, 'I have yet to see a Police Superintendent who has a conscience'. Then, with regard to the Chief Minister's responsibility, he said, 'Mr. Suhrawardy was perhaps the fulcrum. He wanted to show the whole world what he was capable of doing. But he over-reached himself.'

Someone then pointed out to Gandhiji that the Ministry in Bihar had employed Muslim armed soldiers to quell the disturbances, the suggestion being that this was for the appeasement of the Muslims. Gandhiji was clearly of opinion that such a thing, if true, was surely a sign of weakness.

The last point raised was in connection with the Hindu members of the peace committees. Manoranjan Chaudhuri pleaded for postponement, as most of the leading Hindus had left the district and only poor weavers, blacksmiths or farmers remained behind. If these were to be on the committees, they would be no match for the more intelligent and educated Mussulman representatives. Gandhiji said with some warmth that if many had fled, leaving neighbours to their own fate, they did not deserve to be called leaders. The seats would have to be occupied by barbers, washermen and the like, who were as much interested in the preservation of their life and property as the rich. It was not unlikely that they might submit to the influence of Muslim members, but the risk had to be run if true democracy was to be evolved. 'In all preliminary steps in democracy, we have to run tremendous risks.' Gandhiji then referred to the history of democracy in England, and expressed his admiration for the manner in which the common people of England had fought every inch of the ground for the preservation of their rights; and in this connection he mentioned the name of Wat Tyler.

*Srirampur, Friday, 22-11-1946:*

Ever since the 22nd of February 1943, when Kasturba Gandhi laid down for life in prison, the twenty-second of each month has been observed as a monthly day of remembrance for her. The whole of the Gita is recited during the early morning prayer.

Gandhiji himself read the first three chapters and then it was continued by Parasuram, myself and Anukul Chakraverty who had arrived early to join the prayer. Gandhiji finished with the last chapter. Anukul Babu's reading was very hurried, and his pronunciation of Sanskrit was also of a poor quality. When the prayer was over, Gandhiji called all of us together and related how the monthly observance had begun in gaol at the suggestion of Sushila Nayyar. Then, in a tone full of deep feeling, he proceeded, 'I do not know if the departed soul knows what is happening here. I do not know, but I believe that in some way this reading may be of some good to them. It is, at least, good for our own soul. Sanskrit is difficult. Therefore I have taken sufficient pains to learn the pronunciation correctly. Pundits in Kashi or Srirangam read it in a wonderful way; I do not pretend to do it as well as they do. But you must learn both the meaning as well as the correct pronunciation before I permit you to read the Gita any more on a similar occasion. I would far rather that we should keep silent than read it in the present fashion.

'Never slur over a thing. In that case, you succeed in deceiving no one but yourself.'

During the morning walk at 7-35 a.m., Gandhiji visited the house of Maulvi Waliullah Kari. He enquired in detail about the population of the village. Altogether, there are 1,450 Mussulmans and 650 Hindus. Among the Mussulmans, there is one matriculate, while four or five have passed the Middle Vernacular Examination. An equal number can read English. Altogether forty to fifty adults are literate, while the number of boys attending school is 160. About a thousand can read the Koran, but only two or three can follow its meaning. Gandhiji was in Maulvi Sahib's house for a quarter of an hour, and while on his way home he remarked, 'You see how deplorable is the condition of both the Hindus and the Mussulmans. It is awful how both are kept in darkness about the meaning of their scriptures.'

The meeting for the formation of peace committees was scheduled at three in the afternoon at Ramganj. Minister Shamsuddin Ahmed was responsible for making arrangements for transport; but his agent arrived in Srirampur with a boat at 4 p.m., three hours too late. We reached Ramganj at 4-45 p.m. The meeting of representatives of the fifteen Union Boards which constitute the Ramganj Thana, was held in Shamsuddin Ahmed's tent, and it proceeded till 9-30 p.m. Gandhiji spoke for a few minutes, Satish Babu rendered it into Bengali, and we reached home at 11-40 p.m.

*Srirampur, Saturday, 23-11-1946:*
The morning prayer was conducted entirely by Gandhiji; he read out the third, fourth and fifth chapters of the Gita

## CIRCUMSPECTION AND A CALL FOR COURAGE

and asked us to follow the pronunciation carefully with books before us. Instead of the usual music, he himself read out the English hymn, 'O God! Our help in ages past.'

At 7-30 a.m. he went out for a walk and paid a visit to Chhota Maulvi Sahib. The village schoolmaster was also present. Gandhiji related the tale of a *Hafiz*, one who knew the whole of the Koran by heart, but who did not understand the meaning of the verses. Then he remarked, if people had known the true meaning of their scriptures, happenings like those of Noakhali could never have taken place.

Among today's vegetables, there was a *dhundul* (*Luffa Aegyptica*), which, we did not know, was bitter. Gandhiji felt sick, and took an internal wash at 1 p.m. before starting for the meeting at Chandipur which we did at 2-50 p.m. Sailen Chatterji, the representative of the United Press, who has practically become a member of Gandhiji's household, was in the same boat with us. After we had gone some distance, Gandhiji felt very sick and had to be taken to the paddy-fields. He became so exhausted that I proposed he should return home with Sailen Babu, while I should proceed to Chandipur with a written message from him. But he refused to go back. After having taken some rest in the boat, he said, he was feeling better, and remarked moreover that the indisposition was a punishment for his own sin (*yah meri gunah ki saza hai*); and now that the body had expelled the bitter stuff and penance had been done, he felt relieved and must proceed to the meeting, for a promise should never be broken.

We reached Chandipur at 5 p.m. The meeting continued till 8-15 p.m., for several other speakers also addressed the meeting and there was a recess for the Muslim prayer at sun-down. We returned home at 11 p.m.

In the meeting, Sushila Nayyar was present, so was Satish Babu. And as both of them began to take notes when Gandhiji started his address, I naturally refrained. My position, as I had taken it, was that of a *locum tenens*. After the meeting Dr. Nayyar left her report with Parasuram for correction. When Gandhiji was presented with that report on the following morning, he felt irritated and said that I should not have neglected my duty.

A substantial portion of the report is given below in Gandhiji's corrected form:

'Several speakers addressed the audience yesterday; Gandhiji was the last to speak.

'His advice to them was that all must help the work of the peace committees that had been formed and strengthen its hands. They had heard the speeches of Minister Shamsuddin Sahib, the Parliamentary Secretary Hamiduddin Sahib and others. They had requested the evacuees to return to their villages and had assured them that they would guarantee their safety and honour. They should accept the assurance. They might say, all this was mere talk; they had been deceived before. It was beneath one's dignity to distrust a man's word without sufficient reason. If all Muslims were liars, Islam could not be a true religion. But his knowledge of history contradicted such a theory.

'Here were elected Muslims who were running the government of the Province, who gave them their word of honour. They would not be silent witnesses to the repetition of shameful deeds. His advice to the Hindus was to believe their word and give them a trial. This did not mean there would not be a single bad Mussulman left in East Bengal. There were good and bad men amongst all communities. Dishonourable conduct would break any ministry or organization in the end.

'Shamsuddin Sahib had told them plainly that Pakistan could not be achieved by cruel deeds. It was clear to him as daylight that if they kept quarrelling amongst themselves, a third power was bound to rule over them. Whether it was the British or the Allied Powers, it made no difference; they would remain slaves.

'If they wanted real peace, there was no other way than to have mutual trust and confidence. Bihar, they said, had avenged Noakhali. Supposing the Muslims of East Bengal or the Muslims all over India made up their minds to avenge Bihar, where would India be?

'The speaker then referred to a letter that had been handed to him during the meeting. It was said that in

Chandipur, the damage amounted to a crore of rupees and it should be compensated. He did not know whether it was a crore or a lac, but the Government was bound to do what it could in such matters. Where the houses had been burnt and destroyed, the Government was, he understood, raising new ones. If there were any difficulties, if they were harassed in any way after return, they should place their complaints before the peace committees.

'Then it was said in the letter that the Chief Minister's speeches breathed fire. God alone knew the hearts of men. He could not say whether Suhrawardy Sahib was a good man or bad. But he knew that he had been elected by the voters. The Hindus and the Muslims had to live under his Government, just as those in Bihar had to be under the Congress Government. If the people did not like a particular Government, the electorate could change it. It was in their power to do so.

'Then there was a request that the military must stay on. According to the present Constitution the military had to act under the orders of the Ministry. That was democracy. When the Ministers themselves were offering to become their soldiers, why should they ask for military help?

'After all, if the worst came to the worst, they could only lose their lives. Only, they must do so as brave men and women. By running away from East Bengal, they would become worse cowards. He could never wish that for anybody. If all Hindus were bad, Hinduism must be bad. If all Muslims were bad, Islam must be so. But neither Hinduism nor Islam was bad. Christ had said that he alone was His disciple who did His work, not he who merely called him, "Lord, Lord". That applied to all religions.

'If Shamsuddin Sahib and his companions did not mean what they said, they would know. He, for one, did not wish to be a living witness to such a tragedy.'*

*Srirampur, Sunday, 24-11-1946:*
Sarat Chandra Bose arrived in Srirampur at about 7 in the morning. He was accompanied by Chapala Kanta

---

\* See *Harijan*, 8-1-1947, p. 432.

Bhattacharya, Editor of the *Ananda Bazar Patrika*, and Debnath Das, Captain Razvi, Lieutenant Samson of the Indian National Army of Netaji Subhas Chandra Bose, and another local friend. The interview lasted for two hours. The report was prepared by me, but only the first two paragraphs were corrected by Gandhiji. It was not meant for publication in its present form, but a version was prepared by Pyarelal to serve as the leading article in the *Harijan*.\*

Sarat Babu questioned Gandhiji about his immediate plans. Gandhiji replied that he was going to remain in East Bengal until he was satisfied that every single Hindu had found freedom of growth (i.e. live life freely). There was then some discussion on the peace proposal emanating from the side of the Government. Gandhiji's advice was that we should act boldly and on the square. Sarat Babu questioned if it was yet time for peace, should we not rather prepare for war? Without hesitation, Gandhiji replied that it must be peace for which we should work, but failing that it might be war. The world would then know who was really in the wrong. But peace must be with honour. 'Today,' continued Gandhiji, 'I say peace must also be safety for your riches and the honour of your women.' Sarat Babu saw Gandhiji's point and agreed. Then he remarked, the Muslim League could never have joined the Interim Government without the backing of the British Cabinet. Gandhiji assented.

Sarat Babu had met the Chief Minister in Calcutta and had suggested to him that both should go and really do something in Noakhali; then people would gain some confidence and peace committees might function properly. It was premature to set them up under present conditions. The Ministers had lately been talking well, but there was yet no sign of change of heart. Gandhiji said, 'That may be; but it is wise to trust.' Even in the village of Srirampur, he remarked, there was good response, but he was not building upon that.

\*\*Sarat Babu then spoke about the panic from which Hindus were suffering, and described some of the things he

---
\* *Harijan*, 12-1-1947, entitled 'At Shrirampur'.
\*\* From here onwards the report was not revised by Gandhiji.

## CIRCUMSPECTION AND A CALL FOR COURAGE    61

had personally learnt after coming here, the crime against women as well as the monstrous cruelty to which people had degraded themselves. Gandhiji corrected him by saying that we must look at the original fault and need not be concerned so much about consequential developments. These lay, firstly, in the declaration of the 16th of August 1946 as a holiday, and, secondly, in the forcible conversion of non-Muslims. Forcible conversion was the worst thing imaginable; and all that had taken place in Noakhali could be traced to this original sin. It was not impossible that the idea might have emanated from the highest quarters in the League command, the political intention being to free a portion of India from non-Muslims, and if possible even to place India itself under Islamic domination as in Mughal times.*

What had however pained him most was that people here did not take a change of religion as seriously as they should. Personally, he had grown from toleration to equal respect for all religions; but this matter of forced conversion was sickening to him. Conversion was good if it came from within; but what had happened was very far from that. If people degraded themselves in this manner out of fear, then they cut the very root of their life.

Sarat Babu remarked that the Ministers had been saying all along that the Press reports were full of exaggeration, but after having seen things for themselves, they should hesitate to say so again. Gandhiji said that there had been undoubtedly an exaggeration in the number of men murdered; but when the facts themselves were of an exaggerated character, no embellishment was called for. The duty of journalists, he proceeded, should be to serve a cause, rather than to line their own pockets.

Chapala Kanta Bhattacharya now raised the question of the rescue of women and the difficulty with which women workers were being confronted in this task. Gandhiji's advice was that we should not call for military or police aid at all for this purpose. 'We should be consistent all

---

* Here Gandhiji made a personal reference to Jinnah when he said that the latter 'had become like a maniac pursuing an unreal dream'.

along the line. Democracy, if it is good in Bihar, ought to be so in Bengal too. I must, therefore, go to the popularly elected ministers, for they constitute my military. If they fail, the necessary public opinion must be created against them. One must learn also the art of self-defence, and there is no question of violence or non-violence here.'

Chapala Babu now raised a further question. Why could not the Interim Government intervene as in Bihar? Pandit Jawaharlal had threatened to hurl bombs from the air if rioting continued; was he not speaking as the Vice-President? Gandhiji's remark was that it was not right for Jawaharlal to have spoken in this manner, he should have acted more as a Congressman than as Vice-President. Although Gandhiji himself was the author of the idea of acceptance (of the invitation by the British Government to the Congress to join the Interim Government), yet he must confess that the Congress had not yet got power, it was acting as an usurper of power.

Chapala Babu then referred to the widespread feeling in Bengal that this Province was being sacrificed for the sake of India's independence. Gandhiji immediately replied, 'But then Bengal has always been in the forefront. Where else in India, could you get the intellect of Bengal; who else could produce a Rabindranath or a P. C. Ray? And then there were the Chittagong Armoury Raid people. I met one of them recently, but told him that the type of courage which Bengal is expected to show today is of a higher order than that which she had shown before. If Bengal, at this critical juncture, plays the game, the whole of India is saved. That is why I have become a Bengali today. All my old loves, including Uruli\*, have been left behind.

'Today, Noakhali lies bereft of its best men. It is therefore time for the common man to rise and take the place of leadership.' Gandhiji continued that he was not going to shed a single tear at what had already happened; his task was to march forward.

---

\* Uruli-Kanchan in Poona District where Gandhiji had established a clinic for evolving a cheap system of nature-cure within easy reach of the poor.

During the morning walk, in which Sarat Babu and his party joined, Gandhiji explained to him how he proposed to set up one brave Hindu and one brave Mussulman in every riot-torn village, who would be expected to defend, even at the cost of their life, the life, property and honour of the inhabitants. But as he was beginning to feel that Muslim workers would not be forthcoming, he would have to carry on with Hindu workers alone.

In reply to the last question as to what Bengal was expected to do at the present juncture, Gandhiji said that, above everything else, it should work for the removal of untouchability, root and branch. Without this reform, Hinduism could never rise.

Sarat Babu left with his party at about 9 a.m.

Gandhiji started his 24-hour silence earlier than usual so that he might be able to address the meeting on the following afternoon at prayer time. Today's speech was written out in Hindustani and handed over to the Press after translation and correction. During prayer, Sailen Chatterji sang a Bengali song, while Parasuram conducted the service as usual. Only 36 persons attended the prayer meeting.

Gandhiji is feeling much better today, and went to bed early, at about 8 p.m. Twice during the whole day, I heard him muttering to himself, 'Kya karun? Kya karun?', 'What should I do? What should I do?'

*Srirampur, Monday, 25-11-1946:*

As it was his day of silence, Gandhiji did not pay visit to any Muslim house during his morning walk.

We started at 5 p.m. for the Thana Peace Committee meeting at Ramganj and reached there at 7. Shamsuddin Ahmed had not yet arrived, and we had to wait for another 45 minutes. The meeting actually began at 7-50 a.m., and when it was over we started home at 10 p.m. reaching Srirampur at 12-10 a.m.

Gandhiji spoke in Hindustani. He said, 'Brothers, I had no desire to speak to you tonight, for, as you see, my voice is still very weak. Let me hope that your work will proceed well.

'But there are indications that trouble is brewing even

now. I have just received a wire from Sandwip and some more complaints which tend to show that all is not well. I am handing them over to Shamsuddin Sahib for enquiry and necessary action, if the reports prove true.

'With regard to the peace committees formed in villages, a complaint has reached me that some of the Muslim members of the committees are not reliable. The Hindus stand in fear of them but have not the courage to speak out openly. But unless they muster such courage, and if wrong people are left there, the committees will not be able to command confidence. What we really want is the right sort of person. My suggestion is that if two good and brave men, one a Hindu and another a Mussulman, take the responsibility of preventing mischief even at the cost of their life, that would be enough. Why should there be eagerness for entering the committees? It is not a place for acquiring position or honour but a place of service, and if anyone really wishes to serve, he can as well remain outside as on the committee.

'It was only in order to serve the cause of Islam that the Muslims are being called to join the committees. The most important task is to restore the confidence among the Hindus that they would be able to pursue their religious practices in freedom. Mr. Akhil Dutta has lately sent me a cheque for Rs. 850/- and a letter stating that 200 pairs of conch-shell bangles and a pound of vermilion had been despatched to Noakhali.* These are for distribution among women who had suffered during the riots. The best part of the presents is that they were collected by eleven Muslim gentlemen and one Englishman. I have met women who put on the vermilion mark indoors but wipe it off when they stir out in public. Such fear has to be removed by the Muslims. It is not a question of giving money aid, but of restoring confidence by respect shown to the culture of others. I will ask my Mussulman friends to treat this as their sacred duty. The Prophet once advised Mussulmans

---

* A Hindu woman uses these auspicious symbols as a mark of her wifehood. During the riots, the vermilion marks were forcibly wiped away, the bangles broken, when the women had to submit to conversion and worse.

to consider the Jewish places of worship to be as pure as their own, and offer it the same protection. It is the duty of the Mussulmans of today to assure the same freedom to their Hindu neighbours. Qaid-e-Azam Jinnah has said that every Muslim must show by his conduct that not a single non-Muslim need be afraid of him, the latter would be guaranteed safety and protection. For, thus alone can the Mussulmans command honour and respect.'

*Srirampur, Tuesday, 26-11-1946:*
Gandhiji started on his morning walk and visited Ismail Khondkar's house where a child has been laid up with kalazar for the last seven months. He has decided to do something for the child's treatment.

Some members of the Communist Party and of the Students' Federation saw Gandhiji by appointment at 8-20 a.m. As he sat basking in the sun outside his room, they reported that people apprehended fresh trouble on the 9th of December when the Constituent Assembly was to begin work. They had gone to Hamiduddin Ahmed for assurance, but had been advised by him to wait for the direction of the League High Command in this connection. The friends suggested that Gandhiji should convene an all-parties' meeting in the district and co-ordinate the work run severally by various organizations.

In reply, Gandhiji stated that he was personally cast in a different mould; when he had no confidence in a particular step, he never undertook it. Under the present circumstances, he did not think that the step suggested by the friends would be of any use. Personally, he was trying to have everything done through the Ministry. He had also undertaken a programme here, all by himself, and this was without the co-operation of the tallest in Bengal. The Hindu population in Bengal could co-operate by utterly forgetting caste, not as mere lip-profession but in actual practice. They had also to purge themselves of all fear. For, it is only when a man's heart is free from fear, that the flower of religion can find a place in it. Finally, he added, 'I don't want to retire from Bengal as a defeated coward. I would like to die here, if need be, in the hands of an assassin. But I don't want to *court* such death.'

Sushila Nayyar came in the afternoon. She was indisposed, and although Gandhiji asked her to stay on, she left for Changirgaon. Gandhiji is in a strained mood today.

In course of an interview today, someone asked him, why he was keen on burying himself in one village. His reply was, a wise gardener tries to raise up one seedling properly instead of sowing broadcast, and then he is able to discover the exact conditions under which the plant will thrive.

The conversation with some friends who had come on behalf of the Gita Press of Gorakhpur had more than a usual interest. They came with an offer of blankets worth a lac of rupees for distribution among the evacuees. But Gandhiji wished them to hold back the gift for the present. He said, it was the duty of the Government to provide warm covering, and it was within the rights of the evacuees to press their demand. If the Government failed, and confessed that it had not resources enough, then only could private organizations step in to help the evacuees. Unless the people were conscious of their political rights and knew how to act in a crisis, democracy can never be built up.

The conversation then shifted to another interesting matter. Gandhiji had apparently noticed that I had lost a little weight. This was due to nothing more than irregularity of meals, which resulted from the uncertainty of our programme. Curiously enough, he questioned me, if I ate fish. I replied that I was not a vegetarian but had not so far taken either fish or meat in Noakhali.

'Do not members of the family here take fish?' he asked.

'Yes, they do. But we are living here with you, and Parasuram is a vegetarian. If I leave him for taking my meals elsewhere, it won't even look nice.'

Then he advised me to take more milk and fruits. One of the friends then put the question.

'But Bapuji, is it not violence to eat fish?'

'Fish is a common food in Bengal, it is a land of water; so where is the harm?'

'Bapuji, does that not mean destruction of life?'
Gandhiji replied, 'Yes, it does; but it means less harm than what people inflict on others by selling adulterated food.'

*Srirampur, Friday, 29-11-1946:*
This morning, as I was attending him during bath, Gandhiji began to take some personal interest in me. He questioned me about my work in the University.

Some contractor came on behalf of the Government, and set up a tube-well in the courtyard south of Gandhiji's room. It is difficult to secure clean water, it has to be fetched from some distance. The pump would therefore save us a lot of going to and fro.

A letter was addressed by me to Surendramohan Ghosh, Vice-President of the Bengal Provincial Congress Committee, in which I drew his attention to the fact that Ministers Suhrawardy, Goffran and Shamsuddin Ahmed had complained to Gandhiji that the number of persons killed or converted or women abducted, as given in the former's Press statement, was considerably above the mark. Gandhiji wanted him to send relevant cuttings from the Press; and, if there was exaggeration, it was proper to admit the fact, otherwise to take the responsibility of proving its correctness.

*Srirampur, Saturday, 30-11-1946:*
During bath, Gandhiji once more asked me some personal questions. I related to him my experience in constructive work in Bolpur and how I had been drawn into political movements now and then. I told him how scientific research was my true vocation (*Swadharma*), while serving in the political campaign, even when it was by intellect, was no more than an emergency duty (*Apaddharma*). Then he said to me,

'You have drank up all that I have written (*Tumne to mera lekh ghont kar pee gaya*). But it is necessary that you should observe me at work so that you can understand me better. I have called you to my side. You must examine carefully if it was dictated by self-interest. Self-interest may be of two kinds, one is entirely personal, the other is in relation to what one stands for. Even if I call you for help in the execution of my ideas, it would be selfishness in a subtle form. Examine my motives carefully. I do not wish to keep you tied to me selfishly, although you may be bound to me by a promise. You need not forsake the path which you have chosen, for any selfish purpose of mine.'

But Gandhiji probably had forgotten that I had actually given him no promise.

Sushila Nayyar was due at 8 in the morning, but she failed to turn up. So, with a letter from Gandhiji I started at 11-30 a.m. for her camp at Changirgaon and came back with her at 3 in the afternoon.

An American lady married to an Indian who has been working at a relief centre in the district of Tipperah near by, paid a visit to our camp today and brought with her vermilion and conch-shell bangles for presentation to the Hindu women here. Gandhiji advised her to deposit the presents in the centre at Kazirkhil. She then asked Gandhiji, what his plan was. The latter replied that he had yet no fixed plan. A short while before the lady left, she once more asked Gandhiji, how she could help in his mission. Gandhiji was in a slightly irritated frame of mind and curtly replied, 'You can't do anything except save me every minute!'

## X. THE DAILY ROUND

Gandhiji stayed in Srirampur from the 20th of November 1946 to the 1st of January 1947, i.e. for 43 nights. This was his longest stay at any particular place in Bengal; and, in spite of the frequency of visitors or of the numerous political problems with which he was occupied during this period, and in spite of the suspense through which he was personally passing, he did gain a certain amount of physical rest. The climate of this part of the country is damp, the soil remains wet even in January and the sky is thus entirely free from dust. Gandhiji used to suffer frequently from catarrh as it was difficult for him to put up with the damp climate of East Bengal.

Let us now describe how he passed the whole day, what food he ate or how much exercise he took, how he used to cope with such a large amount of work from day to day; as, I believe, there will be many readers who may feel interested in this aspect of Gandhiji's personal life.

When Gandhiji was in Noakhali, the current time was one hour in advance of the Indian Standard Time, but the following routine has been drawn up according to the latter scale for convenience of comparison.

Gandhiji generally awoke at 4 a.m. in the morning. A twig used to be kept immersed in a small bottle of water for his tooth-brush; its forepart was beaten previously into the form of a brush, while a part of the lower half was split for some length to serve as a tongue-scraper later on. While brushing, some powder was also used by him. This was prepared from charcoal usually made from the shells of almonds or walnuts which had been eaten earlier. This was ground into fine powder and mixed with a little amount of salt. Several bottles of water were kept ready at his bedside, and while Gandhiji brushed his teeth—actually his gums, because he had no teeth—he held an old iron bowl on his lap.

Prayer started immediately after. The prayer began with the recitation of a Buddhist formula in Japanese, and some reading of Sanskrit verses. This was followed by a hymn, which was usually in Bengali. Gujarati or English hymns were also sung or recited on special occasions. At the end of the hymn, the name of God was chanted for a few minutes when Gandhiji used to keep time by clapping his hands. When the recital was over, a few chapters of the *Bhagabad Gita* were read. The reading was so arranged that the eighteen chapters of the Gita were completed in the course of one week. It was only on the 22nd of every month that the whole of the Gita was recited; this being in memory of his wife who had laid down her life in gaol on the 22nd of February 1943. The order of reading ran as follows:— Friday, first and second chapters; Saturday, third, fourth and fifth chapters; Sunday, sixth, seventh and eighth chapters; Monday, ninth, tenth, eleventh and twelfth chapters; Tuesday, thirteenth, fourteenth and fifteenth chapters; Wednesday, sixteenth and seventeenth chapters; Thursday, the eighteenth chapter. During the reading of the Gita, Gandhiji used to lie down once more in bed. He listened to the reading in silence; but when there was a mistake in pronunciation, or a line was dropped, he never failed to correct the reader promptly.

When the prayer was over, i.e. at about 4-30 a.m., the mosquito curtain was removed, and a kerosene lamp placed on a stool upon his bed. His day of work thus began. One of us used to prepare some hot water for him. This was mixed with three dessert-spoonfuls of honey and five grains of baking soda. Gandhiji used to sip the water as hot as he could bear, by means of a wooden spoon. Then he sat for his Bengali lesson, with which the day's work actually began. Every morning, he used to spend some time in writing the Bengali alphabet from memory. Sometimes he also took a few lines of dictation from one of us. The book which he personally preferred was a primer in which Bengali was printed side by side with the Devanagri alphabet. He never missed a single day's lesson. Even when the pressure of work was high, it was his rule to spend at least five minutes over his Bengali lesson. He was a believer in absolute regularity of practice. What however impressed me most was that, even when he could spend no more than five minutes for the purpose, the work was gone through without any haste whatsoever. When the watch told him, the time was over, he folded his papers neatly, and passed on to the next item of work in an unhurried manner. Sometimes, Gandhiji spent as much as fifteen minutes over his Bengali lesson. Then he sat down with his correspondence.

At 5 a.m. a glass of fruit juice was served to him. This was usually orange juice or the juice of some other lime like *mosambi* mixed with an ounce of fresh lime juice. If there was not enough of it, we sometimes added freshly expelled pineapple juice with it; but Gandhiji never objected to this strange concoction. Manu Gandhi, his granddaughter, used to remark that Gandhiji had no sense of smell.

Gandhiji continued his correspondence or writing till 6-30 a.m. when he prepared for his morning walk. The winter of Noakhali is very mild, but because the air is wet, one feels the chill much more than in a dry place. Yet, during the walk, he used to cover his body with a very thin cotton sheet, so that the sun's rays might play freely upon his body. Gandhiji covered not much more than a mile during his morning walk. He used to carry a bamboo stick, about 5½ feet long. Noakhali is covered by numerous canals, and one has to cross over slender wooden bridges every now and then. There was one small bridge like that, not more than 6 feet long near our camp, and Gandhiji tried to walk over it unaided every day. The bridge was a collection of round stems of areca palm laid side by side; while Gandhiji's leather sandals were already wet from the dew which had collected on the grass. So, he used to slip frequently; but this never deterred him from trying to cross the bridge unaided. There were other, and longer bridges too, and while climbing one of them, one day he slipped, and had to save himself by leaning against one of his assistants.

During the walk, Gandhiji was accompanied frequently by visitors, and the time was then passed in conversation. The road along which he used to take his walk every morning, carried him by the side of a school for Muslim boys and girls, where they sat in the sun as they recited verses from the Koran in a sing-song manner. Gandhiji sometimes stood near the school and listened to the boys' recitation with interest. Sometimes on his way back home, he paid a visit to some Muslim peasant; and if there was a sick child or any other patient in the house, he not only spent some time in advising the members of the household as to how to take care of the patient but also made adequate arrangements for their treatment, if the family agreed.

On the 2nd of December 1946, Gandhiji thus came across a child suffering from fever and constipation in Ismail Khondkar's house; he decided to administer enema to the patient himself. His argument was, as we had plenty of work on hand, he would attend to the patient personally. But we prevailed upon him to rely on us, and the instructions which he wrote down for us make curious reading today. It reveals an obscure part of his personal character, as well as the meticulous care with which he addressed himself to the details of every little piece of work. The day was Monday, and therefore Gandhiji's day of silence, hence his instructions were all written on small slips of paper.

1. 'You understand what is meant. Mag. Sulph. to one patient, enema to another.

'When he comes here I shall give the enema.'

But Khondkar Sahib hesitated to carry the child to our camp; so the next instruction was,

2. 'In the morning, i.e. now, if he has not eaten anything, I shall bring the enema here and give it. The only thing is that there should be clean hot water.'

3. 'When will the child be ready?

Then we shall come here at 2 o'clock. If he prefers it can be given to-morrow morning.'

4. 'This old man requires an ointment for his skin disease. The ointment will come.'

When we had prevailed upon him to allow us to administer the enema, he wrote,

5. 'The water should be no warmer than the finger can bear. Take ten ounces of such water and mix in it 2 tea-spoonfuls of clean salt, stir well. The enema should be gently administered so that water may be retained for a while. When it has acted and the water is expelled, administer an equal quantity of cold water without salt or

## THE DAILY ROUND

anything else. Examine the stool each time to see whether any worm is expelled. If the 2nd quantity is not expelled in a few minutes, you may leave the patient asking the inmates to examine the stool and report upon the condition of the stool.

'The patient should be given every night until further instructions ½ a dram of *Ajben* seeds (*Carum Copticum*—N.K.B.) properly cleaned.

'Smear the nozzle with vaseline to ensure easy insertion. Boil it after to sterilize it.'

Gandhiji returned home from his morning walk a little before 9. Before entering the room, he used to leave the leather sandals outside and put on wooden ones instead. The former had to be scraped clean of the mud which had collected upon it, and then left in the sun to dry. Occasionally, we forgot about it, and found that the sandals had bent over from being too long in the sun. Then it had to be straightened before Gandhiji once more needed it in the afternoon.

On returning from the morning walk, Gandhiji prepared for his bath. He had to be massaged for about an hour every day in the sun before taking his bath. One ounce of mustard oil mixed with an equal quantity of fresh lime juice was used for this purpose. Gandhiji used to lie completely uncovered upon a table in the courtyard, a portion of which was screened off, and an umbrella was stuck into one of the walls to protect his head and face from the direct rays of the sun.

While the body was being massaged, he used to read some book for about quarter of an hour, after which he went to sleep for about half an hour, when we proceeded to massage the feet and legs gently. After the nap, he used to turn over on his back, when the rest of the massage was gone through.

Gandhiji used to shave on alternate days. This was done in Noakhali by means of a safety razor. He was very thrifty in the use of his blades, and would not allow us to throw one away unless it had become hopelessly blunt. We used to do the shaving for him; but every time, he rubbed his hand over the beard and felt that some part was not clean enough, he would take the razor himself and go on shaving, until he had succeeded in convincing himself that things were better. On several occasions, I distinctly remember, he drew blood from a wart on his chin before the shaving seemed satisfactory enough. So, what I used to do subsequently was, to change the blade as soon as it became slightly dull, and this, without consulting him. And he never objected even when he came to learn about it; he made trouble only when we asked his opinion about the blade.

One day, shortly after Christmas, there was a funny incident when some presents had been sent to our camp by members of the Friends' Service Unit. Among these was a tube of shaving cream. One day I tried this cream instead of the usual soap on Gandhiji. I have forgotten to mention that this used to be an ordinary bath soap and applied to the chin without a brush. When I used the cream instead of the soap, and rubbed it over the face with water, the shaving did not turn out very good. Either the blade was old or I had not lathered his beard long enough. Gandhiji asked me what it was, and when I told him that it was the new cream and I had not found it satisfactory, with a merry twinkle in his eyes, he said, 'That's just as it should be!'

The bath in Noakhali was always in hot water which was mixed with cold until Gandhiji felt it was of the right temperature. During the bath, he used no soap, but rubbed off all the oil with a towel. The feet were daily cleaned with a piece of pumice stone. One day, this was left behind, by mistake, at one of the camps, while Gandhiji was on his march from village to village. And then poor Manu Gandhi had to run all the way back to the last station before she succeeded in recovering it. The pumice stone had been presented to Gandhiji by Mirabehn, and had seen continuous service for the last twenty-five years. It was too precious a thing to be lost through carelessness.*

Gandhiji used to bathe his spectacles also every day.

When the bath was over, he put on clean sheets, and stepped across the courtyard into his room. What impressed

---

\* **Manu Gandhi:** *Bapu—My Mother*, pp. 25-27.

## THE DAILY ROUND

me about the bath was that the massage, or even the cleaning of the oil had to be undergone in exactly the same manner every day; first, one part of the body, then another, following one another in invariable succession.

It took about an hour to finish the bath, so that it was over by about 10 a.m. when he prepared for his breakfast.

The food which Gandhiji ate varied considerably from time to time.* While he was in Sodpur in December 1945, the daily meal consisted of the following:—

    5-30 a.m.—16 ounces of orange or *mosambi* juice.

    7 a.m.—16 ounces of goat's milk and 8 ounces of fruit juice.

    12 noon—16 ounces of goat's milk boiled down to 4 ounces. Boiled vegetables 8 ounces. Raw vegetables, like tomatoes, carrots etc. 8 ounces; salad of green leaves like *palong* or coriander 2 ounces.

    2 p.m.—A glass of milk from a green coco-nut.

    5 p.m.—16 ounces of goat's milk boiled down to 4 ounces, 10 ounces of dates boiled in milk, a small quantity of fruits, including coco-nut.

But in Noakhali, his diet contained less milk and a little more cooked food. The midday meal in Noakhali consisted of 8 ounces of goat's milk, mixed with 1 ounce of fresh lime juice. About an equal quantity of vegetables, including green leaves, were passed through a grater, and then converted into a paste by means of a metate and muller. This lump, along with the milk, were placed in two pots in a steam cooker and boiled without the addition of any salt, sugar or oil. Before eating the boiled vegetables, Gandhiji used to sprinkle several spoonfuls of yeast powder upon it, when he proceeded to eat the vegetable with the help of a spoon or fork. If the vegetable lump was too big for him, he used to set aside a little for us before starting his meals. But we took good care never to eat the stuff in his presence, which we did only after it had been made passable by the addition of salt, spices and some amount of cooking oil.

---

\* For other lists see *Bapu's letter to Mira* (1924-48), pp. 176, 243, 269, 271.

Besides these two articles, Gandhiji also took during his midday meal, one whole grape fruit, over which a few tea spoonfuls of glucose were sprinkled. This was followed by a small quantity of fruits like papaya or a few cashew nuts which had been previously roasted, but without salt. Thin strips of raw radish were also added at times to the dessert.

After some weeks had passed in Noakhali, and the effect of the milkless diet which Gandhiji had imposed upon himself by way of penance for Bihar, had passed off, he added a few pieces of thin bread to the menu. These were prepared by kneading together 5 ounces of flour with 5 grains of baking soda and $2\frac{1}{2}$ grains of salt, to which was added a small quantity of clarified butter prepared from goat's milk. The dough was rolled into thin sheets which were baked on an iron pan, when they became crisp like biscuits. Gandhiji ate as many as he liked, and then left the rest for us.

At 12 a.m. he sipped the milk of a green coco-nut, by means of a glass pipe, after which the nut was opened and the scrapped pulp served in a saucer.

At 3-30 p.m. Gandhiji took his last meal for the day, shortly before starting for the public prayer at 4. This meal consisted of 8 ounces of milk, but without any lime juice in it, boiled vegetables, as in his breakfast, and a fair quantity of fruits like papaya and some nuts.

Gandhiji used to take his meals very slowly. He had a full set of false denture which was used only at meal-time, and he took plenty of time for mastication. While he was at his meals, we used to read out letters to him at Srirampur. Some of these letters were answered by us on his behalf; others were dictated by him, and had to be typewritten before signature, while a few were retained for answering in his own hand.

After breakfast, Gandhiji used to sleep for a short while. During his stay in Noakhali, he used to lie upon his bed near the window with legs stretched out into the sun. In this position, we used to massage his feet with a small amount of clarified butter. This was necessary because his feet were usually cold and the skin used to crack from poor circulation. When the massage was over, the feet had to be wiped clean with a piece of cloth. One day, as he lay asleep, and as

## THE DAILY ROUND

I did not want to disturb him, some portion of the fat remained over between the toes. When he woke up and discovered this, he proceeded to clean the inside of the toes himself. He then asked me not to hesitate to perform my duty thoroughly even though I might awaken him in the process.

When the siesta was over, Gandhiji sat with his correspondence. This work went on till 12 p.m. when, as already mentioned, the milk of a green coco-nut was served to him. Then, he used to lie down with a mud-pack upon his abdomen for half an hour. Gandhiji was a patient of chronic amoebiasis; he had also high blood-pressure, and his veins used to stand out in the temples almost all the time. He therefore took every precaution to keep the body in perfect working condition, and the daily mud-pack was part of that routine treatment. Sometimes, he used to apply another cold mud poultice on the forehead which occasionally used to stretch down to well over the eyes. This comforted his tired eyes and gave him a much-needed rest.

Two in the afternoon, was the time fixed for his daily round of spinning. The wheel was set up and he used to spin half-a-hank, i.e. about 430 yards every day. While Gandhiji sat spinning, we used to read out the daily papers to him, because the post arrived in Noakhali not earlier than midday. We used to read out from the papers the head-lines of the columns and when he wanted to listen to any particular item, we read it out to him.

From about this time onwards, till the moment he sat for his last meal in the day, was also the time fixed for interviews. Intimate co-workers like Kaka Kalelkar or Sushila Pai could come in at any time; but for others, we had to fix appointments and distribute the time in accordance with the importance of the subject concerned. So many had to be accommodated that the time allowed to each was always of the briefest possible duration.

Some persons used to come only for having a *darshan*\* of Gandhiji. With his permission, we used to allow groups

---

\* 'Sight' or 'Vision'. Pilgrims who go to a shrine have a *darshan* or ceremonial view of the idol.

of such visitors into the room even while he was at work on the spinning wheel or at his correspondence. Gandhiji used to return their salutation, and now and then ask a few questions if he was in a mood to do so; and then they departed. But some used to stare at him from outside the door or peep through the window out of sheer curiosity. He disliked this intensely and called into the room anybody whom he happened to notice in this state. One day, at Srirampur, a group of men and women had come on such a visit while he was at work. He had asked them to come into the room, but as they did not understand his Hindustani they stayed on where they were and continued to stare at him from behind the door. Parasuram and I were both away at the time. So when I came into the room a little while later on, Gandhiji asked me if I had spoken to the group standing outside; and when I told him, I would do so presently, he asked me, 'Are they observing my asinine qualities?'

Gandhiji's interviews continued till 3-30 p.m., when he sat for meals.

After this he left for the daily prayer meeting. The latter started at 4 p.m. and continued for an hour or more. After prayer, he used to take his evening walk. If the prayer ground was some distance away, the walk to and for served as his constitutional. When he returned home, he once more sat down to work, on his bed, amidst his multitude of files and papers. In Noakhali, this was the time also when he wished to be left alone and did not need our services, until the moment when he decided to retire. The time for retirement was at about 8-30 p.m. at Noakhali. While he went into the bath-room before retirement, the bed had to be cleared of all papers and writing materials, and made ready for the night. The bedding consisted of a cotton mattress and two pillows. The cover consisted of two or more shawls of wool. Gandhiji's personal mosquito curtain was of a special design. For the sake of economy, somebody had prepared a curtain, more or less, in the form of a low alpine tent. There were two ends, to which strings had to be attached instead of the usual four corners. This curtain was in use in Sodpur in 1945; but at

Noakhali, we secured an ordinary rectangular curtain locally for Gandhiji's use; as far as I can remember, he had given his own away to one of his workers who was without a curtain.

As Gandhiji prepared to go to bed, we had to keep every little thing that he might require in the night or early in the morning in its proper place. The twig had to be thrashed and split for his toothbrush and kept immersed in a wide-mouthed bottle in exactly the same height of water; other bottles of water and the iron bowl had to be kept in their scheduled positions; for, as Gandhiji used to remark, he did not wish to waste a single moment's time in hunting about for anything. And last of all, the pocket watch, with the alarm set at 4 a.m. had to be kept under his pillow.

Gandhiji went to bed at 8-30 p.m. and was soon fast asleep. He usually awoke at 4 a.m., but there were nights when he drafted replies to letters or issued instructions even at 2 a.m.

But this was naturally on very rare occasions.

## XI. DAYS FULL OF DARKNESS

*Srirampur, Sunday, 1-12-1946:*

Gandhiji passed a quiet day. The weekly silence began before prayer time. The weekly market here is on Sunday, when people attend the bazaar at Sonapur. So there were few people during prayer and the written speech was also dispensed with.

Some villagers arrived from the refugee camp at Mashimpur. There is yet water in the fields, and when Gandhiji was told that it would take about $3\frac{1}{2}$ hours to reach the place on foot, he remarked that, when the fields became dry he might have to undertake a tour on foot through the affected parts of the district. This was first said in answer to a question asked by Sailen Chatterji.

Krishnadas who acted as Gandhiji's secretary in 1921 had an exclusive interview, of which he prepared a report and sent it to us for filing on the 6th. A portion of the report, written in the form of a letter to a friend, is given below:

'As desired by you, I saw Gandhiji at Srirampur in Noakhali on the 1st instant. He gave me an exclusive interview for more than an hour and a half when he discussed the situation in the disturbed areas of Noakhali and Tipperah from various points of view.... The problem of the Hindu minority of Noakhali and Tipperah is not an isolated problem but has its all-India implication. He has asked the Bengal Government some crucial questions, on the reply of which will depend his future course of action. If the Bengal Government are sincere when they declare that they are anxious about the welfare of the Hindus of East Bengal, they should give a definite proof of their sincerity by giving distressed Hindus adequate relief and compensation for the loss sustained by them. If the Government are anxious about peace, they should quickly re-establish a peaceful condition in which even a single, poor, helpless Hindu widow living in a remote and inaccessible village will be able to carry on unmolested her peaceful life and observe the practices of her religion uninterrupted by members of the majority community.... If he finds total removal of the Hindus from these disturbed districts unavoidable, he will himself lead them to safer zones and arrange to establish them there.'

*Srirampur, Tuesday, 3-12-1946:*
Early in the morning, Gandhiji went on his usual walk. Now-a-days he does not need our help any longer while crossing the small bridge over the culvert, his legs have become more steady.

Shortly after bath, Prafulla Chandra Ghosh and Mihirlal Chatterji had a long interview with him on the problem of rehabilitation of refugees. There was also some consultation on the Constituent Assembly. Gandhiji expressed the desire that the meeting of the Working Committee of the Indian National Congress might be held in Comilla so that he might attend. A letter to this effect to the Congress President, Acharya J. B. Kripalani, is being carried by Prafulla Babu.

In the afternoon, Amiya Chakraverty arrived here along with Mae Alexandre of the Friends' Service Unit and Prof. Stuart Nelson of the Howard University of Washington. While speaking to Prof. Nelson, Gandhiji repeated his familiar view that for those who were in need, God appeared in the form of bread and of clothes. During prayer, Prof. Nelson read out the hymn, 'Oh God! Our help in ages past.' In his speech, Gandhiji explained the meaning of the verses in Hindustani.

A very important letter was written today to the Premier of Bengal. It is reproduced below:

'Having waited for some time for the return of Shamsuddin Sahib as he had led me to expect, I write this to you and that in English in order the better to enable you to deal with the matter referred to herein.

'1. Somehow or other the committees that were being formed do not appear to be functioning properly. As yet they have failed to inspire confidence.

'2. In spite of all my efforts exodus continues and very few persons have returned to their villages. They say the guilty parties are still at large, some find a place on the peace committees, that sporadic cases of murder and arson still continue, that abducted women have not all been returned, that forcibly converted persons have not all returned, that burnt houses are not being rebuilt and generally the atmosphere of good will is lacking. How far these charges are true or can be proved I do not know.

'My object just now is to bring these to your notice. It might be that a summary impartial inquiry is necessary to restore confidence.

'3. Restrictions are being placed on volunteers irrespective of the organisations to which they belong. I can understand illegal activities being restricted, but no other restriction would be advisable.

'4. Adequate food and warm clothing and fit habitation is surely necessary while there are bonafide refugees. To deny these amenities would create suspicion and defeat the purpose of sending them back to their villages. I am of opinion that if the Government are unable to provide adequate food and clothing, facility should be readily given to benevolent persons to supply them.

'5. As I write this the following letter has reached— (Here followed a letter from a worker dated 1-12-1946).

'6. Another letter says: (Here was a letter conveying news about the situation in Hime Char).'

In the afternoon a note was dictated on the Constituent Assembly for the Working Committee. This is to be sent through Prafulla Chandra Ghosh. Unfortunately, while I was taking down the dictation, there was some noise outside, the burnt hut near by was being dismantled, and the iron sheets creaked loudly as they were being unloosened. I missed Gandhiji's words now and then, and he became irritated. The last three lines of the draft were later written down by Gandhiji in his own hand. The instruction, as given to the Working Committee, ran as follows:

'I am quite clear that if there is a boycott by the Muslim League of the Constituent Assembly, it should not meet under the Cabinet Mission's statement of 16th May. It clearly contemplates the co-operation of two major parties, viz. the Congress and the League. Therefore, if one of them proclaims a boycott, the Constituent Assembly cannot meet with propriety under that paper. If the Government convene the Constituent Assembly in spite of the boycott, they can legitimately do so under some other statement which they can draw up in consultation with the Congress. It should never be forgotten that however powerful the Congress has become, Constituent Assembly as contemplated today can only meet by action of the British Government.

'Even if the Constituent Assembly meets in spite of the boycott, but with the willing co-operation of the British Government, it will be under the visible or invisible protection of the British forces, whether Indian or European. In my opinion, we shall never reach a satisfactory constitution under these circumstances. Whether we own it or no, our weakness will be felt by the whole world.

'It may be said that not to meet as a Constituent Assembly under these circumstances will amount to a surrender to Q. A. Jinnah or the Muslim League. I do not mind the charge because the waiver will not be an act of weakness, it will be an act of Congress strength because it would be due to the logic of facts.

'If we have attained a certain degree of status and strength to warrant us in convening our own Constituent Assembly irrespective of the British Government, it will be a proper thing. We will have then to seek the co-operation of the Muslim League and all the parties including the Princes, and the Constituent Assembly can meet at a favourable place even if some do not join. Thus it may be only the Congress Provinces plus Princes who may care to join. I think this would be dignified and wholly consistent with facts.'

This instruction was despatched on the 4th by a messenger to Prafulla Babu.

*Srirampur, Wednesday, 4-12-1946:*
Amiya Chakraverty had stayed for the night with us. He joined the early morning prayer and during the morning walk had an important interview with Gandhiji. The report was corrected by the latter and then typed. Amiya Babu left at half-past two in the afternoon. A paragraph from the report is given below:

'Some of us who brought to Gandhiji our reports based on recent experiences in the villages, wanted his advice with regard to the technique of approaching wrong-doers so that their resistance could be dissolved. The difficulty with callous perpetrators of crime was that they were not only unrepentant but defiant and even jubilant about their misdeeds. Gandhiji replied, "Yes, they have their own reason to be jubilant, and the only way to meet their attitude is not to succumb to it but to live in their midst and retain one's sense of truth. Goodness must be joined with knowledge, mere goodness is not of much use.... I am groping for light—I am surrounded by darkness—but I must act or refrain as guided by truth. I find that I have not the patience and the technique needed in these tragic circumstances; suffering and evil often overwhelm me and I stew in my own juice. Therefore, I have told my friends that they should bear with me, and work or refrain, guided by the wisdom which is now utterly demanded of us. This darkness will break and if I see light, even those will who created the tragedy of recent communalism in Bengal".'

*Srirampur, Thursday, 5-12-1946:*
Nirmal Chandra Chatterji and Debendranath Mukherjee, President and Secretary of the Hindu Mahasabha, Naren Bose, brother of Suren Bose, the first victim of Noakhali, and a few others had a 45-minute interview when the Mahasabha's project of segregating the Hindu population in Noakhali for purposes of safety was discussed. Gandhiji argued against it and said that it would be an unworkable proposition. 'Put yourself in Mr. Suhrawardy's shoes; do you think he would favour it, or even the Muslim residents of Noakhali? For it would be interpreted as a preparation for war. But if you believe that this alone is the only workable scheme, you can go ahead with it.

'For myself, the path is different. I have become a Bengali to all intents and purposes. Today Nirmal Babu is my ear and is indispensable, but when I learn enough Bengali, he will be free to go.' Then he explained his own plan, how he had already posted one worker in each village, with a Bengali interpreter where necessary, in order to 'steel the hearts of the inhabitants'.

It did not matter if there was only one or many Hindus in a village; his prescription was that they should stick to their posts and even face death, if necessary, with courage and willingness. If they lived in clusters, it would really mean accepting the Muslim League's mischievous two-nation theory. Then he added, 'If there has to be migration at all, it must be complete.' He then proceeded to say, 'I am not going to be a willing party to Pakistan. Even if I fail to prevent it and all Hindus go away, I shall still remain here; and shall not make a single change in my religious practice.'

Nirmal Babu remarked that no one had taken to this advice so far, as the scheme was beyond the strength of the average individual. Gandhiji replied, 'If some could die like this, the few shall become many. I am not a visionary as I am generally supposed to be. I am an idealist, but I claim to be a practical idealist.' Then he continued, 'I have been born a Hindu and I shall die a Hindu, a Sanatani Hindu. If there is salvation for me, it must be as a Hindu. Hinduism absorbs the best in other religions, and there is scope for expansion in it.'

Nirmal Babu thanked him for his kindness in thus taking up the case of Bengal. Gandhiji immediately replied that it was no kindness; and if it was, it was kindness to himself. 'My own doctrine was failing. I don't want to die a failure but as a successful man. But it may be that I may die a failure.'

While taking his bath, Gandhiji said to me that he might have to stay here for several years (*varson tak rahana hoga*), unless, of course, they killed him. He was prepared for that, but believed that neither Suhrawardy nor Jinnah wanted his death; for the latter knew that Gandhi was after all a friend of Mussulmans.

The conversation drifted to the murder of Mahasay Rajpal, Bholanath Sen and Swami Shraddhananda by Muslim fanatics and Gandhiji expressed his surprise that the murderers had been looked upon as martyrs even by men like Fazli Hassan, Muhammad Iqbal or Begum Shah Nawaz's father. Incidentally, he said that if he was assassinated, India, and perhaps also the world, would not forgive the Muslim League.

While I was reading out my typescript of *Selections from Gandhi* to him in the afternoon, we came to the passage, 'Non-violence in the very nature of things is of no assistance in the defence of ill-gotten gains and immoral acts.' I asked him, what he meant by 'ill-gotten gains'; did it include the accumulation of capital? Without hesitation he replied, the accumulation of capital could never take place without exploitation, that was his firm conviction.

Two letters from the Chief Minister came through a special messenger. Its reply was drafted by Gandhiji at night, and I was asked to see if any point had been left unanswered or not.

*Srirampur, Friday, 6-12-1946:*

During the morning walk, Gandhiji paid a visit to the house of Rajendra Nath who is a weaver by caste, and made detailed enquiries about his earning, whether he uses handspun yarn, and so on.

While I was massaging him with oil before bath, our conversation drifted to Ruskin, Tolstoy and Rabindranath. I told him how once Rabindranath had expressed the opinion that Jawaharlal was a truer representative of modern India than Gandhiji. Gandhiji did not agree, and said that Jawaharlal himself would not substantiate that opinion. Jawaharlal was by taste, training and everything else an Englishman, but he had an Indian heart. On the other hand, he personally claimed to be a true representative of the Indian people.

English friends had often told him that he was carrying on the work of John Ruskin and also of Tolstoy. Tolstoy had written letters to him and English friends had also given him credit for what they believed were his merits. When I asked him if all those letters had been preserved or not, he said that they had mostly been destroyed, there was hardly a place where he could keep them, for he was always moving from place to place. Moreover, the letters had become unnecessary for his own sake; it was enough that his life should speak for itself. But he realized after their destruction that they might have been preserved for the use of others.

*Srirampur, Saturday, 7-12-1946:*
Rani Chanda, the artist, had written a letter to me from Santiniketan in which she sought Gandhiji's permission to come and serve as a volunteer in our camp. When I told him about this during massage in the morning, he asked me to write back that she should not come. For he was yet extremely uncertain about his own plans and should therefore not add to his encumbrances. He said, 'Never in my life has the path been so uncertain and so dim before me. If Suhrawardy Sahib had believed half of what I said, and of which I meant everything, a road would have opened up before me. But today my intelligence is beaten (*mera dimag har jata hai*). I do not know how to deal with him. All will depend upon the reaction from the other side; in a few day's time I hope, I shall know what to do.' I heard him muttering to himself several times during the day, 'What should I do! What should I do! (*Kya karun? Kya karun?*)'

He advised me to lighten our luggage as far as possible so that the proposed tour could be undertaken as soon as the ground was sufficiently dry. As all such arrangements are in charge of Satish Babu, I sent a letter to his wife conveying Gandhiji's wishes as expressed today.

*Srirampur, Sunday, 8-12-1946:*
During the morning walk, Gandhiji asked me about the difference between *u* and *oo* when added to letters, for they looked so much alike in Bengali. I explained to him how the two differed.

Arabinda Bose, a nephew of Netaji Subhas Chandra Bose, came with a friend of his and had an interview while Gandhiji was taking his meals. This continued till 1 p.m. in the afternoon. Arabinda Babu was carrying on relief work and had seen the Relief Commissioner. Gandhiji dealt with the problem as a whole and explained that we should proceed in such a manner that the Government might be put in the wrong and the struggle lifted to the necessary political plane. Whatever steps had to be taken, whether it was relief or migration, should be taken only after the Government had been made to confess that they were unable to do anything more for the sufferers, or had failed to restrain the rowdy Muslim elements. If, in the meantime, which he hoped would not be more than a week or so, a few of the sufferers died of exposure, he was hard-hearted enough (*main nirday hun*) not to be deflected from his course by such events. The whole struggle had to be lifted to the political plane; mere humanitarian relief was not enough, for it would fail to touch the root of the problem.

Gandhiji advised Arabinda Babu to demand 'adequate relief' from the Relief Commissioner 'till we can advise the people safely to go back to their homes.' Such advice could not be given at the present moment. He spoke with passion against the timidity and cowardice of our people and related a few instances which had come to his notice.

In the afternoon, as he was spinning, a number of people came to see him from Hajiganj. They related how both the Hindu and Muslim merchants had combined there to maintain peace during the riots, but the feeling between the two communities had not yet become normal. When Gandhiji heard this, he remarked that when snakes and other animals are washed away by a flood, both take shelter in the same tree and forget their enmity. What had happened in Hajiganj was no better than this.

The Government has offered Rs. 250/- to each family for building huts. Volunteers have been asked to prepare an independent estimate of the actual minimum cost. Two volunteers from Chandipur Relief Camp reported today that the lowest cost would be between five and six hundred rupees. Another volunteer came from A. V. Thakkar's camp where Abha Gandhi has been posted. Gandhiji wrote down replies to their letters and asked me to send some old newspapers for them to read.

The old lady of the house, whom we all call *Pishima* (aunt), suffered from a bad fit of asthma last night. She came in the afternoon with a bowl of water and entreated Gandhiji to touch the water with his finger when she would drink it. When I explained what she wanted, Gandhiji asked Parasuram to boil some water for her and advised Pishima to drink nothing but tepid water all through the day. He did not believe in this kind of magical cure nor in blind faith. But Pishima was not to be put off so easily. So, in the end, Gandhiji had to touch the water in the bowl with his clean finger tip, and Pishima went back, happy in the thought that this water would act as a remedy for all her ailments.

*Srirampur, Monday, 9-12-1946:*

Deobhankar, Shridhar Purshottam Limaye and Rai Bajrang Bahadur, Raja of Bhadri in Partabgarh, U.P., came with letters from Acharya Kripalani, Mridula Sarabhai and Ram Manohar Lohia. There was a long interview in course of which Gandhiji said that he had never come against such a dead wall in his life.

\*When Deobhankar asked him as to how the Muslim masses could be won over and unified under the Congress, and if this could not be achieved best through some form of economic struggle along class lines, Gandhiji replied that, so far, such a plan had not succeeded in respect of the people whose communal sentiment had proved too strong. What we had to do was to prevent the Congress from turning into a Hindu communal organization. Anyone who had made India his home should be protected by the Congress. Hindus should never think that Hindustan belonged exclusively to them (*wah unka bapka nahi hai*). The Parsis had come centuries ago, and the Syrian Christians were Christians ever since the time of St. Thomas. Every one of them had to be treated as an Indian enjoying the same rights as any other Indian.

Congressmen should not however approach Muslims in a spirit of appeasement or flattery (*khushamad*). Although something like that had been done, and it might even be justifiably said that he himself had partly been responsible for such an attitude, yet, his eyes were now open and he held that it had been unwise to do so. It was by safeguarding every person's *legitimate interests* that Congressmen could

---

\* Not revised by Gandhiji.

prove their genuine love for nationalism. Gandhiji did not mind even if the Congress were manned by Hindus alone. If its members placed the cause of the whole nation above everything else, then their idealism would ultimately triumph over communalism.

What the Hindus or Mussulmans had exhibited so far in Bengal or Bihar was violence mixed with cowardice; there was no element of bravery in it. To those who did not believe in non-violence, he could hypothetically suggest a more civilized form of revenge than what they had actually been guilty of. Supposing there were a Government in Bihar which believed in violence and not in non-violence, they could have written to the Government in Bengal after the Calcutta riots, 'Now, here are the inhabitants of this province who have returned from Calcutta. They have become furious and are bent upon taking revenge on the 14% of Mussulmans in Bihar. But we will prevent them from doing so, if we can. In the meanwhile, you should do everything to stop the riot which is even now going on in Bengal.'

Along with sending such a letter to the Muslim League Government in Bengal, the Government of Bihar should have kept the Muslims of Bihar informed about their efforts. If conditions in Bengal did not improve, they could have notified the Bengal Government that unless the Bihar Muslims left the province for Bengal within, say, eight days, they would have to send the latter forcibly over to Bengal rather than allow them to be butchered in Bihar. And when the eight days had passed, they might have taken necessary steps for evacuating the Muslims of Bihar.

It is quite likely that the Muslims of Bihar would have refused to move and declared that they were with the Congress rather than with the League in the policy that the latter had been pursuing in Bengal. That would have meant a victory for the Congress not only in Bihar but in all those provinces where the government was run by the Congress.

Such action, though fully violent, would have been better than that to which Bihar had lowered herself today. Violence, when cowardly, only served to degrade and did not yield the desired political result.

Gandhiji lastly said that today he was seeking for a non-violent solution for his own sake alone. For the time being, he had given up searching for a non-violent remedy applicable to the masses. He had yet to see if non-violence would prove successful in the present crisis or not. He expected that things would take a definite turn one way or the other within two months and not remain uncertain as they were at the present moment.

*Srirampur, Wednesday, 11-12-1946:*
Gandhiji has been practising the Bengali alphabet regularly and has been trying to read simple words from a Hindi-Bengali self-instructor. He asked me the meaning of a few words. He also expressed the desire that I should converse with him in Bengali and not in Hindi or English, so that he can learn the language more quickly. He said that Bengali can be easily understood as there are so many Sanskrit words in it. Moreover, as verbs and nouns do not change gender, Bengali becomes an easier language to learn.

During prayer, Gandhiji announced for the first time in public how he had lately been contemplating a walking tour through the villages. His body had become shaky, and difficult bridges had to be crossed in this country of rivers and canals. If the call of God and His service required him to brave these physical obstacles, he would have to do so, however great the risk. If he hesitated, God would not forgive him but rather do without his services.

*Srirampur, Thursday, 12-12-1946:*
A correspondent named Jagneswar Ghosh has sent a letter from Chinsurah in which he proposes that Bengal should be partitioned, because, after all, the culture of the Hindus and Muslims of this province are incompatible with one another. As far as I know, this is the first time that the question of partition has been directly addressed to Gandhiji. He had already expressed himself strongly against the segregation of Hindus in conversation with N. C. Chatterji on the 5th, as that would amount to the acceptance of the mischievous two-nation theory. In accordance

with his instruction, I drafted a reply. Gandhiji skipped through it and said that I should boil it down considerably. Then he told me how, while editing the *Young India*, he used to advise his contributors in the following terms: 'Boil down', 'Boil down', 'Boil it down again'; and he had found that a piece of writing always improved after such treatment.

Some portion of the reply is quoted below:

'Your suggestion is that people of the same culture should be brought together in a common territory and placed under a common government. Of course, for administrative purposes, men have to be divided into groups. This is best done on economic grounds or on the basis of linguistic unity. What Gandhiji objects to is the redistribution of population on the basis of religion. That would mean an admission that people of different faiths cannot live on friendly terms within the same State. The Muslim League has suggested a similar remedy for the present Hindu-Muslim tension, when the minority who remain over in each province will be held as hostages for the good behaviour of the majority in the neighbouring province. This would amount to an armed truce and not peace on terms of equality, friendship and mutual trust. To cut up India into specifically religious zones, and then redistribute population to fit in with such an artificial scheme would, in Gandhiji's opinion, be monstrous. For it will cut across many of the linguistic, cultural and fundamental bonds of co-operation which have held together our people in the past.'

Another significant letter was despatched today to Ramanimohan Sen Sharma, a physician in the affected town of Sandwip in Noakhali.

'Gandhiji can only ask an evacuee to return to his house if he can do so with full reliance upon God. Those who do not feel the necessary confidence in themselves, can certainly not be advised to return.

'Gandhiji keenly feels that any word from his mouth cannot bring courage to anyone; and he would not therefore advise any person to return home by relying upon such a frail reed. If one can put faith in God, let him return.'

*Srirampur, Friday, 13-12-1946:*

Gandhiji confidentially told me that his body was becoming weaker and weaker (*gir jata hai*), so he was not quite sure how far he would be able to undertake the journey on foot. But when the resolve had once been taken, there was no turning back. So far, every one who came on a visit had been asked to leave the camp before night. Usually no arrangements were made for their meals. But today he asked me to make arrangements for the lodging and boarding of visitors. A friend had promised to supply all our wants, and the necessary utensils would come. The food offered to guests should be no more than bread or *khichri* and some vegetables. He then continued to say that even at Phoenix in South Africa, whenever he was there, the place soon became converted into a traveller's inn.

He also asked me to refrain from telling anybody about his physical weakness, particularly to Pyarelal and Sushila Nayyar. But he had already written something to this effect in his personal diary, which was in Gujarati, and which his associates were in the habit of reading when they came here.

While I was massaging him with oil, he felt chilly and said, 'My body has indeed become very sensitive and weak; you should warm the oil slightly from tomorrow.' During bath, he said almost to himself, 'I have not yet developed detachment to a sufficient extent. The happenings in Noakhali succeed in upsetting me; for there are moments when my heart gives way to anxiety (*fikr*) and anger (*rosh*). I have been trying hard to befriend the Mussulmans; let us see what comes out of it.'

*Srirampur, Sunday, 15-12-1946:*

Niranjan Singh Gill, a Sikh leader, had an exclusive interview with Gandhiji. He brought a draft of instructions for members of the Shanti League who have been posted here. Gandhiji added several lines to the instructions, from which extracts are presented below.

In one place he added the following sentence: 'G. gave his approval only when he understood from me (Niranjan Singh Gill, over whose signature the instructions were being issued—N. K. B.) that I had seen our Premier Suhrawardy Sahib and that he had no objection to our working in East Bengal.'

At another place the draft stated, 'All work must be based on the principle of "Love and Courage". Remind them that violence is horrible and retarding, but used in self-defence and honour or for a righteous purpose, is justified.' Gandhiji changed the last line to 'but may be used in self-defence.'

Then the draft proceeded, 'Cowardice is worst. Our workers must be judged by personal character and example.' Here Gandhiji added in his own hand, 'It is not open to our workers to use violence even in self-defence. Their defence consists in cheerfully facing death.'

## XII. THE DARKNESS DEEPENS

*Srirampur, Tuesday, 17-12-1946:*

At 3.20 in the morning, I heard Gandhiji talking aloud to Sushila Nayyar who had stayed over for the night with us. His voice seemed worried.

Some time after prayer, while I was conversing at the door of my cottage with a few friends, suddenly all of us heard a deeply anguished cry proceeding from the main room. It was Gandhiji's voice, and then we heard the sound of two loud slaps given on someone's body. The cry then sank down into a heavy sob. We were all amazed beyond measure and looked at one another. I ran towards the room, and when I reached the doorstep, I saw Gandhiji sitting upon his bed with his back reclining upon the wall, while his eyes were closed and tears were streaming down his face. Sushila was standing near by on the floor. Her face was also bathed in tears, but as she bent forward and tried to say something to Gandhiji, he waved her aside with a strong movement of his arms. This happened more than once.

I did not enter the room but returned to my own and decided that Gandhiji should be left in peace for the rest of the day. The day however proved fairly heavy, for some important matters had to be attended to. But to all those who came, I said that Gandhiji was feeling very much indisposed and it would be best if everyone took as little time as possible.

Gandhiji had already written a letter to Dr. Sarvapalli Radhakrishnan, the Vice-Chancellor of the Hindu University, which was handed over to Omprakash. Sucheta Kripalani had brought a letter from the Congress President; this had naturally to be attended to. Krishnadas had come with a few volunteers engaged in relief work in Comilla. A nationalist Muslim gentleman named Azizur Rahman Kari also came with a suggestion that some nationalist Muslim leader like Hossain Ahmed Madni should be invited to Noakhali for addressing the Muslims and weaning them from the suicidal influence of the Muslim League.

Gandhiji remarked that such an invitation from him was likely to be misunderstood. As things stood, the work here had to be conducted through the help of the League Ministry. It was true, there were numerous difficulties. If Madni Sahib came here he would naturally proclaim that what had happened in Noakhali was contrary to the teachings of Islam, and the League Ministry were to blame. Then, Suhrawardy would say that Gandhi invites people into Noakhali who are inimical to him. As it was, work had to be carried on here in spite of numerous difficulties. He did not want to add to them, because he had yet to try for success through constitutional means.

Asaf Ali, who has been chosen to represent India in the United States, came from Calcutta for advice before leaving the country. Gandhiji spoke to him about the Constituent Assembly, how it should frame a constitution for those provinces and native states which voluntarily wished to join and how no one should be brought under it by compulsion.

The evening walk was taken underneath the open shed where prayers are held. Sushila Nayyar and Sucheta Kripalani were with Gandhiji while he conversed with Asaf Ali during the walk.

Among letters written today, there was one addressed to Sarat Chandra Bose. Just after the early morning prayer, Gandhiji asked me to write a letter in Bengali to Sarat Babu; he had noticed in the newspapers yesterday that Sarat Babu was ill. So this is what he asked me to write.

'Gandhiji is very anxious on your account, and wishes to learn everything about the present course of treatment, and also if there has been any improvement in your condition.

'He said further that it would not do for you to fall ill like this. When one has taken upon oneself the responsibility of serving the country's cause, one has also to master the art of keeping oneself in a workable and healthy condition. However heavy the burden of duties may be, the daily routine for maintaining the body in good order must never be broken. Otherwise one's work is likely to be interrupted.

'He would thank you also for news about Mrs. Bose.'

On the previous day, a letter breathing the deepest of affection had similarly been sent to Haridas Mitra and his ailing wife Bela. Haridas Mitra had been convicted to death for alleged conspiracy with the Japanese during the last war. His wife Bela is Netaji Subhas Bose's niece, and his life had been saved through Gandhiji's intervention. Haridas Babu had recently been set free, and a letter was sent to him by me on behalf of Gandhiji saying that the latter felt very happy on his release and also on the release of his other friends. He might come when he conveniently could. On hearing that Bela was ailing, he hoped that, now that her husband had been set free and her anxiety was over, Bela would recover quickly.

*Srirampur, Wednesday, 18-12-1946:*
During massage, Gandhiji said that he had finished reading the typed copy of *Selections from Gandhi* and wished me to write in the preface how long I had taken to do the work. But this is something which I am not prepared to do.

While on the subject, conversation drifted to the services rendered by Rev. Joseph Doke to the cause of satyagraha in South Africa. Rev. Doke's biography of Gandhiji is one of the best that I have read, and I remarked in this connection that most books on his life were uncritical and contained more effusion than analysis. He usually was painted in high colours. A myth had been created round him, and he was depicted as a man without the traits which belong to common human beings. The result has been that the practice of non-violence itself has suffered considerably in India. Men readily take shelter under the view that while non-violence is good for superhuman beings like Gandhiji, it is beyond the reach of the average individual.

Gandhiji listened in silence, but expressed no remark.

I noticed that Gandhiji has been slightly absent-minded throughout the day. He sent a long letter to Sushila Nayyar.

*Srirampur, Thursday, 19-12-1946:*
This was a very heavy day for Gandhiji. In the morning, Kularanjan Mukherji arrived from Calcutta. He is in charge

of the hydro-therapy section of the Marwari Relief Society's Hospital; and, as Gandhiji takes a keen interest in nature-cure methods, the Society has sent him here for a short time.

Omprakash Gupta conversed with Gandhiji for several hours during the day, and several times the latter had to remind him that he was feeling exhausted. Omprakash Babu wanted to discuss some personal matters with him. At one time, I heard Gandhiji plainly asking him if he had come to dedicate himself wholly to village work here. The real test was this: Was he prepared to continue the work even if Gandhiji were not there? If not, then he had evidently come because the latter's presence provided a sort of intoxication (*nesha*). It was not his business to provide such sop for anyone.

Others also came on interview which were unnecessarily prolonged and left Gandhiji in an exhausted condition. Some of these interviews could not be prevented by me as the workers were old associates who had come from long distances.

Manu Gandhi, daughter of Jaisukhlal Gandhi, Gandhiji's nephew, arrived in Srirampur today.

At prayer time, Gandhiji felt too tired to make any speech.

The news had gone round that he was about to begin a tour on foot through the affected villages of Noakhali and Tipperah, and therefore several Press representatives and photographers arrived here today. I met them in a private conference and communicated to them the following instructions from Gandhiji:

1. They should seek the permission of the villagers before staying anywhere. They should not be a burden to anyone.

2. They should help one another and share news without reserve.

3. They would not be allowed to accompany him in the walking tour, as Gandhiji did not want to travel with a large retinue.

4. He wished that the correspondents should make independent observation in the surrounding villages and try to find out if evacuees were returning home or not, and what

was the effect of Gandhiji's presence on Muslim villagers.

An important letter was sent today to the Secretary of the Bengal Provincial Congress Committee. Already on the 29th of last month, I had written to the Vice-President of the same body to make a public statement to the effect that the number of persons killed was much lower than what had appeared in the Press in October. The latter had said in a contemporary public statement that the figure was nearly five thousand. But detailed enquiries had shown that it was no more than three hundred, although that was not the worst part of the disturbances. The cause of this exaggeration was easily understandable. If there were ten members in a family, and if only one had been murdered when the disturbances took place, then those who survived, escaped in different directions. And when they reached places of safety, each looked upon himself as the sole survivor and gave a high figure for those who had been killed. There was thus a multiplication of error. Now that the real facts were very nearly known, Gandhiji was anxious that the truth should be publicly stated. The Vice-President of the Congress Committee however felt otherwise. He wrote back to say that the figures in his October statement had been described as approximate. Gandhiji had called for the necessary Press cuttings from the Secretary. After going through them, I wrote to him under authority that it was true the figures were approximate, but there was nothing in the statement to indicate, by way of caution, that there might have also been error in the collection of data. A public worker of the Vice-President's standing had to be much more careful in respect of every word in a public utterance.

In the morning, while I was administering his daily bath, Gandhiji spoke to me of his own accord about the happenings of the 17th. Ever since that day, no word had passed on this subject between him and me.

He wished to learn from me as well as from Parasuram 'if Sushila Nayyar had fallen in our estimation' (*Tumhare nazar me gir gai hai?*), on account of that day's incident. I said, I could speak for myself, not for Parasuram. She had undoubtedly fallen, and the reason was this. No person however great had the right to disturb him as Sushila had apparently done. Gandhiji then said, 'Supposing she did so with a good intention, perhaps to help me in my own work? She may have been suggesting certain steps even for my sake, not for her own; even then, would you say she was wrong?'

I said, 'Yes, even then. If she felt that you were contemplating a wrong step, she might have offered her suggestions and then left you free to decide.'

Gandhiji said, 'She is against my plan of tour on foot in the present condition of my health. She thinks that, at least, one old companion who knows all about my personal needs should accompany me, and she offered her own services. She suggested that it would not be safe to depend on new workers like you and Parasuram, who know so little about my physical requirements.'

I said, 'If I had been in her position, I would have placed my views fully before you and left you free to decide. If the decision had not been favourable, I would have waited patiently until you discovered your error.'

After I spoke, Gandhiji repeated the substance of my views in his own language in order to make sure that he had understood me rightly.

*Srirampur, Friday, 20-12-1946:*

The work in Srirampur was becoming heavier and heavier every day. So, when Manu joined us permanently, both Parasuram and myself felt greatly relieved. She has taken charge of the bath and much of the cooking, with the result that we can devote more time to office work.

When I reached Gandhiji's room even before 4 in the morning, I heard him talking to Manu in a low voice in his own bed, where she had gone to sleep at night. After prayer, Gandhiji called me and said that I should get ready a report on recent happenings in Noakhali. Things looked as if he would have to engage in a battle with the League Government in Bengal. He admitted that the non-violence which the whole country had so far evinced was non-violence of the weak. But he had cherished the hope that people would realize from experience that the non-violent method

## THE DARKNESS DEEPENS 101

was more effective than violence in actual practice. This expectation had, however, not materialized. The path which henceforth lay before him was the path which could only be trodden by the brave. Gandhiji mentioned the name of Jesus Christ, and said that Jesus was the 'Prince of passive resisters'. Indeed, there was no passivity in Him and His whole life was an epic of intensely heroic action.

Referring to Manu, he said, that he had been telling her how he personally felt that he had reached the end of one chapter in his old life and a new one was about to begin. He was thinking of a bold and original experiment, whose 'heat will be great'. And only those who realized this, and were prepared to remain at their posts, should be with him. Manu would look after his personal needs, while one more worker would be needed to deal with the Urdu correspondence and that would complete his new staff.

During bath, I said to Gandhiji, 'You have drawn me into your company and given me many liberties. If you pardon me, may I ask you a question? Did you slap Sushila the other day?', for I had not been able to get over the painful recollection of the two sharp sounds which had proceeded from within the room.

Gandhiji's face wore a sad smile and he said, 'No, I did not beat her, I beat my own forehead. When I was twenty-five years old, I once beat my own son; but that was the last time.

'Sushila is a gifted girl, and is of service to me in many ways. When she learnt about my proposed journey on foot, she began to argue against it. We had been talking ever since 2.30 in the night. I explained to her how my mission was going to take me to a lonesome journey through the Muslim villages. Muslims had been taught to regard me as an arch-enemy of Islam. If I was to overcome that feeling, I could only do so by entering into their midst in the most unprotected condition possible. I would have to depend upon them completely for all my needs and they would be free to do with me what they liked. But she was insistent that some old companion who knew about my personal requirements should be in my company. Then I grew impatient. If I could not convince one like her, who has known me for years, that the step was right, how could I hope to convince others? And I beat my own forehead as I wept.'

During midday, as Gandhiji lay resting with a mud-pack over his forehead and his closed eyes, a French journalist came along and sought an interview. I spoke to Gandhiji about him, when he agreed to give him a few minutes. He however asked me to explain to the visitor why he was lying down, and if he was prepared to meet him in that condition and not take it as an insult.

When Raymond Cartier entered the room and was announced, Gandhiji greeted the former with a 'Comment allez-vouz?' Cartier was agreeably surprised and replied in French. Gandhiji broke into a hearty laughter and said that that was all the French which he remembered. He had read French at school but had managed to forgot all of it.

When Cartier introduced himself by saying that he was a journalist by profession and came from Paris, Gandhiji told him how he was an admirer of *Les Miserables*, and how Valjean still appeared to him 'in an unfading light'. The picture of Valjean crawling through the drains of Paris came back to him. He had himself visited Paris, and while returning from the Round Table Conference had wanted to find lodging in the poorest quarters. But this had not been possible. He had however seen the slums, and it was humiliating to see the picture of poverty in the heart of a city which claimed to lead the world.

Cartier asked him what he thought about the present condition of Europe. Gandhiji said that he felt miserable about it, for the last war had apparently failed to disillusion men with regard to violence. 'If this dependence upon violence continues, the world will end by destroying itself.'

'Would you advise us, Europeans, to follow non-violence; we who are the children of violence?'

Gandhiji replied that if Europe did not change its path, humanity was faced only by the prospect of destruction. But even in Europe, there was an undercurrent of thought which was against war.

Cartier then asked him, how could France survive if it did not defend herself against the Germans? Gandhiji retorted by saying that the Maginot Line had failed in its purpose. Cartier remarked that the fault was not in the principle but in some technical imperfection. 'Yes,' Gandhiji quickly replied, 'that is what I mean. Unless you can beat Hitler by superior violence, you cannot obtain victory. But then Hitlerism wins. That can be liquidated only by something which is its opposite in character, not by superiority of arms.'

*Srirampur, Sunday, 22-12-1946:*
This being Kasturba Day, Gandhiji was up at 2.30 a.m. and worked till prayer time. Prayer began at 4.15 a.m. Sushila Nayyar, Manu Gandhi and Parasuram did the reading of the *Bhagabad Gita*. While this was going on, Pyarelal dropped in with an English friend. Sushila left at about ten.

The Provincial Muslim League of Bihar has sent a printed report of the riots in that province. I went through a substantial portion of it before Gandhiji's bath, while he has already finished reading the report. Later on, he told me that even if half of what was written in that report were true, and if the Congress Ministers of Bihar had actually concealed anything from him, then it meant that the end of his life had been reached (*meri zindagi chali gai*). He would, in that case, have to go to Bihar and fast unto death. He had already lived a long life and had done more than an average man's share of work; it did not matter if the time had come for him to depart.

I argued with him that as Jawaharlal Nehru was coming soon, there should be no hurry, for he would get all the facts in a few days' time. But Gandhiji was restless. He said, the visit was yet a week away, and that was a long way off. The Musim League had made conditions hot, and the iron must be struck while it was yet hot. The Congress Ministers of Bihar ought to have taken up the challenge of the League immediately; but they were procrastinating.

He then said that if he left for Bihar, it would mean a great blow to Noakhali. 'I do not know', he continued, 'what the Hindus will do then. Even if it comes to wholesale migration, let them do it. My place is now in Bihar. I shall go there practically as a representative of the Muslims to find out the truth.'

Today, I received a touching letter from Sushila Nayyar in which she tried to explain, from her own point of view, what had happened in the morning of the 17th. The letter is reproduced below in part:

'At night while reading Bapu's diary I read "I had a curious dream". I casually asked him what it was. He did not say and I kept quiet.

'At three o'clock the next morning, I woke up with the noise of Bapu jumping in bed. He said he was very cold and was taking exercise to warm up. After that, he asked me if I was awake and started telling me of his curious dream. After the dream he started explaining how his present step was a *tapascharya* (penance) for him, and how he was going through inconveniences. On the previous day, I had remarked that God did and would send him helpers in whatever he did.... In a short note I asked him if I would be allowed to come with him. I mentioned that what he had said about *tapascharya* and what I had said about God sending him help were not contradictory and tried to explain it. He answered with irritation that he had tried to explain things to me but had not succeeded. ... I could see that he was getting worked up. So ... I walked away. Suddenly I heard him slap his forehead. I rushed back and stopped him....

'I am completely unnerved.... I came yesterday with great trepidation. Bapu had asked me to come for Gita.... He again raised the topic this morning and I found that my self-control has not returned as yet.'

Sushila had left Srirampur in the morning in tears.

*Srirampur, Monday, 23-12-1946:*

Early in the morning, at 5 o'clock, Gandhiji handed a note to me. It was Monday, his day of silence. He had written, 'I do not know what God is doing to me or through me. If you have the time and inclination I would like you to walk to Sushila at daybreak and return after passing some time with her and learning all about her requirements and her health. You can give her the whole of our conversation about her without reserve. The rest you will know from her if she cares to tell you. You can show this to her if you wish. If you propose to shoulder this burden, you will act as the spirit moves you. Don't work beyond your capacity.'

I made ready to go. In the meanwhile, Arun Datta a volunteer had come from the Nandigram refugee camp where out of 1,800 evacuees, Government rations had been stopped for 300. The Government were trying to force the evacuees to return home. Gandhiji gave them the following instruction, 'I do not want them to hunger strike at present. Let there be a full cause ready for such a strike. The question therefore is, are those who get their rations prepared to share with those (300) what they get? If they are, these should take their share while the matter is being prosecuted.'

The party then left for Nandigram in order to carry out Gandhiji's instructions.

I started for Changirgaon where Sushila is posted at 7.30 a.m. with some fruits for her and returned at eleven.

*Srirampur, Wednesday, 25-12-1946:*

A telegram came from Jawaharlal Nehru in which he said that he would reach Srirampur on the 27th evening.

Members of the Friends' Service Unit have sent a bag of Christmas presents to us. The bag contained cigarettes, playing cards, a pair of canvas slippers, a towel, soap etc. Gandhiji seemed to be in a happy and playful mood today. He asked us to spread our gifts on the mat and then started distributing them among the volunteers here and elsewhere. The packet of cigarettes was a problem; but then suddenly Gandhiji asked me to keep it for Jawaharlal Nehru.

Rabindramohan Sengupta, Trailokya Chakraverty, Ananta De, Santimoy Dutt and Pratul Chaudhuri of the Revolutionary Socialist Party of India paid a visit to Gandhiji and wished to place their services at his disposal. Trailokya Babu confessed that, so far, all of us had failed to find a way out of the terrible fear which held the common man in its grip. It was time therefore to try Gandhiji's method of instilling courage before the country could earn its right to freedom.

Another visitor named Sisir Kumar Ghosh presented a purse of a hundred rupees to Gandhiji and asked him how courage could be instilled in the heart of the common man without, at the same time, antagonizing the Muslims. Gandhiji advised him to experiment along the pure non-violent way. He said, any organization along lines of violence would succeed in creating a race for armaments even if it were on a small scale. This would prove disastrous for India in the end. Bengal had tried the method of violence for a long while. The bravery of the revolutionaries was beyond question, but it had failed to instil courage in the mind of the common man. But although the non-violence of the past twenty-five years had been of an indifferent quality, yet nobody could deny that it had succeeded in elevating the character of the whole nation to a certain extent. The only way he could suggest was organization along non-violent lines.

The Muslim League seems to be carrying on a systematic campaign for driving Gandhiji out of Noakhali. A post card reached us today from the 'Office of the Feni Sub-divisional Muslim League', which contained a copy of the resolution passed by that body. It said, 'It is appreciated that Mr. Gandhi's presence in Bihar is much more useful than at Noakhali where the situation is normal. He is therefore requested to leave for Bihar.' Gandhiji wrote back in reply:

Gentlemen,

I have just received your post card scribbled out in ink and thank you for your advice. I am unable to follow your advice which is definitely based on ignorance of facts. In the first place, I know that the situation is not normal here and that in so far as I can contribute to the Bihar problem I have to inform you that such influence as I have on Bihar can be and is being efficiently exercised from Srirampur.

Yours sincerely,
M. K. Gandhi.

*Srirampur, Thursday, 26-12-1946:*
The Secretary of the Ramganj Relief Committee came to report that very bad rice was being issued to the refugees that day, and many had refused to accept rations. When samples of the rice were produced, Gandhiji asked the old lady of the house, our 'Pishima', to cook it and give us her opinion. The latter did so, and when we tried to eat the rice we found it impossible, for many of the grains were rotten and black. A sample had, in the meanwhile, been sent for examination to the Superintendent of the Government Auxiliary Hospital at Ramganj, from where the report came that it was 'quite unfit for human consumption'. Gandhiji then expressed his opinion that if all the rice supplied was of this character, it had to be refused. There was no question of hunger strike; the refugees should approach the authorities concerned, try to find what their difficulties were and then demand a supply of rice which could be eaten. Even if the Government failed to supply sufficient rice of good quality, then the refugees should accept as much of it as available, provided it sufficed to keep body and soul together, and give the Government a chance of mending matters within a fortnight. But if things did not improve, then there would be valid reason for protest in the form of complete refusal of rations.

*Srirampur, Friday, 27-12-1946:*
The following letter was handed over to me for immediate despatch to Calcutta:

Dear Hamiduddin Sahib,
Nirmal Babu read to me your writing in the *Azad* of the 14th instant. It staggered me and I asked him kindly to give me its literal translation. If there is any incorrectness you will please send me your correction. I say it staggered me, because you had left an impression on me that you had entirely realised my sincerity and my usefulness not merely for the Hindu inhabitants of the district but equally for the Muslim inhabitants. Assuming the accuracy of the translation, your article is an indictment against me. Indeed, most of us were under the impression that while Shamsuddin

Sahib was leaving for a few days to meet the Chief Minister, you would be staying behind to continue his work and help the peace committees that were just then being formed. But the next day, I learned with sorrow that owing to some affliction of your eyes you had to leave abruptly with Shamsuddin Sahib. What had happened in the meanwhile to warrant what I have called your indictment I do not know. Why do you in common with many advisers advise me to leave Noakhali and go to Bihar or somewhere else?

I have not come to East Bengal to hold an enquiry. I have come to make my humble contribution to a lasting and heart peace between the two communities. I think that I made this statement during the speeches I had made in your presence. Why then the sudden change betrayed by the article in question? Do you not think that after the exuberant regard you showed for me, I had the right to expect from you a friendly and personal enquiry from me to inform me of the change and giving the grounds for the change? Perhaps on reflection, you will discover in your very article valid reason for my longing to be in Noakhali in preference to Bihar. How can I test the efficacy and soundness of my *ahimsa* except in a place where even the loudest protestations of trust in my professions can be so short-lived as in your case?

You are right when you say, 'In Mr. Gandhi's opinion, the condition in Noakhali is not yet such that Hindus can shoulder the responsibility of returning to their homes.' I have chapter and verse to show why the Hindu refugees who proved themselves deficient in personal courage are reluctant to go back to their homes. The peace committees which you left in the process of formation are not in working order.

The Ministers and Parliamentary Secretaries would not return to their work of seeing the committees doing their duty. I urge you for the sake of the League Ministry in whose efficiency and goodness I am at least as much interested as you ever can be. Believe me, I have not come to East Bengal for the purpose of finding fault with the League. I have come in order to induce it by my conduct to shed its complacency and give solid work for the sake of itself and

India. For I believe that if you and I can produce in Bengal the right atmosphere, the whole of India will follow.

You say again, 'If he (Gandhi) had issued a statement about the real nature of the happenings, perhaps the atmosphere would have cleared to a large extent. His silence with reference to this matter raises suspicion in the minds of many.' Why this insinuation when the fact stares you in the face that I am not in a position to speak in praise of what has been and is being done on behalf of the Bengal Government? If you will care to study the thing, you will appreciate restraint instead of coaxing me to speak.

You are again right when you say, 'Mr. Gandhi does not wish to leave for Bihar.' But your reasons for reluctance are wholly wrong. 'My trusted Bihari followers' have indeed kept me informed of the happenings there. The information they give is wholly contrary to what you believe. In common with all, the Bihar Government deplore the tragic happenings. But they claim that they have acquired control over the turbulent elements and are straining every nerve to give satisfaction to the afflicted.

It will not serve the cause of peace if I went to Bihar and found the Bihar Muslim League's report to be largely imaginary and the Bihar Government's conduct substantially honourable, humane and just. I am not anxious to give them a certificate of good conduct as I am to give you, much though you may not want it. My spare diet and contemplated fast, you know well, were against the Bihar misdoings. I could not take such a step in the matter of Noakhali misdoings. It pains me to think that you a seasoned lawyer should not see the obvious.

I assure you that I am not guilty of 'importing numberless volunteers from outside to serve his (mine) object'. In the first place, I have not imported numberless volunteers. In the second place, my object is not what you have been pleased to insinuate in the same paragraph. Let me tell you that for the fulfilment of my object, I do not need any volunteers here except myself. If you really think that their presence is a menace to the peace of Noakhali, the Government have but to say that they are a danger and to ˑrve a notice on them to quit, and I assure you that without a murmur they would leave this district. From this undertaking, I and one of my company, whose name I need not disclose at this stage, are excepted. You will be astonished to learn that, dear as they are all to me, and valuable as I count their services to the nation, I told them in this mission of mine, I had no need to have any associate with me, for the quickest way to fruition required no protection or co-operation save what God sent. Such is my conception of the working of *ahimsa*. I hope that before the Government takes the adumbrated action they will depute an officer of their choice or trust to find out from me or them the kind of work they are doing. Their life is an open book. There is nothing hidden or underground about their activities.

Permit me to give you my impression that your writing bristles with unprovable and reckless statements without regard to facts. I have noticed only some of them.

As it is, my letter has become much longer than I had sketched in my mind but as I proceeded I could not shorten it if I was to give you some conception of my deep grief. If you will know more, I suggest to you that you should take the trouble of coming to me and passing with me half an hour or so and cross-examine me on the charges you have framed against me.

This letter is not an open letter as yours is. I have written only for you, cherishing the hope that it may perhaps appeal to you as coming from a well-wisher open to conviction.

Yours sincerely,<br>M. K. Gandhi.

I left Srirampur for Ramganj early in the morning and handed over the above letter to the Deputy Superintendent of Police for despatch to Calcutta. Then I went to the officer in charge of relief and rations. We went together with a few representatives of the public to inspect the bags of rice in the godown. The public representatives were invited to choose the lowest grade of broken rice which could be accepted as an emergency measure for the current fortnight. The Officer was prepared to supply that grade of rice as far as possible from his stock and supplement it with wheat flour. It appears the matter will be set right soon.

While I was away, Parasuram approached Gandhiji and unburdened his mind on certain private matters. It will be remembered that Gandhiji had asked for his opinion regarding the happenings of the 17th morning just as he had done from me.

Jawaharlal Nehru, Acharya Kripalani, Sucheta Kripalani, Shankarrao Deo and Mridula Sarabhai arrived between half-past eleven and half-past twelve at night.

*Srirampur, 28th to 30th December 1946:*
Crowds have been gathering ever since early morning and special arrangements have been made for regulating them. Jawaharlal Nehru and the rest sat in conference with Gandhiji till eleven. They left at 12.45 and came back again at 2. The conference continued till prayer time. Prayer had been arranged in the grounds of the school. The crowd was fairly big for these parts. Gandhiji spoke on the ideals of the Indian National Congress and how it differed from the ideals of the Muslim League and the Hindu Mahasabha.

Jawaharlal, Kripalani and others left Srirampur after seven on the 30th. They proceeded to Madhupur on foot, from where jeeps carried them to Feni, the airport.

During these three days, the Congress leaders held long discussions with Gandhiji. I kept myself away for most part of the time, as Pyarelal had come and was in attendance. On one occasion when I was in the room for a short while, I heard Jawaharlal saying, 'There is now a Hindu political India just as they have made a Muslim political India.' He further said with emphasis that almost everyone, including Gandhiji and himself, had been forced almost into a communal position. I heard Kripalani flinging back, 'What are you talking! You know in your heart of hearts, we are not communal. Then why should you talk like that?'

After discussion with the leaders, Gandhiji prepared an instruction for the Working Committee. This was typed by me instead of Parasuram and copies handed over to Jawaharlal Nehru and others.

Gandhiji wrote:

'During its unbroken career of sixty years the Congress has been invariably and progressively representative of all the communities—Hindus, Muslims, and others. It has been also progressively representative of the masses. That it has always had a number of hypocrites is but an ode to these two among its many virtues. If those who represent these two virtues are found to be in a hopeless minority, they should lodge their protest and leave the Congress and influence public opinion from outside. Then only will they be true servants of the nation. Therefore at this critical period I hold it to be necessary for the Working Committee to give the proper, unequivocal lead to the Congress by laying down these propositions:—

1. It is now perhaps late to cry off the Constituent Assembly though I hold it still to be the best course to make the Congress position absolutely clear.

2. The second best is to accept the Cabinet Mission Statement with the joint interpretation of it between themselves and Qaid-e-Azam Jinnah.

3. It must be clearly understood that it is open to any Congress individual or unit to declare his group's or province's secession from the Congress stand, which the Congress should be free to accept whilst still openly guiding the seceding element. This will be in accordance with the Cabinet's position that they will not compel any group or province.

'The result of this would be that the members of Section A would prepare a full constitution in terms of the Cabinet Mission's Statement and B and C Sections would have to frame what they can in spite of the seceders as at present conceived. Assam in the east and Frontier Province in the west, the Sikhs in the Punjab and may be Baluchistan.

'It may be that the British Government will recognise or set up another Constituent Assembly. If they do, they will damn themselves for ever. They are bound when a constitution is framed in terms of the Cabinet Mission's stand to leave the rest to fate, every vestige of British authority being wiped out and British soldiers retiring from India never to return.

'This position of the Congress is in no way to be interpreted as playing completely into Qaid-e-Azam Jinnah's hands. And if this he considers to be what he meant, the Congress will be thanked by the world for giving Qaid-e-Azam Jinnah a universally acceptable and inoffensive formula for his Pakistan. The Congress dare not shirk the right thing because it completely coincides with his creed.

'The Constitution will be for whole India. It will have to contain a specific clause showing in what way it will be open to the boycotters to avail themselves of the Constitution.'

## XIII. A FRIEND'S PARTING

*Srirampur, Tuesday, 31-12-1946:*

Yesterday, when I was away from the camp, Parasuram had spoken for an hour with Gandhiji on a certain private question. He had also told Gandhiji that I held a similar view to his own, but had refrained from giving expression to it because I did not, in any way, 'wish to disturb him in the work he had undertaken for the sake of Bengal'. At seven in the evening, Gandhiji therefore sent for me and asked me if Parasuram's report was correct. We were together till 8-30. I began to speak as usual in Hindi, but with Gandhiji's permission soon slipped into English. The following is a revised translation of my Bengali diary of that date.

I said to Gandhiji, I have deep reverence for you from a particular point of view. I have always looked upon you as one of the great pathfinders in human history. Men have been groping for ages past for some effective means of bringing about social change without recourse to violence. You are one of the pioneers in this respect. For many years I have read your writings with care and have formed a more or less concrete picture of your thoughts on the subject. I have also tried to observe how it works out in collective practice in which common men are involved.

There are in Bengal numerous workers who try to follow your teachings. They spin regularly, practise all kinds of austerities in personal life, but, instead of being able to conduct experiments in collective non-violence, often settle down into an individualistic practice of a set of non-violent rituals. They thus lose all effectiveness in the social or political field.

Those who thus practise austerities have not often taken to it because it is necessary in the pursuit of an ideal; but, in at least some cases, it springs from a mere love of austerities, or from the desire of finding favour in your eyes. As such, the austerity and humility which they exhibit before you become false. Repression does good only when it is a joyous enterprise undertaken for a noble cause. But under the above circumstances, the end becomes vague and over-shadowed by the means; with the result that such persons try to find compensation through other channels. A morbid hankering after fame and public approval may step in, or the personality may begin to crack under a load which nobody called upon it to bear. Thus, your love for asceticism results in an injury to the personality of those who do not know how to preserve a sense of social responsibility, which you personally never lose sight of.

Secondly, I have seen you lose temper and become sentimental at times; and have felt drawn closer to you on that account. If you had been completely free from all weaknesses, I would have perhaps revered you from a distance but would never have felt drawn close to you as I do today.

Parasuram has a complaint against the way in which you deal with different workers, how you seem to have personal preferences and fail to chastise when necessary. He has made this a cause of complaint against you. I do not do so. I have looked upon this part of your life as a necessary element of play to save you from the influence of the cold and barren atmosphere in which you have to work in the rest of your life. If you had tried to root out every trace of softness from your character and even succeeded in doing so, you would have become more distant from us from the human point of view. So, when you hold the reins a little loose, and give way to anger, for instance, I do not look upon it as a matter for complaint.

But there is another side of the picture too.

There are many women, who, when they are in love, try to convert their object of love into a plaything. Sometimes they deal hard blows upon the object and sometimes they invite similar blows in return. There is a secret satisfaction in such play and in exclusive possession. That is an expression of our sexual instinct.

Among the women who are associated with you in social work, I have observed an attitude bordering on this kind. When women love men in normal life, a part of their psychological hunger is satisfied by the pleasure which they derive in the physical field. But when women pay their homage of love to you, there can be no such satisfaction, with the result that when they come close to you personally, their mind becomes slightly warped. Of course, all of us are neurotics to a more or less extent. But the effect of your contact has an undoubtedly dangerous influence upon some of your associates, whether male or female.

Parasuram is a simple, straightforward man. He has told you from his own point of view what he considers wrong. Although I do not share his opinion about right or wrong, yet I felt sympathy for his point of view.

Gandhiji listened in silence and when I had finished said, 'Your hint is that—should be sent away from here.' Of course, that was never my intention although that was an important item in Parasuram's demands.

Parasuram broke in by saying that whatever Gandhiji's attitude may be, as a common man he would say that he should give no occasion for any one to misunderstand him. If reflections were cast on Gandhiji's personal character, the cause for which he stood would itself suffer. This was something he could not bear personally. While at school, he had once come to blows with mates when they had cast aspersions against Gandhiji's character. Moreover, had he not himself promised to his co-workers in Sevagram that he would keep women workers away from his immediate company?

In explaining his position, Gandhiji said that it was indeed true that he permitted women workers to use his bed, this being undertaken as a spiritual experiment at times. Even if there were no trace of passion in him of which he was conscious, it was not unlikely that a residue might be left over, and that would make trouble for the girls who took part in his experiment. He had asked them if, even unconsciously, he had been responsible for evoking the least shade of evil sentiment in their heart. This 'experiment', as he called it, had been objected to by distinguished co-workers like Narahari (Parekh) and Kishorlal (Mashruwala); and one of their grounds of complaint had been based on the possible repercussions which the example of a responsible leader like him might have upon other people.

When Gandhiji finished his personal explanation, I ended by saying that unless I had known how great he was, and unless I had a purely objective attitude towards his life, I might have given way to sentimentality and subscribed to some of the charges laid against him by Parasuram.

Gandhiji then asked me to help Parasuram in framing his complaints in writing.

*Srirampur, Wednesday, 1-1-1947:*
Parasuram typed out an enormous letter running over ten foolscap pages, in which he expressed his views with great clarity and suggested certain changes in our life here.

As this was the last day of our stay at Srirampur, I got up at two and wrote out my personal diary which has been quoted under yesterday's date. A pretty large amount of correspondence had accumulated, and all through the day, I tried to clear up the arrears of work.

Charu Chandra Chaudhuri of the Khadi Pratisthan came with a statement of accounts in which it appeared that more than one lac of rupees had been subscribed by the public for Gandhiji's work in Noakhali. The expenses incurred up to date, amounted to a little over Rs. 8,000 in all. This had been advanced by the Khadi Pratisthan of Sodpur. Gandhiji did not wish to burden the Khadi Pratisthan with these expenses and made arrangements for repaying the advance out of the sum contributed by the public.

*Chandipur, Thursday, 2-1-1947:*
Early in the morning about a dozen volunteers arrived in order to carry all our belongings to the next halting station at Chandipur. All the things had already been made up into packages.

Just before Gandhiji left, the members of the household gathered together and bade him farewell. We started at 7-30 a.m., and as Gandhiji walked across the paddy fields recently laid bare after the harvest had been gathered in, he halted for a few minutes at the residence of the Chakraverty family in the southern extremity of Srirampur. In that house, not a single hut had been left standing by the miscreants. Chandipur was reached at about 9 a.m., although the distance was no more than 3 miles.

The day was spent in arranging our things at the residence of the Mazumdars. Prayer was held in the open space north of the tank at 4-30 p.m. Gandhiji took his meals after this, and then proceeded towards Changirgaon where Sushila Nayyar is posted.

Before leaving Srirampur, Gandhiji had written a reply to Parasuram's letter, in which he said·

'I have read your letter with great care. I began it at 3 a.m., finished reading it at 4 a.m. It contains half-truths which are dangerous. You wronged me, the parties you mention, yourself and the cause by suppressing from them and me your opinion about them.

'I cannot concede your demands. The other points you raise do not make much appeal to me.

'Since such is your opinion and there is a conflict of ideals and you yourself wish to be relieved, you are at liberty to leave me today. That will be honourable and truthful. I like your frankness and boldness. My regard for your ability as a typist and shorthand writer remains undiminished and I was looking forward to taking a hand in bringing out your other qualities. I am sorry that it cannot be.

'My advice to you is that you should confer with Pyarelalji and Sushilabehn. You should take Kanubhai's guidance in shaping your future. I shall always be interested in your future and shall be glad to hear from you when you feel like writing to me. Finally let me tell you that you are at liberty to publish whatever wrong you have noticed in me and my surroundings. Needless to say you can take what money you need to cover your expenses.'

A few days later, Gandhiji perhaps did an injustice to Parasuram, when in a letter to another friend, he wrote, 'Parasuram has left... because he did not believe in my ideals.... The immediate cause I think was that Manu shared the same bed with me. He thought that it was improper not because, as he said, there was anything wrong with me or Manu, because he knew that she was in the place of grand-daughter to me, but because it would be a bad example for young men, for example, like himself.... I believe that everybody in the camp knows that Manu is sharing my cot and, in any case, I do not want to do anything in secrecy. I am not advertising the thing. It is a sacred thing to me. But those who want to see everything wrong about me are at liberty at any time they like to advertise the fact and give it what colour they like.'

This was completely unfair to Parasuram, because Parasuram's complaint as summarised in my own diary or in his subsequent letter was quite different and it was inspired by the deepest of loyalty to the cause for which Gandhiji stood. Only, his point of view was the point of view of the common man; he did not realize how contact with men and women on a common level might be a spiritual need for Gandhiji. My belief is that while writing the above letter, Gandhiji did not perhaps have Parasuram's letter before him and was evidently reporting from memory, which did not serve him right at least on this particular occasion.

## XIV. THE PILGRIMAGE

AFTER his stay at Srirampur for nearly a month and a half, Gandhiji began to feel that the next step which he should take was to try and live among the Muslim peasants in their own villages and convince them by his friendly acts that he was as much concerned about their welfare as of the Hindus. His original idea was to set forth on a walking tour unaccompanied by any of his companions and depend upon what help might actually be given to him by the villagers themselves. But as this was likely to be too uncertain in character, it was decided that he should travel on foot from village to village, meet people in their own homes and in his prayer meetings, and see what came out of it ultimately.

With this end in view, he left Chandipur on the 7th of January 1947, to encamp at one village for one night and carry with him his message of peace and goodwill among men. During the early morning prayer on that day, Gandhiji asked Manu to sing his favourite Gujarati hymn entitled *Vaishnav jana to tene kahiye*: 'The true Vaishnav is he who feels the sufferings of others'. He also said that the word Vaishnav should be replaced by Muslim, Isai (i.e. Christian) now and then during the chorus. As the little group sang, we suddenly heard Gandhiji himself joining the chorus from within his curtained bed. The pitch of his voice was low, but the tune was quite correct. His voice could be heard above our own.

A few days before Gandhiji thus started on his tour on foot, he had received a letter from Sarojini Naidu who had come to Santiniketan in Bengal, but had left without even trying to meet him, for it was Gandhiji's express desire that he should be left alone as far as possible.

Sarojini Devi wrote:
26-12-1946

"UTTARAYAN"
Santiniketan, Bengal.
This is not a letter, it is an affirmation of love and faith.

Had it been possible I should have tried to reach you if only for a moment. You will I know approve of my leaving Bengal without even making the effort. I neither need to see you nor speak with you, because you dwell in my vision and your message sings itself to the world through my heart.

Beloved Pilgrim, setting out on your pilgrimage of love and hope, 'God with God' in the beautiful Spanish phrase. I have no fear for you—only faith in your mission.

Sarojini.

Many weeks afterwards, when Gandhiji discovered this letter among his old papers, he forthwith wanted to destroy it, but I held him back and begged the letter from him. He agreed, but on condition, it would never be published; for, as he said, the letter was no more than praise for his work, which he did not need. But I took it away from him with the assurance that it would not be published during his life-time without permission.

This act of Gandhiji reminded me of what he had once said with reference to his old correspondence. He had destroyed many letters in South Africa, because when he depended upon the opinion of others in order to assure himself about the rightness of his path, it was like depending upon an adventitious aid. Truth had to stand on its own strength; and so he had burnt the letters just as he had removed many an impediment which had likewise come in his way.

The pilgrimage which Gandhiji thus undertook, carried him from village to village where he met Hindu men and women and also some Muslims, who, on the whole, avoided his prayer meetings except in certain localities. Gandhiji's advice to the Hindus uniformly was that they should purify their own hearts of fear and prejudice, and also set right their social and economic relations with others; for only could this internal purification give them adequate courage, as well as the moral right, to live amidst a people who now considered them to be their exploiters and enemies.

The Hindus had, first of all, to remove the taint of untouchability, and to this end, he advised every woman to have her food and drink consecrated by the touch of a so-called untouchable before she partook of her meals everyday. This was the least penance we could do for having sinned against one section of our brethren. In the same manner, he advised them to fraternize with Muslim women and rescue them from the thraldom of the purdah. For, as he said, true purdah resided in the heart and had little to do with its external observance. If half of a population remained paralysed through an ignorant and evil custom, how could we ever aspire to be free and great?

In a speech on the 4th of January, he said that he had not come to talk to the people of politics, nor to weaken the influence of the Muslim League and increase that of the Congress, but in order to talk to them of little things in their daily life. Ever since he had come to India thirty years ago, he had been telling people of these common, little things which, if properly attended to, would change the face of the land and create a heaven out of the pitiable condition in which we found ourselves living today.

Even to the evacuees, Gandhiji's message was uniformly one of courage and fortitude. He said that he held very strong views on the question of charity and thought that it was wrong both to accept as well as to offer a free gift to anyone. If the evacuees got into the habit of dependence on public charity, it would prove disastrous in the end. They might, of course, ask the Government to provide them with manual work of one kind or another against the food which was being provided for them, but it was below human dignity to accept any aid without labouring for it.

On the 8th of February 1947, when there was a proposal for closing down refugee camps, Gandhiji woke up at night and wrote the following letter to the Magistrate of the district:

'This is the letter I promised you when you were good enough to see me yesterday.

'I am quite clear that you should not abruptly stop rations until due notice (at least one month) of their stoppage is given to the refugees that they will be stopped unless one of the specified items of work is done by them against the rations which should be adequate and medically fit for consumption. The items should include:

(1) Road construction or road repair for at least two hours per day, Sundays excluded.

(2) Removal of water hyacinth for the same period as in (1) under supervision.

(3) House building on their own vacated land for the same period as in (1), with material and tools supplied by the Government.

(4) Village reconstruction for the same period as in (1).

(5) Cleaning of tanks for the same period as in (1).

(6) Hand-spinning for four hours per day, cotton and wheel or takli being supplied by the Government; spinning to include ginning, carding or *tunai* or *punai*.

(7) Weaving for the same period as in (6), tools and accessories and yarn, double-twisted in the case of handspun, being supplied by the Government.

(8) Dhenki husking, same period as in (1), dhenkis being supplied by the Government.

(9) Oil-pressing out of cocoanut or seeds supplied by the Government.

(10) Any other village craft chosen by the Government or refugees approved by the Government for the period as in (1) or (6) as the case may be.

'Efficient working of the foregoing is wholly dependent upon a well-thought-out scheme capably managed by the Government. This is no famine measure. It is conceived wholly in the spirit of the maxim, no labour no food.

'No breakdown in transport or other Government machinery should stop the supply of rations to the helpless unfortunate sufferers.

'I would suggest that refugees who are not willing or otherwise incapable may be supplied rations against payment at fixed rates.

'The time for ploughing for the next crop is soon ebbing away. Therefore agricultural implements, bullocks and seeds have to be supplied at once or disaster may have to be faced.

'This was written at 2 a.m., and has not been seen by Shri Satish Chandra Dasgupta of Khadi Pratisthan. I would suggest your seeing and consulting him, since I am wholly ignorant of local conditions.'

To the refugees, he said again that it did not matter if their homes had been burnt or property looted, so long as they had the will to face the calamity with courage and determination. They should build up their lives anew on the foundation of their own labour. The refugees should bravely face the reality and learn some craft by which they could earn their bread and maintain their families. Those who did not labour but lived on the toils of others were thieves. No one was free from the obligation of voluntary labour in order to support himself.

One might feel tempted to ask, what could a few individuals do? The answer was that even if a few began to do the right thing, their example would prove infections and spread among the rest. If 40 crores of small bits of wood were tied together, it would be enough to build a bridge over which the mightiest army could pass. Similarly, if in India, forty crores of men developed new bonds of sympathy and mutual aid, they would be able to build up a new life in which every man, woman and child would prosper. The fear of hard work and of sudden calamities being thus removed, they would march a long way towards freedom. Then it would be said that their adversity had been converted into a gateway of freedom and prosperity.

Another day, his advice was with reference to the inhabitants of the district who had left their homes for better prospect in towns. They had received education and had become educators, doctors, engineers or traders. But what did the common villager gain from them, although they were the people who really paid for that type of education? He therefore wished that all villagers who had left for the towns should spend some weeks every year in serving their more unhappy brothers and sisters in the villages. The engineer should come and teach the people how to make cheap and healthy homes, how to clean the tanks and keep the roads in good repair, with resources within the command of the villagers themselves. The doctor should tell the people what to eat and how to avoid disease. And if everyone thus repaid his debt to those who were their very own, then the poor Muslims would no longer look upon them as men belonging to a different faith, but as friends whose presence enriched their lives instead of rendering them poorer.

One evening, the question was asked of him if the technique of non-violence could be employed for the defence of all kinds of property, whether morally or immorally acquired. The question arose because, in November, he had said in an interview with Sarat Chandra Bose that the Government should guarantee the safety of life, honour and also of the possessions of the Hindus. His answer was clear and he said that a moral weapon could only be employed in a moral cause, not elsewhere. The actual report is given below:

'Q. Is it possible to defend by means of non-violence anything which can only be gained through violence?

A. It followed from what he had said above that what was gained by violence could not only not be defended by non-violence, but the latter required the abandonment of ill-gotten gains.

Q. Is the accumulation of capital possible except through violence whether open or tacit?

A. Such accumulation by private persons was impossible except through violent means, but accumulation by the State in a non-violent society was not only possible, it was desirable and inevitable.

Q. Whether a man accuculates material or moral wealth he does so only through the help or co-operation of other members of society. Has he then the moral right to use any of it mainly for personal advantage?

A. The answer was an emphatic No.'

The implication of this brief answer was that anybody who lived in Noakhali, not on the goodwill of the common people but by dependence on exploitation, could not employ the instrument of non-violence for his own protection. He could do so *pari passu* with a transformation of his relations with his neighbours. Courage was needed for such a daring enterprise. This courage was moral. But physical courage was no less needed by the men and women in Noakhali, if they wished to live here in safety and honour, even if they did not belong to the exploiting class.

O the 1st of February 1947, Gandhiji wrote in reply to

the request of a friend who had asked him to send a 'trainer':

Dear ———,

I have no such trainer you ask for. My work lies in the opposite direction. Non-violent defence is the supreme self-defence, being infallible. No trainer is required for the purpose. And in this part of the country self-defence through some kind of arms is suicidal. Anyway, I am the wrong person to look for the purpose,

Yours sincerely,<br>M. K. Gandhi.

This point came out very well at a place called Jagatpur on the 10th of January 1947. There was a women's meeting in the afternoon when Gandhiji spoke to the audience about courage and the need of never surrendering one's honour even on pain of death. A gruesome sight was encountered at this meeting. A lady who had become slightly demented had come to attend the meeting. Her husband had been murdered during the disturbances along with several others, and then the bodies had been buried by the Muslims. She had recovered one long bone of her husband's body from the grave and carried this thing with her as she came to meet Gandhiji.

When the meeting was over, Gandhiji asked me to record the statements of some of the women who had been carried away during the disturbances. There was one brave girl who gave her whole story without reserve for Gandhiji's sake. What surprised me most was that the women of the Muslim household where she had been taken, seemed to have enjoyed the sight of a helpless woman being dragged into their midst. They had spoken encouragingly to the girl and asked her to become one of themselves, instead of exercising any control on their own men-folk.

On the following morning, I went to see the mother of this girl in the house of a neighbour. Their own home lay deserted after having been burnt. For some time past, the girl's mother had been trying to arrange the marriage of her daughter with a young man, and it was this man who had given the family shelter after the disaster. On questioning the mother, I learnt that there would be no difficulty about the marriage of her daughter in spite of what had taken place. The difficulty lay with regard to their house, which had to be all built up before they could think of the marriage ceremony.

With the mother's permission I then took the girl to the deserted home. On reaching the site, we saw nothing but denuded plinths and a few pieces of charred wood strewn here and there. The iron sheets had all been carried away by Muslim villagers. The place where two of her brothers had been thrown into the fire after murder lay beside the wall in the garden, and there I picked up charred bits of bone from among the charcoal. The girl described to me how the rioters came, what they did and so on; and then I put her the following question. Would she be able to come back here and live once more in the midst of scenes she could never forget? The girl remained silent for a little while, and then, with her eyes fixed in gaze on the distant fields, she calmly said, 'Yes, I can. What can they do to me now? They have done all that was in their power to do, and if they come again, perhaps I shall know how to save myself by dying.'

Weeks afterwards, I asked myself, where did this woman gain the strength which she displayed? She had come in contact with Gandhiji only once and had heard from him how a woman should lay down her life rather than surrender her honour. But could that speech have produced the courage which I witnessed on that winter morning? Personally, I would love to answer the question in a different manner. This unhappy girl was however fortunate in one respect. In spite of her accident, she had not forfeited the respect of one whom she loved; and it was perhaps this love, more than anything else, which gave her the courage to face the future bravely in spite of the fact that her past had been filled with sorrow and suffering.

Gandhiji's call for courage for the sake of re-ordering one's life as a preliminary step in the practice of non-violence, did not seem to bear much fruit. Perhaps the time at the disposal of the sufferers was too short, perhaps the claim upon their courage, whether physical or moral, was too great. Yet, Gandhiji hoped that if a few were forthcoming, the few in time would become many.

On the 1st of March 1947, someone asked him:

Q. Those who have lost their dear ones, or the homes which they built up through years of patient labour, find it extremely difficult to forgive and forget. How can they get over this feeling and look upon the community from which the miscreants came with a feeling of brotherliness?

A. The one way to forget and forgive was to contemplate Bihar which had done much worse than Noakhali and Tipperah. Did they want Muslims to take dire vengeance for the Hindu atrocities there? They could not. From this they should learn to forget and forgive, if they did not wish to descend to the lowest depths of barbarity.

They must not harbour inferiority complex. They should be brave. And forgiveness was an attribute and adornment of bravery. Let them be truly brave. Bravery refused to strike, it would suffer all infliction with patient cheerfulness. That would be the truest way of disarming opposition.

In the meanwhile, the economic boycott of Hindus by Muslims with which Gandhiji first became acquainted from some fishermen at Jayag on the 29th of January 1947, began to mount in intensity. It not only affected the landowning Hindus but poor peasants, fishermen and artisans as well. The condition became rather acute by about the middle of February 1947, when scores of people reported to him instances of such boycott from many parts of the district. At Raipur on the 6th of February, he said that he had heard of the boycott before. But he uniformly asked people to ignore such events if they were isolated instances. If however they were on an extensive scale, it was the Government's duty to deal with the situation.

If, unfortunately, boycott became also the policy of the Government, it would be a serious matter. He could only think non-violently. If the Government, under such circumstances, gave proper compensation, he would probably advise acceptance by the Hindus. He could not think out there and then the pros and the cons. If, on the other hand, they resorted to no compensation, he would advise people to stand their ground and refuse to leave their homesteads even on pain of death. He however hoped that no Government would be mad enough to subscribe to the policy of boycott whether with or without compensation. Those who belonged to the land for ages could not be removed from their homesteads for the simple reason that they found themselves in a minority. It was intolerable.

On the 19th of February 1947, the question was raised again at Birampur.

*Q.* You have advised evacuation if the majority become irrevocably hostile. But you have also maintained that a truly non-violent man should never give up the hope of converting his opponent by love. Under these circumstances, how can a non-violent man accept defeat and leave his home?

*A.* In answer, Gandhiji said, it was perfectly correct that a non-violent man would not move out of his place. For such a one, there would be no question of compensation. He would simply die at his post and prove that his presence was not a danger to the State or the community.

He knew however that the Hindus of Noakhali made no such pretension. They were simple folks who loved the world and wanted to live in peace and safety. Such persons would consult their honour if the Government honourably offered them compensation in order to see the majority living in peace. If the mere presence of Hindus irritated Muslims who were the majority community, he would consider it to be the duty of the Government to offer compensation, as it would be of the Government in Hindu majority provinces to offer compensation to the Muslims if their presence irritated the majority community.

But whilst he examined and admitted the possibility of evacuation, his experience of all India told him that Hindus and Muslims knew how to live at peace. He declined to believe that people had said goodbye to their senses so as to make it impossible for them to live at peace with each other as they had done for generations. For he believed with the late Poet Iqbal that the Hindus and Muslims who had lived together long under the shadow of the mighty Himalayas and had drunk the waters of the Ganges and the Jamuna had a unique message for the world.

Whatever might have been the result of Gandhiji's appeal to the Hindus, his appeal to the common Muslims seemed to bear even less fruit.

On the evening of the 17th of February, a Muslim divine named Khalilur Rahman paid a visit to Gandhiji at a village called Devipur. It was reported that this divine had been responsible for the conversion of a large number of Hindus during the disturbances. When Gandhiji asked him if this was true, the divine said that the conversion should not be taken seriously, it was a dodge adopted to save the life of the Hindus. Gandhiji asked him if it was any good saving one's life (*jan*) by sacrificing one's faith (*iman*)? It would have been much better if, as a religious preceptor, he had taught the Hindus to lay down their lives for their faith, rather than give it up through fear. The divine continued to argue that such false conversion for saving one's life had the sanction of religion, when Gandhiji grew impatient and, in an almost angry tone said, if ever he met God, he would ask Him why a man with such views had ever been made a religious preceptor. The divine became silent, and after an exchange of courtesies, left.

In the meanwhile, Muslim opposition to Gandhiji's continued presence in Noakhali became still more acute. Beginning from the Chief Minister of Bengal down to the lowliest educated and politically conscious Muslim in Noakhali, everyone demanded that Gandhiji should go to Bihar and take up the cause of the Muslim sufferers there if he were to prove his claim of impartiality.

Indeed, on the 14th of January 1947, Gandhiji had written the following letter to H. S. Suhrawardy:

'Sardar Niranjan Singh Gill had told me of all the talk he had with you. He says whilst you do not mind his men working in Noakhali, you would doubt his *bona fides* until he with his men worked in Bihar just as assiduously as in Noakhali. In the circumstances, I have told him that he should first go to Bihar and work there and, in order to be able to do so effectively, he would take from you a note of recommendation to the leader in Bihar of the League Party.

Unless he is so armed, I have told him, his work might, from the League point of view, fall flat. I added that he should keep himself in touch with you regarding the work there.

'As to his work in Noakhali, I have told him that, regard being paid to your views as interpreted by the Sardar, he should withdraw his men from Noakhali unless you approved of his work in Noakhali. It is not enough that you tolerate his men's work but it should have your written approval. His men can only be here as accepted friends of both Hindus and Muslims. I cannot entertain them on any other term. I have told him too that he should find financial support not from private sources including funds at my disposal but he should, in order to be above board, depend upon open public support. Therefore, I have suggested to him that, if you approve of his activity here, you should subscribe to his appeal even if it be a token rupee. But there may be difficulty in this of which I could have no knowledge even though you might approve of his activity in Noakhali.'

On the 8th of February 1947, Gandhiji wrote to Niranjan Singh Gill on the subject of Bihar:

Dear Sardarji,

I have your letter and enclosures. The Chief Minister's letter seems to meet the case. You will now go to Patna and see what the League members have to show and meet the members of the Ministry. Please do not fail to see Dr. Mahmud, Prof. Bari and the other Muslim Minister. Make written notes of what they say. Test accurately what the refugees are getting in the way of food and clothing. Examine the conditions of the sanitation of the refugee camps. Thus you will be able to prepare a fairly exhaustive report. Do not make any statement to the Press. Do not be in a hurry to return, nor take unnecessary time over the work.

Hazara business is a sorry affair.* I have not reached the bottom yet. But of this when we meet.

---

* Hazara district in the North-West Frontier where extensive anti-Hindu riots had broken out.

Things here are not as they should be That too later.

Yours,
Bapu.

The opposition to Gandhiji's stay in Noakhali began to take a vulgar turn towards the end of February 1947. The roads over which he walked from village to village were deliberately dirtied every day, while Muslim audiences began to boycott his meetings more persistently. Gandhiji tried to bear all this with calmness and patience. For he held stubbornly to the view that it would never be right for him to surrender his own love for men even if they were erring. The anxiety and anger which occasionally assailed him in the earlier days of Noakhali were replaced by an active and a deeper concern for the Muslim community wherever it was subjected to suffering.

He was exactly in this mental state, when one day a messenger arrived with a letter from his friend Syed Mahmud, Congress Minister of Bihar, who thought that his presence in that province would do real good to the suffering Muslim minority there. This confirmed an earlier message from Niranjan Singh Gill who had written to say that the progress of rehabilitation in Bihar was not proceeding satisfactorily. It did not therefore take more than a few minutes for Gandhiji to decide that the tour in Noakhali and Tipperah should be interrupted for work in Bihar. He sent an urgent telegram to the Chief Minister of that province, and even before a reply came, it was decided that he should proceed to Patna, accompanied by Manu Gandhi, Deo Prakash, Muhammad Ahmad Hunar, the Urdu Secretary, and myself. Volunteers like Ajit De who had been looking after Gandhiji's personal requirements or those who had originally accompanied him from Delhi were not permitted to leave their posts of duty. When it came to Ajit De, I explained to Gandhiji how helpful he had proved himself to be, and how, if he were with us, we would at least be free on one account. But Gandhiji insisted that he would do with whatever help came to him in Bihar and would put up with personal inconveniences if necessary rather than increase his entourage. So Ajit was left behind.

## XV. INTERNAL STRAIN

The reader will remember how Parasuram left after a difference of opinion with Gandhiji. But the matter for which he left, did not die with his departure. Fresh objections poured in, and this time it was from some of Gandhiji's closest and most respected co-workers.

The fact that some women workers were in company with Gandhiji and were even allowed to use his bed, seems to have been objected to by the latter; and, therefore, on the 1st of February, at a village called Amishapara, Gandhiji himself raised the question in his prayer meeting. He stated that he was in the midst of so much suspicion and distrust that he did not want his innocent acts to be misrepresented. He had his grand-daughter with him. She shared the same bed with him. The Prophet had discounted eunuchs who became such by an operation. He welcomed eunuchs made such through prayer by God. His was that aspiration. It was in the spirit of God's eunuch that he had approached what he considered was his duty. He felt constrained however to refer to this very personal matter because he did not like small talks, whispers and innuendoes. They would not expect him to go into the why and wherefore of his action. All they needed to know was that it was an integral part of the *Yajna* or sacrifice which he was performing. And he invited them to bless the effort. He knew that his action had excited criticism even among his friends. But a duty could not be shirked even for the sake of most intimate friends.

While translating the speech into Bengali, I left out the portion summarized above; there were other more important matters in the rest of his speech. But as we were walking back home, Gandhiji said to me that he 'did not like my omission', it had displeased him. I did not however reply but decided to place my views before him in writing, as I had done previously in the first week of January.

On the 3rd of February 1947, he referred to the same question once more in his prayer meeting. He said that what he had said about his private life was not for blind imitation.

He never claimed to have extraordinary powers. What he did was for all to do if they conformed to the conditions observed by him. If that was not done those who pretended to imitate his practice were doomed to perdition. What he was doing was undoubtedly dangerous, but it ceased to be so if the conditions were rigidly observed.

Satish Chandra Mukherji of Banaras, the founder of the Dawn Society, was one of the men whom Gandhiji held in high esteem. On the day he made his first reference in the public meeting, Gandhiji also wrote to Satish Babu a letter, towards the last part of which the following paragraph appeared: 'And now I put before you a poser. A young girl (19) who is in the place of grand-daughter to me by relation shares the same bed with me, not for any animal satisfaction but for (to me) valid moral reasons. She claims to be free from the passion that a girl of her age generally has and I claim to be a practised *brahmachari*. Do you see anything bad or unjustifiable in this juxtaposition? I ask the question because some of my intimate associates hold it to be wholly unjustified and even a breach of *brahmacharya*. I hold a totally opposite view. As you are an experienced man and as I have regard for your opinion, I put you the question. You may take your own time to answer the question. You are in no way bound to answer it, if you don't wish to.'

On the following day, Gandhiji despatched the following telegram to Kishorlal Mashruwala at the Harijan Ashram, Sabarmati: 'Your letter. See public statement made yesterday. Writing. Bapu.'

Here let me give below a small portion of my personal diary once again.

*Sadhurkhil, Tuesday, 4-2-1947:*
There were a large number of interviews on this day. Gandhiji gave more than half an hour to a retired official of the Postal Department in explaining certain nature-cure methods for an old ailment of his. This solicitude for anyone suffering physically or mentally, is an important characteristic of Gandhiji; he seems to take an almost motherly interest in anyone who is ailing and seeks his help.

But my experience during the present week has been that this attitude occasionally makes him indulgent towards some of his associates. He puts them under severe spiritual strain, and then, in a fit of exaggerated tenderness, even becomes party to causing injury to others for the sake of his beloved ones. This has been worrying me for some time past, for a recent case has cropped up in relation to one of the volunteers serving here. In fact, I had to draw his attention to this event one day.

A careful perusal of the letter quoted below will show, with what tender care he addresses himself to the personal problems of those who come close to him. Incidentally, it also proves to men like us, how, after a life of prolonged *brahmacharya*, he has become incapable of understanding the problems of love or sex as they exist in the common human plane.

7-2-1947

Chi. Nirmal Babu,

I never succeeded in writing to you on your first personal letter. The second on B's relation with A now comes. I must undertake this second today. I sent your letter to A, you left it open for me to do so. My loyalty to him demanded that I should.

B has led you into doing an injustice to A. I discussed it with her. She saw the truth of it. A's love is wholly free from animal passion. I have called it poetic. It is not a perfect adjective but I can find no better. He loved once a girl with the same passion with which he loves B. In either case, it was philanthropic. The first came in a flash, the second took practically two years to discover. He thought he would give B the best of him in point of education. In his opinion both cases went wrong because of my initial aversion. In the first, I relented when as A thinks it was too late. In the second, it is almost too late. The first girl is married. He is entitled to hope till B is married elsewhere, if she is. So far as B knows herself, it is a sealed book. Now mark the beauty of it. A says so long as B does not change her mind, she will be as sister or daughter to him and would never make any other advances to her. B believes this assurance, what she objects to is his shadowing her as she calls it.

If he does not get B as wife, he will never think of making love to another woman. He is too pure to think of any such thing. If you accept any analysis, you will render justice to A and lead B aright.

I do wish you could see that in non-violent conduct, whether individual or universal, there is an indissoluble connection between private, personal life and public. You may be as generous and charitable as you like in judging men, but you cannot overlook private deflections from the right conduct. If you are convinced about this proposition, you should pursue my connection with Manu and if you find a flaw, try to show it to me.

I have written in order to save your time and to let you think. But I shall welcome discussion, if you like it.

Asirbad,<br>Bapu.

It was late at night on the 9th of February 1947 that two telegrams reached Gandhiji from our headquarters at Kazirkhil. One of them ran as follows:

'Your letter first instant. We relinquish charge Harijan papers and correspondence. Charge against Jaisukhlal withdrawn in second letter on learning our misunderstanding. Writing. Kishorlal Narahari.'

To this and to another, Gandhiji sent the following replies:

'Kishorlal, Harijan Ashram, Sabarmati. Sorry your decision. You are entitled. Regard it hasty. Any case, you will render necessary help till new arrangement made. Wired Jivanji. Bapu.'

Wire to Jivanji D. Desai:

'Similar wire received from Kishorlalbhai. Sorry, but helpless. Sure they will give necessary help till new arrangement made. You are a Trust. You and trustees have to decide whether my help can be taken conduct Navajivan papers. I shall not misunderstand any of you dissociate from my activities. If you and Trust conscientiously desire my association I shall resume editing from here. Show this trustees, others and wire. Bapu.'

On the 14th of February, Sudhir Ghose came to see Gandhiji with a number of letters from Delhi. Gandhiji had a long conversation with him. The fact of his breach with old and respected friends, seems to be hanging heavily on his mind, though he hardly gives any expression to it. But during the conversation with Sudhir Babu, I heard him say: 'Even if my nearest and dearest leave me, I do not want to be cowed down. I do not want to prove a coward.' Physical courage of a very high order, he said, was even to be found among ruffians. The courage which made a man risk public disapproval when he felt that he was right, was undoubtedly of a superior order. The work in Noakhali was the most difficult he had undertaken in life. He then continued, 'I do not want to die a discredited or defeated man. So I have kept one loophole, I have said that I would rather die in Noakhali than go back a defeated man. I do not want to die by inches, as a paralytic for example. An assassin's knife may put an end to my life, but what I would welcome is that I shall breathe my last even in the midst of work. But I do not know what God has in store for me. I am trying to reach the state described in the Gita. I get impatient and worried when I am confronted with silly arguments, but I have no right to be angry on that account. Why should I get worried about it either? I sometimes flare up in anger. This should not be so. I am afraid, I am yet far from the state of *sthita prajna*.'\*

On the same evening, in course of his speech after prayer, Gandhiji quoted the following saying of the Prophet Muhammad, 'Be in the world like a traveller, or like a passer on, and reckon yourself as of the dead.' He commented, how good it would be if all regarded themselves as of the dead. They knew that death might overtake them any moment. What a fine preparation for the event if all became as dead.

In the last week of February, while we were having some rest at Haim Char, a letter arrived from Kishorlal Mashru-

---

\* The condition of the man who has completely mastered himself, as described in the *Bhagabad Gita*, II, 54-72, a text which was read daily morning and evening in Gandhiji's prayers.

wala. Gandhiji called me to his presence and said how differences had developed between him and some of his closest associates. He referred to Manu's practice of sleeping with him and asked for my opinion regarding the question raised by his friends. Naturally I needed some time to gather all the facts. Manu translated K. G. Mashruwala's letter to me as the original was in Gujarati. The main charge seemed to have been that Gandhiji was obviously suffering from a sense of self-delusion in regard to his relation with the opposite sex. Manu then related to me the details of what Gandhiji described as his *prayog* or experiment or self-examination.

But, of this, later.

In the meanwhile, preparations were made for leaving the camp at Haim Char. This was done on the 2nd of March 1947, when we left by jeep for the steamer station at Chandpur. The road all along was lined by eager crowds of men and women.

At Chandpur, we boarded a special steamer offered by the Steamer Company for Gandhiji's service. But the latter insisted on our payment of the regular fare to the authorities. So we purchased two first-class and half a dozen second-class tickets from the Company's agent who was on board with us and left Chandpur the same evening.

## XVI. THE FIRST FORTNIGHT IN BIHAR

THE train by which we travelled from Calcutta reached Fatwah station near Patna early in the morning and Professor Abdul Bari, the President of the Provincial Congress Committee, Srikrishna Sinha, the Chief Minister, and others welcomed Gandhiji on the platform. As soon as Gandhiji saw Bari Sahib, he laughed and said, 'How is it that you are still alive!' (*Kya abhi tak zinde hain?*), for Professor Bari is a Mussulman.

Gandhiji was then driven in a car straight to Patna while we proceeded with the luggage by train. At Patna we were all accommodated in the palatial residence of Syed Mahmud on the bank of the Ganges. The whole day was passed in company with Rajendra Prasad and the Congress Ministers. When Gandhiji learnt that Abdul Aziz, an influential leader belonging to the Muslim League, was ailing in bed, he paid a visit to the latter.

The prayer meeting was held in the lawn which is close by. But the crowds were so heavy and so unorganized that the car could proceed to the prayer ground only with the greatest difficulty. At the end of prayer, Gandhiji refused to take the car and decided to walk back home. The crowds became almost unmanageable and plenty of time was taken in reaching Mahmud Sahib's residence. Gandhiji had a talk with Prof. Bari about this and said that henceforth he would not use the car while going to the prayer ground and Congress volunteers must work and bring order among the crowd.

Prayer meetings were held in the lawn from the 5th to the 11th, while the whole of each day was mostly passed in listening to Muslim sufferers and their complaints or in conference with Rajendra Babu and the Ministers of the province. As the speeches were in Hindi and I had no need of translating them as I used to do in Noakhali, I had only to prepare the prayer reports and have them revised by Gandhiji for the Press. Mridula Sarabhai took charge of the interviews while Deo Prakash and Hunar looked after most of the correspondence in Hindi and Urdu. My work thus became light, and I asked Gandhiji what I should do now. I suggested, at the same time, that there was one thing to which I could devote myself; I could meet different political parties in Patna and gather from them independent accounts and opinions regarding the riots and allied questions. Gandhiji agreed readily, and for the next few days, I met the Provincial Secretary of the Communist Party of India, the Royists, prominent members of the Bengali community in Bihar like P. R. Das and P. K. Sen, and also a number of high Government officials. Reports of these conversations were submitted duly every day.

During prayer, the main burden of Gandhiji's speech was that the people of Bihar should feel sorry for what they had done by way of reprisal against innocent Muslims for what some of their misguided co-religionists had done in Noakhali. This was not only cowardly but also suicidal for the whole nation. Gandhiji wanted them to return all the looted property, to restore such abducted women as were still alive, and, last of all, to show real repentance by contributing their mite and actively helping in the rehabilitation of the Muslim evacuees.

Extracts from some of his speeches delivered during this week will illustrate how his mind was working at the time.

He knew that what the Hindus of Bihar had done towards their Muslim brethren was infinitely worse than what Noakhali had done. He hoped that they had done and were doing all the reparation possible, and that was, in magnitude, as great as the crime. The Congress, which rightfully claimed to represent the whole of India, had to make itself responsible for the misdeeds of all communities and classes.

He was grieved to find that there were thoughtless Hindus in all parts of India who falsely hugged the belief that Bihar had arrested the growth of lawlessness that was to be witnessed in Noakhali. It was a cowardly thing for a man to believe that barbarity could ever protect a civilization or a religion or defend freedom. The way to make reprisals for Noakhali was to learn how not to copy the barbarous deeds such as Noakhali had proved itself capable of, but to return barbarism by manliness, which consisted in daring to die without a thought of reparation and without in any way compromising one's honour.

Gandhiji expressed his surprise that he had received a telegram warning him that he must not condemn Hindus in Bihar, for what they had done was purely from a sense of duty. He had no hesitation in saying that the writer did no good to India or to Hinduism by issuing the warning. He spoke as a Hindu having a living faith in his own religion and he claimed to be a better Hindu for claiming to be a good Muslim, Christian, Parsi or Jew, as he was a Hindu. And he invited every one of his audience to feel likewise. As such, he felt that he would forfeit his claim to be a Hindu if he bolstered up the wrong-doing of fellow Hindus or any other fellow being.

On the 12th at Patna City, he said, 'Should we forget our humanity and return blow for blow? If some misdirected individual took it into his head to desecrate a temple or break idols, should a Hindu in return desecrate a mosque on that account? Did it in any way help to protect the temple or to save the cause of Hinduism?' Personally, said Gandhiji, he was as much an idol worshipper as an idol breaker, and he suggested that the whole of the audience whether Hindu, Muslim or other were also so, whether they admitted it or not. He knew mankind thirsted for symbolism. Were not musjids or churches in reality the same as mandirs? God resided everywhere, no less in stock or stone than in a single hair on the body of men. But men associated sacredness with particular places and things more than with others. Such sentiment was worthy of respect when it did not mean restriction of like freedom in others. To every Hindu and Mussulman, Gandhiji's advice was that if there was compulsion anywhere, they should gently but firmly refuse to submit to force. Personally, he himself would hug an idol and lay down his life to protect it rather than brook any restriction upon his freedom of worship.

Gandhiji referred one day to a certain letter he had received from a very frank and honest friend. The latter had reminded him that the efforts for religious toleration that he had been making were all in vain; for, after all, the quarrel between the Hindus and the Mussulmans was not on account of religious difference but was essentially political in origin; religion had only been made to serve as a label for political distinctions. The friend had expressed the opinion that it was a tussle between United India on the one hand and of India Divided on the other.

Gandhiji confessed he did not yet know what the full meaning of dividing India was. But what he wanted to impress upon the audience was that, supposing it were only a so-called political struggle, did it mean that all rules of decency and of morals should be thrown to the winds? Human conflicts divorced from ethical considerations could only lead to the use of the atom bomb where every trace of humanity is held completely in abeyance. If there are honest differences, could they not agree to settle their differences decently and in a comradely spirit? If they failed, only slavery of an unredeemable character could await them at the end of the road.

As an instance of non-violent resistance, Gandhiji referred another day to the question of Pakistan. He said that if some one asked him under threat of violence to admit such a claim, he should not immediately rush to return the violence thus offered. In all humility, he would ask the aggressor what was really meant by the demand and, if he were really satisfied that it was something worth striving for, then he would have no hesitation in proclaiming from the house-top that the demand was just and had to be admitted by every one concerned. But if the demand was backed by force, then the only course open to the non-violent man was to offer non-violent resistance against it as long as he was not convinced of its justice. Such resistance required courage of a superior order to that needed in violent warfare.

The true meaning of non-resistance had often been misunderstood or even distorted. It never implied that the non-violent man should bend before the violence of the aggressor. While not returning the latter's violence by violence, he should refuse to submit to the latter's illegitimate demand even to the point of death. That was the true meaning of non-violence.

If we returned blow for blow between ourselves at a moment when the British nation out of a strong sense of reality had decided to quit India, we would only succeed in tearing up our motherland into bits which went by the name of Hindustan and Pakistan, Brahministan and Acchutistan (Land of the Brahmins and Land of the Untouchables). What more madness could there be than what had taken place in Bengal and Bihar, or what was taking place even then in the Punjab or the Frontier Province?

Sometimes, in these speeches, Gandhiji spoke not to men collectively, in political terms, but his appeal was directed towards the individual; and then his speeches touched the heart of the audience more readily and gave rise to a new sense of personal responsibility.

Thus, in a written speech on his day of silence on the 9th, he said that with those who had been guilty, he would plead for repentance and for discovering themselves. While for those who had not personally participated in the shameful killings, his advice was that they should purify their own thoughts. When thoughts are not pure, one's actions can never be purified. Pure action can never come from imitation. If one tries to become good by merely imitating the good conduct of others, such conduct never succeeds in radiating any influence upon others, because it is after all not the true stuff. But one whose heart has become really pure along with his actions, can at once sense the true character of the thoughts which influence the behaviour of his neighbours. When thought and action have both become pure, there can be no repetition of the deeds which have marred the fair face of Bihar. But the world never progresses in a straight line. The thoughts and actions of men never follow a parallel and uniform course. For all men, these two can never be completely purified at any single point of time.

'Therefore I would wish to indicate to you tonight only that ideal of duty which workers should keep before themselves. If workers are available in sufficient numbers, they should first explain clearly to the miscreants the full consequences of their misdeeds. It should be explained to the wrong-doers that such deeds can never be of any good to them personally nor can it serve the cause of Hinduism or of the country in general. It should be explained to them that they have not been able to harm those whom they intended. They should also be induced to come forward and make an open breast of their misdeeds before the public. They should also restore looted property and abducted women to the proper quarters.

'A change of heart can never be brought about by law, it can only be effected through inner conversion. When that is accomplished then there is no longer any need of compulsive laws.

'I had asked you to help in the relief of Muslim brothers and sisters who have suffered during the last riots. Yesterday you did not come prepared for that purpose. I expect of you today to contribute your mite in this noble cause.'

From the 9th onwards, collections began to be made for relief and rehabilitation of the sufferers. One day he referred to a question whether Muslims had contributed similarly for relief in Noakhali. It was indeed true, he said in reply, that little had come to him from that quarter. But the reason, he believed, had been that he was now looked upon as the Enemy No. One, rather than a friend by the majority of the Muslim community in India. Yet, even in Comilla, there had been a case when some Muslim and Christian friends had contributed more than Rs. 800 along with a parcel of conch-shell bangles and vermilion for distribution among Hindu women from whom such ceremonial marks had been forcibly removed during the disturbances.

Incidentally, on the 7th of March 1947, Gandhiji said that he had been seriously thinking if he should not march from village to village as he had done in Noakhali, so that what little power his thoughts contained might be conveyed directly to the most distant villager who had done a wrong to his brother Mussulman.

And thus began his new programme, in which, with headquarters in Patna, he went everyday to some village to hold his prayer meeting in the evening. His body was too tired, and the crowds of Bihar too unmanageable for him to undertake a walking tour through the affected parts of the province. The prayer meetings were accordingly held from after the 9th in different villages within several miles of Patna. The crowds swelled as the days rolled by, and the

## THE FIRST FORTNIGHT IN BIHAR 145

Government also made good arrangements for regulating them. Loudspeakers were fitted in generous numbers everywhere, while strongly built platforms were set up from which Gandhiji addressed the meetings. There used to be a shade on the top, all the sides being kept open, so that he could be seen in full from every quarter. At the end of the meeting, he used to sit at the edge of the platform and receive contributions personally while volunteers moved about among the crowd to make further collections. The fact that most people wanted to place their little contribution in Gandhiji's own hands made it difficult for us to control the crowd when the meeting was over, for everyone tried to push his way to the dais; and this was always dangerous.

On the 10th, Gandhiji paid a 'courtesy' call to the British Governor of the province. He referred to the visit in his prayer speech and said he could not go to the Governor expecting any favours or solaces. He could expect services or favours only from the Ministers who were representatives of the people.

Khan Abdul Ghaffar Khan had joined us in Patna, and on the 16th of March, he made an impassioned appeal to Hindus, Muslims and Sikhs to realize the consequences of the present fratricidal war. He confessed he did not yet see any light through the dark clouds which had spread from Calcutta and Noakhali to Bihar and then to the Punjab and the Frontier Province. The spectre which loomed before him was of India burning. He asked all to ponder over its terrible consequences. Pakistan, he said, could be established through love or non-violence. He did not know if it were possible to do so through force; but if it were, then it could not be lasting or of any good. It was the duty of every one, he held, to change the poisoned atmosphere of the country through love, to prepare the country for enjoying the fruits of real freedom in peace and amity.

On the 17th, we started for a village named Masaurhi by train. We reached there in the afternoon, and after inspecting the damaged houses of the Mussulman inhabitants, Gandhiji held his prayer meeting in a spacious lawn. He stayed at Masaurhi for three days and then returned to Patna to continue his tour in other villages.

For some time past, I had been asking for his permission to leave. He was however reluctant to let me go, but in the end I left on the 18th of March 1947 by the afternoon train for Patna, from where I proceeded once more to my work in the University of Calcutta.

## XVII. TILL WE MEET AGAIN

THE events which led to this parting were of a rather painful character. Yet they have to be recounted as faithfully as possible, because they throw an unexpected light on some corners of Gandhiji's personality as well as on his relation with those who lived and worked with him.

The reader will remember that although our original party during Gandhiji's pilgrimage in Noakhali had consisted of Parasuram and myself, Parasuram had left and Manu had taken his place. She had come partly because she wanted to serve Bapu, and partly also because he wished her to come. The other co-workers of Gandhiji like Kanu and Abha Gandhi, Pyarelal, Sushila Nayyar and others had each been posted in one village or another and had been ordered to be at their posts till the fruition of the peace mission. Pyarelal's brother Deo Prakash had joined us later on, not on Gandhiji's invitation but on his own; and he continued to be of help in dealing with interviews and part of the correspondence. For dealing with Urdu correspondence, there was no capable assistant after Pyarelal's departure. Pandit Sunderlal of Allahabad had suggested to Gandhiji the name of Muhammad Ahmad Hunar, a young writer who knew both Hindi and Urdu very well, and Hunar accordingly had become a member of our party towards the latter part of Gandhiji's stay in Noakhali.

While we were leaving Noakhali, the reader may perhaps remember that a volunteer named Ajit De, who looked after Gandhiji's personal requirements along with Manu, was left behind, as Gandhiji said that he would manage to do with whatever help came to him in Bihar. In Bihar, the Government had made more than adequate arrangements for secretarial work. There were plenty of stenographers and clerks, as well as volunteers to look after the personal requirements of the camp.

Five days after we reached Patna, the feeling began to grow upon me that there was little to which I could devote myself exclusively for Gandhiji's sake. One member of our party whom I shall call R began to take more and more interest in secretarial work, and at Gandhiji's suggestion, he began to learn from me how I used to keep indexes of letters, interviews and events. Card-indexing is no difficult job, and R did not take very much time in learning the method; yet, he did commit a few mistakes now and then as all apprentices usually do. There was nothing to worry about that; and I tried patiently to pass on more and more work to him. But in course of my five months stay with Gandhiji, I felt occasionally that he had a tender corner for various persons in his heart. And for those for whom he had a feeling of tenderness, he often went to great lengths to keep them pleased.

In fact, a great friend of Gandhiji once wrote to me explaining how he looked after the personal needs of those who worked with him and whom he loved. Thus he wrote: 'If you accept that X must stay with Bapu, then all those conditions which will keep him "efficient" must be fulfilled. And that is how so many things come in train, whether they be good lights, torches, fountain pens, stationery... or now and then some children or kitten to play with. Bapu has strength of mind enough not to feel helpless by being deprived of any associate or thing of comfort. He can raise new associates and improvise new means. But X would break down. He (the latter) needs props both in men and materials.'

Now this is a point which had been worrying me for some time past. Why should a fountain pen or, for that matter, a kitten or a human being be sacrificed for the sake of one man, particularly if the kitten or the pen or the person in question does not feel an eagerness for being so offered? Gandhiji might not force the person into a bout of self-sacrifice, but why should he or any of his companions encourage anyone to be such a sacrifice for the sake of another, who, in turn, might thus be maintained at a level of efficiency for Gandhiji's service?

Men and women undoubtedly do things of this kind in life. Women with a motherly feeling for those whom they love, may find recourse to such an action justifiable; but I had somehow gathered from Gandhiji's writings that he was above this tender care for people. He had, of course, every right to be tender to whomsoever he liked, and to any degree that suited him; but somehow it hurt me somewhere. I felt, it was subordinating a human being to a purpose not determined independently by the person concerned.

And so, on the 11th of March in Patna, I conveyed to Gandhiji the desire to be relieved of my duties by the end of the month. This I told him while I was shaving him in the morning; and I also reminded him that he had said in Noakhali that his entourage would consist merely of those who were indispensable. But now, he had allowed more persons to be with us than were actually needed; and the reason was not always their indispensability. He defended himself by saying that he did not ask anyone to come, but took only such help as came along. I retorted by saying that, at Noakhali, he had been very strict and had once said to Manu that he was going to turn a new leaf in his life in this most difficult enterprise of his, but that strength was not in evidence consistently all along. Why should he display a softness even when the political mission in which he was engaged suffered to some extent thereby? For these personal preoccupations sometimes wasted his time and left his temper in a none too balanced condition all through the day.

In the meanwhile, the breach between him and some of his co-workers had remained unbridged. And, in order to discuss matters, Swami Anand and Kedar Nathji came to Bihar on the 14th of March 1947. Their discussion was entirely private, and continued through the 15th and the 16th when they left. On the 15th and the 16th, both of these old associates of Gandhiji also tried to ascertain from me what views I held with regard to the question on which differences had developed between them and the latter. I placed my viewpoint orally before them, and also wrote out a letter for communication to other friends. All this had become necessary because Gandhiji had said to Kedar Nathji and Swami Anand that his views regarding *brahmacharya* were of an unorthodox kind; he had been partly influenced by the writings of some Western writers on this subject, and also that his immediate personal associates did not see anything wrong in his acts. The last was a reference to me, and that was the reason why the two friends from Gujarat had wanted to ascertain my views on the subject.

A substantial portion of that letter is reproduced below after necessary changes:

Patna, 16-3-1947

My dear—,

Swami Anand and Nathji have heard from me my reaction to the problems they came to discuss with Gandhiji. They are also carrying copies of three letters which will help to make my position clear. Swami Anand asked me this morning if he could say to his friends that I disapproved of Gandhiji's action. It is with reference to this question that I should try to make my position clear. Hence this letter.

Swami Anand told me in the morning that during the discussion last night, Gandhiji had said to Nathji that his ideas on *brahmacharya* were not of the orthodox kind, and they had been modified by his long contact with the West. This was an agreeable surprise to me; as I personally belong to a rather unorthodox frame of mind. Yet the surprise was there, because from a serious study of Gandhiji's writings I had formed the opinion, which was perhaps not unjustified, that he represented a hard, puritanic form of self-discipline, something which we usually associate with mediæval Christian ascetics or Jain recluses.

So, when I first learnt in detail about Gandhiji's *prayog* or experiment, I felt genuinely surprised. I was informed that he sometimes asked women to share his bed and even the cover which he used, and then tried to ascertain if even the least trace of sensual feeling had been evoked in himself or his companion. Personally, I would never tempt myself like that; nor would my respect for woman's personality permit me to treat her as an instrument of an experiment undertaken only for my own sake.

But when I learnt about this technique of self-examination employed by Gandhiji, I felt that I had discovered the reason why some regarded Gandhiji as their private possession; this feeling often leading them to a kind of emotional unbalance. The behaviour of A, B or C, for instance, is no proof of healthy psychological relationship. Whatever may be the value of the *prayog* in Gandhiji's own case, it does leave a mark of injury on the personality of others who are not of the same moral stature as he himself is, and for whom sharing in Gandhiji's experiment is no spiritual necessity.

This has been the reason why I have sometimes spoken or written strongly to Gandhiji on the subject of repression and its effects upon those who come under his influence either in private or in public life. But, you will see, this charge is quite different from the one to which you or your friends subscribe. This is also the reason why I have drawn a distinction in the case of Manu, whose relation to Gandhiji is of a completely different order.

I hope my position is quite clear. But if it is not, please do not hesitate to write.

Yours sincerely,<br>Nirmal Kumar Bose.

*Post-script.* Even with regard to the 'experiment', I would stand by Gandhiji, if—
(1) the other party were a willing agent, voluntarily entering into the experiment with a knowledge of the possible consequences upon her own personality;
(2) and the public knew about the experiment and expressed their mind over it.

The second is otherwise unnecessary, but has only been called for because Gandhiji himself invited public opinion on this subject twice in his prayer speeches in Noakhali. He expected the public to express an opinion even when they did not know the entire details of the situation. But, even if after knowing everything, the public thought that Gandhiji was in the wrong, while he considered himself to be right, I would stand by him.

After Swami Anand and Kedar Nathji left on the 16th, I placed before Gandhiji a copy of the letter written for them along with the post-script which I wanted to post.

It was Monday, the 17th, his day of silence. So he wrote to me on a slip of paper:

'You may post it if you wish. There are errors of facts in the letter. There are other defects to which I would draw your attention. I would therefore advise you to wait till you have seen my opinion. But do just as you please.'

This post-script was therefore actually posted by me only on the 21st from Tipperah district, while the original letter had been carried by hand by Swami Anand.

As we left by train for Masaurhi on a three days' tour, the crowd kept swelling round the train. But amidst all the noise and disturbances created by the crowd, many of whom stepped upon the footboard to have a view of Gandhiji, he sat calmly near the window, busy writing on slips of used paper. When the writing was over, he handed over the slips to me, and I found it was a letter meant for me. It is given below with the personal names of persons suppressed:

Chi. Nirmal Babu,

Your letter is full of inaccuracies and unwarranted assumptions. I had asked you to discuss the thing with me. You could not do it. The result is bad. I do not mind what opinion you hold, only it must be well fortified.

You should have ascertained my views from me before accepting second-hand evidence however honest it might be.

I go beyond the orthodox view as we know it. My definition does not admit of laxity. I do not call that *brahmacharya* that means not to touch a woman. What I do today is nothing new for me. So far as I know myself, I hold today the same view I held when about 45 years ago I took the vow. Without the vow in England as a student, I freely mixed with women and yet I called myself a *brahmachari* for the period of my residence there. For me, *brahmacharya* is that thought and practice which puts you in touch with the Infinite and takes you to His presence. In that sense Dayanand Saraswati was not. Most certainly I am not. But I am trying to reach that state and in accordance with my belief, I have made substantial progress in that direction.

I have not become modern at all in the same sense you seem to mean. I am as ancient as can be imagined and hope to remain so to the end of my life. If this displeases you, I cannot help it. Let me appear to you and others as naked as I can.

You have not done justice to A, B or C. You do not know them fully. Have you any right to judge them before you have taken the trouble of knowing them as fully as possible? That you may not want to or that you have no time, I would appreciate. But that very fact should prevent you from passing judgement on them.

I am amazed at your assumption that my experiment implied any assumption of woman's inferiority. She would be, if I looked upon her with lust with or without her consent. I have believed in woman's perfect equality with man. My wife was 'inferior' when she was the instrument of my lust. She ceased to be that when she lay with me naked as my sister. If she and I were not lustfully agitated in our minds and bodies, the contact raised both of us.

Should there be difference if it is not my wife, as she once was, but some other sister? I do hope you will acquit me of having any lustful designs upon women or girls who have been naked with me. A or B's hysteria had nothing to do with my experiment, I hope. They were before the experiment what they are today, if they have not less of it.

The distinction between Manu and others is meaningless for our discussion. That she is my grand-daughter may exempt me from criticism. But I do not want that advantage.

'Experiment' or *prayog* is an ill-chosen word. I have used it. It differs from the present\* in the sense that the one could be stopped by me, the other being *dharma* could not be. Now comes the stop.

That I should take the public in my confidence before I do anything new is novel to me. In the present case there is nothing new.

Bapu.

---

\* The knotty question, namely, whether Manu should be allowed to use his bed or not in contrast to his self-examination, which was considered part of his religious or spiritual practice or *dharma*.

After having received the letter, I began to frame an answer in mind. In the meanwhile, I told Gandhiji that I might have to leave him earlier than by the end of the month. He asked me in writing: 'When must you go? There is no immediate hurry, is there? Let us wait till the 3 days' tour is over.' That same night, I asked Gandhiji a few questions regarding facts connected with the subject of my letter. I also arranged my few things in a small package, for the feeling grew upon me that the time had come for me to depart.

On Tuesday the 18th, while I was shaving him, I had a long conversation with him bearing on the subject, and later on, I wrote out my views in the form of a letter which I handed over to him. A portion of that letter is reproduced below:

Masaurhi, 18-3-1947

Bapuji,

After receiving your letter written yesterday in the train, I had about an hour's talk with you in which I tried to refute the charge against me that I had formed judgement hastily without giving A or others any chance of presenting their case fully.

If you please refer to my letter of the 2nd of January 1947, you will find in line 14 that I have connected by implication X with you in your experiment. It was just because of that that last night I first ascertained from you if she had had any connection with the experiment, and you replied in the affirmative. I had a suspicion when she told me some time ago that she had had nothing to do with your *prayog* that she was screening facts, may be even from herself. And when it came to that, where was the point in trying to gather more facts from her by direct interrogation?

Personally, I have practised the Freudian technique of dream analysis on myself and have derived immense benefit, as it has helped to bring to the surface submerged desires which had been causing trouble, and thus helped me to deal with them satisfactorily. That method was inapplicable in the case of X. As her conscious and unconscious thoughts were beyond direct approach, I had to depend on outside observation of behaviour, which I did.

And, as I told you in the January letter, my charge against her was that she had become nearly neurotic and had been taking away a considerable portion of your time when all your services were needed almost exclusively in the national cause. Thus I based my judgement on personal observation of behaviour. I admit it was not wholly adequate. But then, I was sitting in no public judgement over her, and also wanted no more than to prevent her from wasting your time over personal matters. I was encouraged to do so particularly because every time she was with you, you were left in a disturbed frame of mind which definitely interfered with your capacity for work. All that I want to tell you is that I did not base my judgement on 'second-hand' evidence; but on another type of observation, which is valid to the extent it goes.

It was likewise in the case of A. I do not ascribe any impure motive to him. But if his love for B is of the poetic variety, why should he need B's physical presence even within several miles of himself? I have not yet been able to reconcile myself to the belief that A's first love in life is village-work and all else takes second place. If I had been in A's position, I would have returned to some place of rest, taken time to discover myself, settled down as a householder after marriage and tried to do no more than what I was honestly capable of. But if the need of my service to the country were so urgent that I could not afford that pleasure to myself, I would have swallowed the bitter pill in a sporting spirit, tried to develop my devotion to work and left it at that.

But you must not take any of this as an indictment against either X or A. It only means that we poor mortals are often motivated and carried away by unconscious desires in directions other than those to which we consciously subscribe.

In your own case, I have observed that you try to defend your close associates in discussions regarding them, rather than place the cause of reality above everything else. It is perfectly natural for a man to place his loyalty to comrades above many other things, but then I expected more than a gentleman's behaviour from you.

Now for a personal matter. Bapuji, you originally called me to service under you while you were in Bengal. The University gladly granted me indefinite leave so long as you needed my services. But the interest of my students has also been suffering. When I have to choose between the amount of service I can render to you here in Bihar and for science in the University, I would place the latter first. But if it had been in Bengal, I would have sacrificed the latter interest, because I would then have known that so far as translating your speeches into Bengali was concerned, I would have been more useful than most of your other assistants. But now that you are in Bihar, men like Pyarelalji or others would be in their elements with their mastery over Hindustani and their undoubtedly great ability for secretarial work. So I would love to make room for anyone whom you may choose.

When once more you are in Bengal and feel the need of my services, the University will gladly grant me leave for service under you without hesitation.

Hence my plan is to leave for Calcutta even tonight if you do not object.

Yours affectionately,
N.K.B.

To this he replied:

Chi. Nirmal Babu,

If you must leave today I must not stand between you and your duty as you conceive it. You have made me so used to you that I shall miss you. Pyarelal I cannot have just now. He must be in his place. If you leave today, I suppose you have arranged to hand over all papers in perfect order. The only one who can take charge is Deo.

Your explanation does not give me satisfaction. But I must not argue. If you want me to do so, I could do it through correspondence which perhaps better suits your nature. Of course you are at liberty to discuss the whole of me and my writings with anybody you like. This applies equally to the three letters. I simply drew your attention to what appeared to be hasty decisions and that too in order to see as much perfection in you as possible.

'Haste is waste.'

Bapu's blessings.

At a quarter to three in the afternoon I bade good-bye to Bapu with the words, 'Bapuji, I have always been a wanderer like this in life.' He blessed me and said, 'You have taken your decision in haste.' And so I left for the train which was to take me to Patna and thence to Calcutta.

On the 19th of March 1947, Gandhiji wrote to Satish Chandra Dasgupta from Patna:

Chi. Satish Babu,

I must dictate this to save time. The dictation can only be in English because Rangaswamy is not an efficient Hindustani writer.

The first thing is to give you the sad news that Nirmal Babu abruptly left yesterday. He had prepared me for the news two days ago. He was wanted by his University. He had some private work too. And so he was to leave. But he suddenly took it into his head to leave yesterday. I had not the heart to detain him and what he thought was his *dharma* at the time.

Kaka Sahib wrote to me three days ago that he would like me to have Bishen by my side. I was thinking what to do and though I know that he could not in any way be a substitute for Nirmal Babu, the latter's absence has made me come to a hurried decision that if Bishen is not wanted by you he should join me.

I am here touring Patna district and looking at the awful scenes of destruction wrought by human beings gone mad. I had hoped that I would be able, at the outside, in a fortnight to go back to Noakhali and its velvety earth and soft grass.

I very much fear that I must now do Noakhali work from here as I had flattered myself while in Noakhali that I was doing Bihar work. Having come here I see how vitally necessary it was for me to come. I do not know that I won't have to undertake pilgrimage on foot here also. Probably I shall not be able to do so on foot. But everything is in the lap of God.

It is quite clear to me that, whatever be my fate, you should all, including the Sevagram party, stick to your posts.

Bapu's blessings.

On the same day, Gandhiji wrote me the following letter from a village named Bir:

Bir, 19-3-1947

Chi. Nirmal Babu,

Now that you are gone, I must say I did not like your abrupt departure. Manu was disturbed and Y asked if she had been the cause of your sudden departure. I told her, I did not think so; but there was an uncertain ring about my 'no': If you went without any other cause than the call from the University, I have nothing to say.

What is Freudian philosophy? I have not read any writing of his. One friend, himself a Professor and follower of Freud, discussed his writings for a brief moment. You are the second.

I do not want to emphasize my impression that you jump to hasty conclusions. You ought to know the three more fully. You are not just to them.

Have you in the light of my letter and discussion accepted my position that I am not guilty of modernity? If you hold on to the view you have expressed in your letter to K, you owe it to me to explain your standpoint and enable me to understand myself more fully than I do.

Bapu's blessings.

To this I replied from Calcutta on the 6th of April:

Calcutta, 5th/6th April, 1947.

Bapuji,

I have returned to Calcutta only this evening. Your letter dated the 19th of March was awaiting me here, as my sister did not know when and where I might be. So please pardon me for the delay. In this letter I shall try to confine myself to one question only, viz. why I came away. The others raised by you, like the philosophy of Freud, I shall reserve for future treatment.

It is perfectly natural that you should not like my abrupt departure, nor have I myself felt very happy about it. Let me now state the reasons why I left.

1. On the 18th of November 1946, you wrote to me at Kazirkhil, 'I want you, if you can and will, to be with

me wherever I go and stay *while I am in Bengal*. The idea is that I should be alone with you as my companion and interpreter...'

On 20-12-1946, while I was massaging you, you said that during the early hours of the morning, you had been telling Manu how your old life had ended and a new chapter had begun. You were going to conduct a new experiment in non-violence of the brave, for hitherto the non-violence displayed by the nation or in evidence in the institutions built up under your inspiration had only reflected non-violence of the weak.

Under these circumstances, I determined to serve to the best of my ability in this new experiment, and although my scientific work has always been very dear to me, I decided to hold it back for the time being so as to serve the present cause without any interference from my old self.

2. But I began to feel uneasy in Srirampur soon after the 17th of December when the incident took place in which Dr. Sushila Nayyar was involved. She used to come frequently, maybe generally on account of her patients. But each time she came, we found you no longer in an unruffled or happy state, and fits of impatience used to be often in evidence. They might never have reached a high pitch, but they were there all the same.

3. A also came quite often. I have no grouse against him and can have none. But when I found he needed B's love even when she was clearly unwilling, and that you were personally also trying to convince her of the genuineness and disinterested character of his love in the face of her clear refusal, I could not like it either. I asked myself, why should you involve yourself in such a task when other and more urgent matters were awaiting your attention? You know how our arrears of work often mounted high and you were worried at the files which were growing fatter every day.

4. With regard to Z also I should say that she was not always disinterested in her relations with you. If she had placed the work of Hindu-Muslim unity above everything else, why could she not have subordinated her interest in who was and who was not serving you? Did she not succeed in ruffling your temper even at Haim Char? If her

case had been one of single-minded devotion to unselfish service, what reason was there for you to be ruffled or even angry with her at times?

5. The developments noted in paras 2, 3, 4 above showed me that your past associations were clearly pursuing you without remission. They do so in the case of every man. Most people succumb to them. You did not; yet you were not as relentless in severing the old ties as you had led me to expect from the letter quoted in para 1.

6. When we reached Bihar, you could naturally feel that things were not running as smoothly as they should have done. One day I suggested certain changes to you. In my opinion, Deo Prakash, in spite of all his goodness and sincerity, was clearly a liability rather than an asset. Hunar had been entrusted with part of your cooking, but it would have been better if he had been left absolutely free to work only at your reports in Hindi and Urdu and the task of tackling such correspondence as he could manage. And when I referred the matter of Deo Prakash to you, you said that your claim was that you never called anybody to your help but managed to work with those whom God sent, as best as you could.

Yet this was only partly true, for did you not ask people also *to go away*? Let me remind you of the case of Ajit who served splendidly in the kitchen and left every one of us free on one account. You were insistent in his case that he should be left behind, and you would manage with such help as might be vouchsafed to you in Bihar. That was all right; but then one expected the same spirit in other instances also. In the case of R, I felt clearly that you placed personal considerations above the interest of the work *on hand*. I did what I could by bringing things to your notice; but beyond that I could not go. I was myself working as your secretary, and the suspicion might be there that I was trying to get rid of someone ostensibly on account of his inefficiency. So it was not possible for me to press the point, although I knew work was suffering and you also felt the same about it.

7. The fact is that these small but significant series of events led me to believe that you did not want to cut

yourself away from your old moorings as much as I had been led to expect. I saw your strength come back in flashes when you rose to heights no one else has reached in our national life. But the fact also remained that you permitted yourself to be weak in respect of particular persons. Hence I did not feel the same joy in work, however heavy it might be, as I had experienced in Noakhali.

8. When my mind was thus wavering, and faith shaken in your statement that a completely new chapter had opened in your life, I tried to find out clearly what my duty was.

For one brief moment, the temptation came to me that in spite of what had happened, I should remain with you in these momentous days of our national history. Perhaps the temptation came from the desire to share in reflected glory. Immediately I felt ashamed of myself and said, 'Here you are losing faith in what was described as the great venture. The experiment in non-violence of the brave Gandhiji promised you in Noakhali has been eclipsed for the time being, and yet you wish to remain for considerations other than the original one. It is a shame that you should stick to Gandhiji for the sake of fame.' There I was, and I had to quit, because the wanderer in me would not allow me to build a house like that for myself.

9. As soon as my faith in your ability or perhaps desire to shake off the old completely and be true to the bold future was weakened, the scales in my judgement turned in favour of my scientific work in the University. In the meanwhile, I had received a letter from the University that work was suffering on account of my absence. I would have put up with that if the call for adventure in non-violence had not dimmed. But now I clearly felt that the quality or quantity of work I was doing in Bihar was less than what I would be able to put in at the University. Hence I came away on that ground.

Besides that, there was also some amount of personal work awaiting me here. While I felt that I was doing little effective work in Bihar, this gained in weight just as the University work had also done, and for the same reason. So altogether, I decided to come away.

10. I have now placed before you everything without reserve. My services are still at your command. And if you feel you need them, all that you have to do is to write to Syamaprasad Babu who is the President of our Board of Studies. I do not wish to sever my connection permanently with the University, except for reasons which call for such a sacrifice. But then please call me only if you feel you have cut asunder your old moorings for the sake of adventure in a new life altogether, as you wrote to me and as you spoke to Manu on the fateful day when you asked her to think before she took the final plunge.

Yours affectionately,<br>Nirmal.

The reply came about a week afterwards:

On the train,<br>13-4-47

Chi. Nirmal Babu,

Your letter is frank. It does you credit on that account, but it makes me sad.

On your own showing, you were less than truthful. Had you shown the requisite courage and spoken out, I would not have let you go so abruptly as you did.

I see that I have lost caste with you. I must not defend myself. If we ever meet and if you would discuss what I consider to be your hasty judgement, we shall talk.

My Bengali continues, though slowly. Love.

Bapu.

## XVIII. AN EXCURSION IN PSYCHOLOGY

THE separation which thus took place between Gandhiji and myself were, as the reader will have observed, on grounds other than those which had led to his breach with either Parasuram or some of his intimate co-workers in Sevagram. The questions raised by the latter had been two. One was: barring the needs of nursing in illness or other occasions of helplessness, may one needlessly appear in a nude condition before man or woman, if one does not belong to a society in which nakedness is customary? Secondly, should people of opposite sexes share the same bed, assuming that they were not husband and wife, or people openly living as such?

After the events of March 1947, although Gandhiji was in the midst of the devastation in Bihar and although threatening clouds were already breaking upon the political horizon of India, he felt it his duty to explain clearly his views on *brahmacharya*. This led to a curious series of articles in the *Harijan* of June 8, 1947 ('How did I begin it?'), June 15, 1947 ('Walls of Protection'), June 22, 1947 ('Who and where is God?'), June 29, 1947 ('Towards Realization'), July 6, 1947 ('A Perplexity') on the practice of continence. Readers did not know why such a series suddenly appeared in the midst of intensely political articles, but the roots lay in one of the most critical events of Gandhiji's personal life when he had to differ from those whom he respected greatly for their independence of opinion.

There are many who were close to Gandhiji and who knew about these happenings, but who, out of a fear of misrepresenting him, have thought it wise to leave out this portion of his life from any critical consideration at all. But the present writer has always felt that such an attitude is not justified. Perhaps away at the back of our minds there is a lurking belief that what Gandhiji did was not right; and, in an apparent effort of avoiding injustice to his greatness, we may perhaps decide to draw a veil over certain events of which we have personal knowledge. But this can only be achieved by sacrificing what I believe to be one of the most important keys to an understanding of this unique personality of our age.

Even if we fail to approve of certain things, that is no justification for sitting in judgement over them and deciding, according to the stature of our small minds, what should or should not be said about Gandhiji. We can only bear testimony to what we have witnessed; and, in a spirit of utter truthfulness, describe it with the utmost fidelity possible. Perhaps we may be pardoned if we put our own construction upon events; but then the facts and the opinions must be clearly distinguishable from one another; so that when our age has passed away and many of the values for which we stand have been relegated to the lumber heap of history, men may have the means of knowing all that is possible about a man who once stood towering like a mountain above those who lived beside him.

As I left Gandhiji in Bihar, I wandered for weeks from place to place, and constantly pondered over the experiences of my five month's lonely but very intimate association with Gandhiji. It gradually dawned upon me that although I had felt hurt by his overshadowing concern for the private welfare of individuals which occasionally led him to allow these concerns to interfere with his larger public interests, it had been wrong on my part to have expected an absolute abandon for any particular aspect of life at the cost of more humble ones. He was not like a star in heaven by which men guide their pathway in life and which professes neither love nor hatred for those who tread upon the earth with their weary footsteps. He was more like a giant banyan tree which rears its head high in the heavens, but which, at the same time, spreads its branches in all directions, and from those branches it throws down newer roots to grip the earth once more in its embrace. This symbol of the tree, I felt, was more characteristic of the life of Gandhi than anything else. He stood in daily need of a contact with the earth of humanity from which he had sprung, and the sap of life which was thus gathered coursed through his veins and kept him evergreen. He would have been nothing without these roots which he dug into the earth; the barrenness of the titanic battles which he waged against political or social evils of tremendous magnitude would have otherwise dried up the sap of life which flowed within him. A mere voyage in high heavens would have meant for him an utterness of selfish indulgence from which his mind recoiled in horror. The earth with its lowly creatures was as much part of Truth for him as the high heavens with their immaculate dustlessness.

And when I gradually realized the truth of this, I appreciated the need which he felt for his sacred bath in the stream of earth-bound human life. I felt also how he was justified in his own way even while violently differing in either thought or action from his most trusted and loving comrades, who were undoubtedly right from their own point of view.

This led me to enquire closely into the origin of Gandhiji's character and whatever little I achieved in this respect, is being presented here for what it may be worth.

The point which we should never permit ourselves to forget is that even when Gandhiji's associates failed to approve of certain things connected with him, yet the latter consistently held that his relation with members of the other sex was something 'sacred', and though he did not 'advertise' it, there was no 'secrecy' about it either. On 3-2-1947, again, Gandhiji had said, 'What he was doing was not for blind imitation. It was undoubtedly dangerous, but it ceased to be so if the conditions were rigidly observed.' Why then should we draw a veil over them even when we try to understand the uniqueness of Gandhiji's personality? A bias never helps one to *understand*, even when it springs from a feeling of worshipfulness for one's object of study. It is better perhaps to err than not attempt at all, or start by censoring with the help of values which have mostly been picked up by us without question from the market place.

One can perhaps make the best attempt to understand Gandhiji's attitude towards womankind by a consideration of his relation with his mother. It is well known what a deep influence this devoutly religious woman exercised over her son in his boyhood days. The love for saintliness, for hard vows and an unflinching adherence to them even in the midst of severe trials, in other words, a heroic devotion to high ideals, were all apparently imbibed by Gandhiji from the example of his mother's life. For these very traits in his mother's character had evoked the deepest admiration within his soul while he was yet very young.*

It is also well known that before he started on a voyage for studies in England, it was at the instance of his mother that Gandhiji took a solemn vow before a Jain monk saying that he would never touch 'wine, women and meat'. It was only then that he could secure the blessings of his mother in undertaking a journey which was still considered taboo for members of his caste.**

Besides this, Gandhiji's relations with his wife whom he had married even at the age of thirteen also exercised a profound influence upon his life and opinions on the question of sex. An event of very great significance had taken place during the illness of his father when he was sixteen years of age. A little while before his father breathed his last, Gandhiji had retired to his own room where his wife lay asleep. Within a few minutes, a servant knocked at the door to announce that his father was no more. In profound sorrow he wrote later on how deeply ashamed and miserable he felt. He ran to his father's room. He saw that if 'animal passion had not blinded him, he should have been spared the torture of separation from his father during his last moment'. Commenting on the event, he wrote again: 'The shame of carnal desire even at the critical hour of my father's death... is a blot I have never been able to efface or forget, and I have always thought that, although my devotion to my parents knew no bounds and I would have given up anything for it, yet it was weighed and found unpardonably wanting because my mind was at the same moment in the grip of lust. I have therefore always regarded myself as a lustful, though a faithful husband. It took me long to get free from the shackles of lust, and I had to pass through ordeals before I could overcome it.'

\* *Autobiography*—2nd edition 1950, pp. 12-13.
\*\* *Ibid*, p. 56.

It was in the year 1906, when he was 37 years of age, that he took the vow of continence or *brahmacharya*. Ever since that date, his relation with members of the other sex was progressively 'purified' and he felt that he was becoming a fitter instrument for the practice of the highest virtues of non-violence. We may be permitted to assume that the repression of the sexual instinct was not only a means to a lofty end, but it was also the penance which Gandhiji voluntarily imposed upon himself for having proved untrue to his father during the last moments of his life.

Long afterwards, the question of Gandhiji's relationship with the other sex came up for some amount of hostile criticism; and, in order to explain his stand, he wrote several articles and also made some public statements, a few of which bear reproduction and analysis. In the *Harijan* of September 21, 1935, there was an article entitled 'A Renunciation', which is reproduced below in full.

'In 1891 after my return from England I virtually took charge of the children of the family and introduced the habit of walking with them—boys and girls—putting my hands on their shoulders. They were my brother's children. The practice continued even after they grew old. With the extension of the family, it gradually grew to proportions sufficient to attract attention.

'I was unconscious of doing any wrong, so far as I can recollect, till some years ago at Sabarmati an inmate of the Ashram told me that my practice, when extended to grown-up girls and women, offended the accepted notions of decency. But after discussion with the inmates it was continued. Recently two co-workers who came to Wardha suggested that the practice was likely to set a bad example to others and that I should discontinue it on that account. Their argument did not appeal to me. Nevertheless I did not want to ignore the friends' warning. I, therefore, referred it for examination and advice to five inmates of the Ashram. Whilst it was taking shape a decisive event took place. It was brought to my notice that a bright university student was taking all sorts of liberties in private with a girl who was under his influence, on the plea that he loved her like his own sister and could not restrain himself from some physical demonstration of it. He resented the slightest suggestion of impurity. Could I mention what the youth had been doing, the reader would unhesitatingly pronounce the liberties taken by him as impure. When I read the correspondence, I and those who saw it came to the conclusion that either the young man was a consummate hypocrite or was self-deluded.

'Anyway the discovery set me athinking. I recalled the warning of the two co-workers and asked myself how I would feel if I found the young man was using my practice in his defence. I may mention that the girl who is the victim of the youth's attention, although she regards him as absolutely pure and brotherly, does not like them, even protests against them, but is too weak to resist his action. The self-introspection induced by the event resulted, within two or three days of the reading of the correspondence, in the renunciation of the practice, and I announced it to the inmates of the Wardha Ashram on the 12th instant. It was not without a pang that I came to the decision. Never has an impure thought entered my being during or owing to the practice. My act has always been open. *I believe that my act was that of a parent and had enabled the numerous girls under my guidance and wardship to give their confidences which perhaps no one else enjoyed in the same measure.*\* Whilst I do not believe in a brahmacharya which ever requires a wall of protection against the touch of the opposite sex and will fail if exposed to the least temptation, I am not unaware of the dangers attendant upon the freedom I have taken.

'The discovery quoted by me has, therefore, prompted me to renounce the practice, however pure it may have been in itself. Every act of mine is scrutinized by thousands of men and women, as I am conducting an experiment requiring ceaseless vigilance. I must avoid doing things which may require a reasoned defence. My example was never meant to be followed by all and sundry. The young man's case has come upon me as a warning. I have taken it in the hope that my renunciation will set right those who

---

\* Italics, present author's.

may have erred whether under the influence of my example or without it. Innocent youth is a priceless possession not to be squandered away for the sake of a momentary excitement, miscalled pleasure. And let the weak girls like the one in this picture be strong enough to resist the approaches, though they may be declared to be innocent, of young men who are either knaves or who do not know what they are doing.'

If anybody questioned Gandhiji's purity in respect of sex, he could fly into an anger; and an article written almost in an angry mood appeared in the *Harijan* of November 4, 1939. It was entitled 'My Life', and is reproduced below:

'The following from its Allahabad correspondent appears in *The Bombay Chronicle*:

"Startling revelations have come to light regarding what has been going round the House of Commons about Gandhiji. It is reported that Mr. Edward Thompson, the British historian who visited Allahabad recently, threw some light on the curious mentality prevailing in England. Mr. Thompson, who met some political leaders here, is reported to have told them three things going round the House of Commons regarding Gandhiji:

1. Gandhiji was for unconditional co-operation with the British Government.
2. Gandhiji could still influence the Congress.
3. There were various stories about Gandhiji's sensual life, it being the impression that Gandhiji had ceased to be a saint.

Impressions about Gandhiji's 'sensual life', it appeared to Mr. Thompson, were based on some Marathi papers. He spoke about them, I understand, to Sir Tej Bahadur Sapru, who repudiated them. He spoke about them to Pandit Jawaharlal Nehru and Mr. P. N. Sapru also, who strongly repudiated them.

It appears Mr. Thompson, before leaving England, had seen several members of the House of Commons. Mr. Thompson, before leaving Allahabad, sent a letter to Mr. Greenwood, M.P., on the suggestion of Pandit Nehru pointing out that the stories regarding Gandhiji were absolutely baseless."

'Mr. Thompson was good enough to visit Segaon. He confirmed the report as substantially correct.

'The "unconditional co-operation" is dealt with in another note.

'The country will presently know the influence I have over the Congress.

'The third charge needs clearing. Two days ago I received a letter signed by four or five Gujaratis sending me a newspaper whose one mission seems to be to paint me as black as it is possible for any person to be painted. According to its headline it is a paper devoted to "the organization of Hindus". The charges against me are mostly taken from my confessions and distorted from their setting. Among many other charges, the charge of sensuality is most marked. My brahmacharya is said to be a cloak to hide my sensuality. Poor Dr. Sushila Nayar has been dragged before the public gaze for the crime of giving me massage and medicated baths, the two things for which she is the best qualified among those who surround me. The curious may be informed that there is no privacy about these operations which take over $1\frac{1}{2}$ hours and during which I often go off to sleep but during which I also transact business with Mahadev, Pyarelal or other co-workers.

'The charges to my knowledge began with my active campaign against untouchability. This was when it was included in the Congress programme and I began to address crowds on the subject and insisted on having Harijans at meetings and in the Ashram. It was then that some Sanatanists,* who used to help me and befriend me, broke with me and began a campaign of vilification. Later, a very highly placed Englishman joined the chorus. He picked out my freedom with women and showed up my 'saintliness' as sinfulness. In this chorus there were also one or two well known Indians. During the Round Table Conference American journals indulged in cruel caricatures of me. Mirabai who used to look after me was the target of their attack. As far as I could understand Mr. Thompson, who knows the gentlemen who have been behind these charges,

---

* Sanatanists or orthodox Hindus.

my letters to Premaben Kantak, who is a member of the Sabarmati Ashram, have also been used to prove my depravity. She is a graduate and worker of proved merit. She used to ask questions relating to brahmacharya and other topics. I sent her full replies. She thought they might be of general use and she published them with my permission. I hold them to be absolutely innocent and pure.

'Hitherto I have ignored these charges. But Mr. Thompson's talks about them and the importunity of the Gujarati correspondents, who say the indictment sent by them is but a sample of what is being said about me, impel me to repudiate them. I have no secrets of my own in this life. I have owned my weaknesses. If I were sensually inclined, I would have the courage to make the confession. It was when I developed detestation of sensual connection even with my own wife and had sufficiently tested myself that I took the vow of brahmacharya in 1906, and that for the sake of better dedication to the service of the country. From that day began my open life. I do not remember having ever slept or remained with my own wife or other women with closed doors except for the occasions referred to in my writings in *Young India* and *Navajivan*. Those were black nights with me. But as I have said repeatedly God has saved me in spite of myself. I claim no credit of any virtue that I may possess. He is for me the Giver of all good and has saved me for His service.

'From that day when I began brahmacharya our freedom began. My wife became a free woman, free from my authority as her lord and master, and I became free from my slavery to my own appetite which she had to satisfy. No other woman had any attraction for me in the same sense that my wife had. I was too loyal to her as husband and too loyal to the vow I had taken before my mother to be slave to any other woman. *But the manner in which my brahmacharya came to me irresistibly drew me to woman as the mother of man. She became too sacred for sexual love. And so every woman at once became sister or daughter to me.*\* I had enough women about me at Phoenix. Several of them

---

\* Italics, present author's.

were my own relations whom I had enticed to South Africa. Others were co-workers' wives or relatives. Among these were the Wests and other Englishmen. The Wests included West, his sister, his wife, and his mother-in-law who had become the Granny of the little settlement.

'As has been my wont, I could not keep the new good thing to myself. So I presented brahmacharya for the acceptance of all the settlers. All approved of it. And some took it up and remained true to the ideal. My brahmacharya knew nothing of the orthodox laws governing its observance. I framed my own rules as occasion necessitated. But I have never believed that all contact with woman was to be shunned for the due observance of brahmacharya. That restraint which demands abstention from all contact, no matter how innocent, with the opposite sex is a forced growth, having little or no vital value. Therefore natural contacts for service were never restrained. *And I found myself enjoying the confidences of many sisters, European and Indian, in South Africa. And when I invited the Indian sisters in South Africa to join the civil resistance movement, I found myself one of them. I discovered that I was specially fitted to serve womankind.*\* To cut the (for me enthralling) story short, my return to India found me in no time one with India's women. The easy access I had to their hearts was an agreeable revelation to me. Muslim sisters never kept purdah before me even as they did not in South Africa. I sleep in the Ashram surrounded by women for they feel safe with me in every respect. It should be remembered that there is no privacy in the Segaon Ashram.

'If I were sexually attracted towards women, I have courage enough, even at this time of life, to become a polygamist. I do not believe in free love—secret or open. Free open love I have looked upon as dog's love. Secret love is besides cowardly.

'Sanatanist Hindus may abhor my non-violence. I know many of them think that Hindus will become cowards if they remain under my influence. I know of no man having become a coward under my influence. They may decry my

---

\* Italics, present author's.

non-violence as much as they like. But they ill serve themselves or Hinduism by indulgence in palpable lies.'

It is interesting to observe in this connection how Gandhiji regarded the slightest trace of sexual excitement on his own part as a fall from the vow of brahmacharya,* and how he considered public confession as the proper means of punishing himself for the lapse and also of relief from the feeling of sin which oppressed him. During a convalescence in 1936, there was an occasion when, while asleep, he had felt momentarily excited. This forthwith led to a confession entitled "Nothing without grace" in the *Harijan* of February 29, 1936, a part of which is being quoted below.

He wrote:

'I have been trying to follow *Brahmacharya* consciously and deliberately since 1899. My definition of it is purity not merely of body but of both speech and thought also. With the exception of what must be regarded as one lapse, I can recall no instance during more than thirty-six years' constant and conscious effort, of mental disturbance such as I experienced during this illness. I was disgusted with myself. The moment the feeling came I acquainted my attendants and the medical friends with my condition. They could give me no help. I expected none. I broke loose after the experience from the rigid rest that was imposed upon me. The confession of the wretched experience brought much relief to me. I felt as if a great load had been raised from over me. It enabled me to pull myself together before any harm could be done. But what of the Gita? Its teaching is clear and precise. A mind that is once hooked to the Star of Stars becomes incorruptible. How far I must be from Him, He alone knows. Thank God my much vaunted Mahatmaship has never fooled me. But this enforced rest has humbled me as never before. It has brought to the surface my limitations and imperfections. But I am not so much ashamed of them, as I should be of hiding them from the public. My faith in the message of the Gita is as bright

---

* The reader will recall how Gandhiji once said that his aspiration was to become 'a eunuch not through operation but to be made such through prayer to God' (Prayer meeting, 1-2-1947).

as ever. Unwearied ceaseless effort is the price that must be paid for turning that faith into rich infallible experience. But the same Gita says without any equivocation that the experience is not to be had without divine grace. We should develop swelled heads if Divinity had not made that ample reservation.'

This violent reaction against any physical manifestation of sex and his psychological effort to become as pure as his mother, led Gandhiji into a profoundly significant attitude in public life.

He was the fashioner of the instrument of non-violence in public life. All social evils need remedies; and the remedy can be either violent or non-violent. The essence of violence consists in inflicting punishment upon the wrong-doer, which may eventually lead to his destruction if he does not correct himself. The essence of non-violence, on the other hand, consists in resisting the evil of the wrong-doer so that he is forced to shower punishment upon the non-violent man for his resistance or non-co-operation with evil. If the latter does not bend, then his heroic suffering in a just cause is likely to evoke respect for him in the heart of the wrong-doer, and the process of conversion begins. If it fails, the non-violent man takes more drastic steps, intensifies his non-co-operation, invites more suffering; and eventually this may lead to his own destruction in contrast to the destruction of the evil-doer under violence. The way of non-violence thus becomes the way of heroic self-suffering in which the fighter never surrenders his respect for the personality of the opponent, and aims at his conversion rather than destruction. He tries to bring about a cessation of evil even with the co-operation of the erstwhile wrong-doer.

This deep respect for human personality coupled with infinite capacity for self-suffering was regarded by Gandhiji as a characteristic specifically associated with the nature of woman.

In 1940, he wrote:

'My contribution to the great problem lies in my presenting for acceptance truth and ahimsa in every walk of life, whether for individuals or nations. I have hugged the hope that in this woman will be the unquestioned leader and, having thus found her place in human evolution, will shed her inferiority complex.

'I have suggested that woman is the incarnation of ahimsa. Ahimsa means infinite love, which gain means infinite capacity for suffering. Who but woman, the *mother of man*,* shows this capacity in the largest measure? She shows it as she carries the infant and feeds it during nine months and derives joy in the suffering involved. What can beat the suffering caused by the pangs of labour? But she forgets them in the joy of creation. Who again suffers daily so that her babe may wax from day to day? Let her transfer that love to the whole of humanity, *let her forget she ever was or can be the object of man's lust. And she will occupy her proud position by the side of man as his mother, maker and silent leader. It is given to her to teach the art of peace to the warring world thirsting for that nectar.*\* She can become the leader in satyagraha which does not require the learning that books give but does require a stout heart that comes from suffering and faith.'\*\*

'Woman is more fitted than man to make explorations and take action in *ahimsa*. For the courage of self-sacrifice woman is anyday superior to man as I believe man is to woman for the courage of the brute.'\*\*\*

It follows from all this that, according to Gandhi, progress in civilization consisted in the introduction into human life and social institutions of a larger measure of the law of love or self-suffering which woman represented best in her own person. This was a profoundly transformed projection on the broad canvas of social life of an attitude which had come into being in the privacy of his personal life.

In private life, too, Gandhiji's relationship with individuals was deepened and modified in the same direction in which it moved in public. Thus we read in Manu Gandhi's *Bapu—My Mother*, how he said to her:

'Have I not become your mother? I have been a father to many but only to you I am a mother. A father does pay

---

\* Italics, present author's.
\*\* *Harijan*, 24-2-1940, p. 13.
\*\*\* *Harijan*, 5-11-1938, p. 317.

attention to the bringing up of his children but the real education of a girl comes from mother.' (p. 3).

'Ever since then,' writes Manu Gandhi, 'Bapu began to bring me up just as a mother would bring up her own daughter of 14 or 15. A girl of that age is generally near her mother and her development requires the company of her mother. Bapu also began taking interests in the minutest details of my life, such as my food, attire, my sickness, my visits and companions, my studies, right down to whether I thoroughly washed my hair every week and he continued to do so still his last moment.' (p. 8).

Gandhiji used to sleep under the open sky or in an open room if the weather happened to be cold. There was no privacy about him because other men and women also slept near him and some even on the same bed. At an age bordering on eighty, his circulation became poor, his feet had to be massaged every day with clarified butter, otherwise it tended to crack. On cold nights, he had occasional tremors which were difficult to control. These fits might continue for several minutes, and then it was the practice of his attendants to hold him tightly clasped to their bodies so as to restore warmth to his shivering frame.

On other occasions, too, Gandhiji's body might have come in contact with other persons; and it is curious that he tried to ascertain from them if any impure feeling had, even momentarily, assailed their minds. It was his belief that if he was not wholly free from sensualism, it would not fail to evoke a kindred feeling in those who attended him. He held firmly that if his mind was completely free from lust, such an experience would spiritually prove elevating to both parties. He made a reference to this in his letter to me dated the 17th of March 1947.

Personally, I have had the *feeling* that the question which he asked those who shared in his 'experiment' was whether they did not feel the same about him as they felt in respect of their mother. In such experiments, sex, which had so long acted as a barrier to that complete identification which exists between a mother and child, was laid low and the experimenter became free to enter upon a new relationship with men and women which was completely pure', and therefore spiritually elevating.

Gandhi's concern about the private, personal life of individuals, whether men or women, sprang from the same attitude of mind. This domestic concern had repelled me originally and made me leave him for the time being; but it was a deep, spiritual attitude on his part which was the by-product of his attempt to conquer sex by becoming a woman. The intense concern which he evinced in the lives of men and women, and his ceaseless efforts at manipulating them, whether in the case of individuals or of communities, is therefore comparable to the manipulating technique exercised by Leonardo da Vinci after the sublimation of his sexual impulse. Only, in the case of Leonardo da Vinci, it was exercised in respect of physical material, while in the case of Gandhi, it was in respect of human lives whether in the private or the public sphere.

Saints have lived in India who have been able to rise above the impulse of sex by identifying themselves with those belonging to the opposite sex. In the case of the mystic Shree Ramakrishna, it is said that this psychological identification reached such a high degree that somatic changes followed, and discharges of blood through the pores of the skin appeared periodically during one phase of his life, as in the case of women.*

But Gandhiji, even within the secret recesses of his heart, never gave himself up to such an absolute abandon to an intensity of feeling. He was less of an introvert, more closely bound to the world of sense-experience to develop such total exclusiveness of certain experiences as we observe in the case of Shree Ramakrishna. The bridge which held him on to the world of common men remained unbroken till the end of his days. If he had given way to an abandon as in the case of Shree Ramakrishna, we would have lost a leader of men, and the world would probably have been poorer thereby.

In spite of that, this mother-cult of Gandhi's boyhood

---

* *Shree Shree Ramakrishna Leelaprasanga, Sadhak Bhava*, Sixth Edition, B.S. 1344, pp. 216, 250, 259, 261, 266, 352.

days remained throughout his life a very strong element in his philosophy, and he tried to enlist men and women in private as well as in public life to his cult of purity, love and self-suffering. This mission of civilization, which was Gandhi's greatest contribution to modern life, was thus, in the last analysis, an external projection on the larger canvas of the world's life of the saintliness which was embodied in that noble woman who shone like a pole star over her son's great life.

This projection again had become possible only because the son was a genius of action and organization and retained to the end of his days the deep influence he had imbibed from the West during the formative period of his life. A typical Indian, without Gandhi's history of Western contact, would have given way to individual exclusiveness. He would undoubtedly have risen higher in the spiritual plane than Gandhiji, but would have done so by the sacrifice of his beneficial personal influence upon the lowlier lives of his fellow men.

The above analysis does not however mean in any way that Gandhi's cult of non-violence can be dismissed as the idle fancy of a private individual. The world has profited immensely by the physical investigations of Leonardo da Vinci even though they sprang from the humble depths of his personal history. In a similar manner, although the origin of Gandhi's desire to purify and civilize mankind lay within the depths of his personal relationship with his mother, or to certain events of his boyhood days, yet the objective result does not lose any value thereby. His gift to mankind in the shape of a civilized form of collective action in satyagraha as a substitute for warfare, which is helplessly looked upon as the last instrument for the resolution of conflicts of interest in human society, will have to be experimented upon and judged on its own merits and not dismissed on account of its humble, personal origin.

## XIX. DARK CLOUDS OVER BENGAL

THE pilgrimage in Bihar continued as before. In the meanwhile, Jawaharlal Nehru had called an Inter-Asian Relations Conference in Delhi which was to be held there on the 1st of April 1947. Gandhiji's presence was indispensable, so he left Bihar by train on the 30th of March 1947. The reason why he went to Delhi was given by him during his visit to the Conference on the first day. In answer to a question with regard to his views on the proposed Asian Institute, he said:

'The question is certainly very nice. Let me confess my ignorance. I have really to apologize to you. Pandit Nehru had asked me long before this Conference was scheduled to take place whether it would be possible for me to attend it. It has proved to be a much more important conference than it was expected to be. I was obliged to say at that time that I was very sorry and would not be able to come. When Lord Mountbatten, the new Viceroy, invited me to meet him, however, I could not say "No." It would have been foreign to my nature to do so. The Viceroy had already told me that the credit of bringing me to Delhi during the Asian Conference was really his. And I told the Viceroy: "I am your prisoner. But I am also Pandit Nehru's prisoner, for, after all, he is your Vice-President." '\*

In course of his speech after prayer he said on the same day, that the Asian Conference was a big thing and their jewel, Jawaharlal, was very beloved of the delegates because of his love for them and his dream of a United Asia. Only, however, if India was true to her traditions could she be worthy of the role she ought to play. It would be cruel to spoil Jawaharlal's dream of a United Asia by internal strife in this land.

It should be recalled here that, as a reaction against the attitude of the Muslim League, Hindu communalism was also becoming more and more insurgent and almost every

---

\* *Harijan*, 20-4-1947, p. 113.

evening at Delhi someone or other in the audience used to protest against the recital of verses from the Koran which was a regular feature of Gandhiji's prayers. On the 3rd, Gandhiji therefore made a pointed reference to this and said that 'he would ask those who were against his holding the prayer meeting not to come or if they did, they should come by themselves and kill him if they wanted to. Even if he was killed, Gandhiji said, he would not give up repeating the names of Rama and Rahim, which meant to him the same God. With these names on his lips he would die cheerfully. If he refrained from repeating the names of Rama and Rahim, how could he, Gandhiji asked, face the Hindus of Noakhali and the Muslims of Bihar?'*

Riots of a very serious character had, in the meanwhile, started in different portions of India; and even while Gandhiji was in Delhi, the new Viceroy persuaded him as well as Qaid-e-Azam Jinnah to sign a joint statement to the following effect:

'We deeply deplore the recent acts of lawlessness and violence that have brought the utmost disgrace on the fair name of India and the greatest misery to innocent people, irrespective of who were the aggressors and who were the victims.

'We denounce for all time the use of force to achieve political ends, and we call upon all the communities of India, to whatever persuasion they may belong, not only to refrain from all acts of violence and disorder, but also to avoid both in speech and writing, any incitement to such acts.'

| | |
|---|---|
| M. A. Jinnah | M. K. Gandhi |
| 15. 4. '47 | |

Gandhiji returned to Bihar on the 14th of the month and on the same evening made a reference to the disturbing news from Noakhali. There was an exchange of telegrams between him and co-workers in Bengal which was released for the Press. The correspondence was also published in the *Harijan* of 20-4-1947 under the heading 'About Noakhali'. It ran:

* *Harijan*, 20-4-1947, p. 118.

'Gandhiji received the following wires about the Noakhali situation to which he has sent the following replies:

Shri Satish Chandra Dasgupta in his wire dated Ramganj, April 2 says:

"This is a quick post information. I have sent the following telegram to the District Magistrate, Police Superintendent and Chief Minister.

"There have been five cases of arson between March 23 and yesterday. Yesterday's case happened at Mohammadpur in Ramganj *Thana*. It was an attempt to burn alive three families consisting of twenty-one persons male, female, children of the house who for safety slept all in one room. This room was fastened from outside and this thatched hut and other huts of the house simultaneously set on fire. The inmates escaped by breaking through mat wall."

In another telegram dated Ramganj, April 5, Shri Dasgupta says:

"I have sent the following telegram to the Chief Minister and local authorities:

'Have to bring your notice another case of arson last night April 4, at Changirgaon near Ramganj *Thana* where also like the last case the inmate Haralal Bhowmik found himself locked from outside in his sleeping room while all structures including sleeping room were burning. Thank God, Haralal could escape by cutting open corner of stout reed wall of his corrugated sheds. Request you think over these gruesome attempts of burning alive the Hindus and shape Government policy by shaking off inactivity.'"

Gandhiji's reply to the above wires:

"All your precise but painful wires also from Haran Babu. Case seems to be for exodus or perishing in flames of fanaticism. Hope you will not advise my coming to advise on choice. Hold council with workers and act promptly."

Shri Haranchandra Ghosh Choudhury, M.L.A. (Bengal) in his wire dated Chaumuhani (Noakhali), April 6 says:

"Rehabilitation in Noakhali is becoming increasingly difficult. Lawlessness, theft, burglary, house-breaking, night raids, burning of houses, hay-stacks, becoming common.

"Ploughing of fields in some areas obstructed. In about five hundred cases involving loot, arson, murder, final reports submitted on plea of non-availability sufficient evidence which under present circumstances can be had from riot victims alone. Absconders and culprits moving freely reported holding meeting now. People suspect foul play in original cases as all Hindu officers in charge of affected *Thanas* transferred. Those officers who have timely submitted charge sheets against good number of offenders also transferred. Proceedings drawn against officers who attempted quell riots or arrested large number of culprits of whom ninety per cent now bailed out. More than hundred counter cases against workers. Hindu police and army staff are seriously enquired into and in some cases summoned or otherwise harassed."

Gandhiji's reply to the above wire:

"If what you say is true, clear case for exodus or perishing in the flames of madness and fanaticism. Consult Satish Babu and act unitedly."

Gandhiji has sent the following wire to the Chief Minister, Bengal, Mr. H. S. Suhrawardy:

"I continue receive doleful wires about increasing lawlessness Noakhali. I suggest prompt attention wires of Satish Chandra Dasgupta and prompt action. Am publishing wires."*

On the 18th of April 1947, a personal letter was also written to the Chief Minister of Bengal which is reproduced below:

Patna, 18-4-1947

Dear Friend,

Many thanks for your letter of the 9th instant.

I cannot endorse your insinuations, I have never subscribed to hush-hush policy. Publication of false news I hold to be a crime against humanity. If true news gives rise to conflagration there is something wrong with society and its leaders.

I began publishing the wires received from Noakhali when I despaired of getting a hearing from you and when living outside Noakhali, I felt helpless. Probably my presence

---

* *Harijan*, 20-4-1947, p. 115.

in Noakhali would have made no difference in the situation. Only I would have derived satisfaction from the fact that I was in Noakhali sharing the trials of its people and my co-workers.

It surprises me that you should discount the statements of facts supplied by Shri Satish Chandra Dasgupta. The culprits may never be traced but the facts of arson and loot could not be disputed, nor could the community from which the culprits are derived be disputed.

The rulers whether democrats or autocrats, whether foreign or indigenous, forfeit the right to rule when they fail to deal properly with crimes even when the culprits are able to defy detection.

Yours sincerely,<br>M. K. Gandhi.

On the 7th of May 1947, the Chief Minister of Bengal issued a statement to the Press in course of which he said:

'It is perhaps natural, after what has taken place, that the minority community should take alarm at the slightest incident. It is a matter of regret that there are organizations working there that consider it their duty to spread alarm and to keep people in a ferment of fear and panic, as unsettled conditions help them in their political game.

'I deprecate the ease with which reports of alleged oppression by Muslims are accepted as true even by well-meaning people working there, and worse still are circulated in the form of leaflets amongst Hindus increasing their panic and their fear, except of course amongst those who know that the reports are not founded on facts. These reports are also passed on to the local authorities who have investigated them and found most of them to be false, some exaggerated, some twisted and only a few based on facts.

'Unfortunately, therefore, due largely to the activities of well-meaning or ill-meaning organizations or volunteers of the Hindu persuasion in Noakhali, there is still apprehension amongst the Hindus which I must consider genuine, but based on very slender foundations. To the extent that these organizations give encouragement to Hindus to induce them to return and settle in the land of their birth, I value their services and their co-operation, but I must condemn the activities of those that propagate and keep alive hatred and suspicion, and even if they do not go the length of framing cases as alleged by Muslims, their activities have had a very unfortunate effect on rehabilitation as they have kept up the tension.'

It was by a stroke of luck that we were able to secure about this time another version from the side of the Government with regard to the situation in Noakhali. A report dated the 13th of May 1947 had emanated from the office of the Commissioner, Chittagong Division, and it was addressed to the Home Department of the Government of Bengal. It is reproduced in the appendix in full, and gives at least an honest picture of the situation which public statements from the Government never succeeded in doing.

## XX. DARKER CLOUDS OVER INDIA

IN the meanwhile the communal situation in the North-West Frontier had worsened considerably; and everywhere there was talk of partitioning the country into two. Gandhiji had returned to Bihar from Delhi on the 14th of April but had to hasten back to the capital after a fortnight's stay. In his post-prayer speech on the 1st of May 1947 in Delhi, he referred to the violence that was taking place in the Frontier Province, in the Punjab and in other places. The audience might well ask, he said, why in spite of the joint appeal by Qaid-e-Azam Jinnah and himself for peace in the country and the declaration in the appeal that use of force should be eschewed for all time for gaining political ends, the appeal seemed to have been entirely defeated in practice.

In his opinion, the honour both of the Viceroy who was instrumental in bringing about the joint appeal and of Qaid-e-Azam Jinnah was involved in the failure of the appeal. He held that it was not open to Jinnah Sahib to plead that his followers did not listen to his (Jinnah Sahib's) appeal. That would be cutting the whole ground from under his feet because he was the undisputed President of the All India Muslim League which claimed to represent the vast bulk of the Muslim population of India. Where was the authority of the League, if the Muslim resorted to violence for gaining the political aim which was summed up in the word Pakistan? Was the British Government to yield to the force of arms rather than the force of reason?

The speaker had expressed his doubts as to the wisdom of issuing the joint appeal unless it was certain that it meant for both the signatories all that the words thereof conveyed.*

On the following evening he said again:

'Was Pakistan to be seized by terrorism such as they seemed to be witnessing in the Frontier Province, in the Punjab, in Sindh and elsewhere?

'People had suggested that everything would be alright

\* *Harijan*, 11-5-1947, p. 147.

and non-Muslims in the Muslim majority provinces would be put on absolute equality with the Muslims if not specially favoured as against them. He suggested that it was an impossible dream. If the Muslims were taught otherwise while Pakistan was not established they could not be expected to behave better after Pakistan had become a settled fact. It was up to Qaid-e-Azam and his lieutenants to inspire trust in the minds of the minorities in the provinces or parts which were designed for Pakistan. Then there would be no longer fear of Pakistan-cum-Partition.'*

On the 6th of May, Gandhiji had a fairly long interview with Qaid-e-Azam Jinnah to which he made a reference on the 7th when he said that the conversations were carried on in a friendly spirit even though there could never be agreement between them on the question of the division of India. He could not bear the thought of it and so long as he was convinced that it was wrong, he could not possibly put his signature to the scheme. He held that it was not only bad for the Hindus but equally so for the Muslims.** To an interviewer in Delhi Gandhiji said, 'Can you describe Pakistan to me? I have tried to understand what it is and have failed. And if the Punjab and Bengal today are hall-marks of Pakistan, then it can never exist.' His own view regarding the division of India had not undergone any change. He stood for a United India as firmly as ever and as he said more than once to friends, 'To ultimate decision of division or partition of provinces and all such matters are for the people to settle among themselves after the British have withdrawn their power.'*

On the 5th of May, Doon Campbell, Reuters' special correspondent in New Delhi, put a certain question to Gandhiji. The question and reply were both published in the *Harijan* of 18th May 1947 (p. 156).

Q. Is the communal division of India inevitable? Will such division solve the communal problem?

A. Personally, I have always said No, and I say No even now to both these questions.

---

\* *Harijan*, 11-5-1947, p. 148.
\*\* *Harijan*, 18-5-1947, p. 155.
\* *Harijan*, 18-5-1947, p. 153.

In answer to another question regarding the British Government's resolve to withdraw all vestiges of British rule in India by the end of June 1947, Gandhiji said again:

'I have never appreciated the argument that the British want so many months to get ready to leave. During this time all parties will look to the British Cabinet and the Viceroy. We have not defeated the British by force of arms. It has been a victory for India by moral force. Assuming, of course, that every word of what has been said is meant to be carried out, then the British decision will go down in history as the noblest act of the British Nation. That being so, the thirteen months' stay of the British power and British arms is really a hindrance rather than a help, because everybody looks for help to the great military machine they have brought into being. That happened in Bengal, in Bihar, in the Punjab, and in the North-West Frontier Province. The Hindus and Muslims said in turn: "Let us have the British troops." It is a humiliating spectacle. I have often said before but it does not suffer in value through repetition because every time I repeat it, it gains force: the British will have to take the risk of leaving India to chaos or anarchy. This is so because there has been no Home Rule; it has been imposed on the people. *And, when you voluntarily remove that rule there might be no rule in the initial state. It might have come about if we had gained victory by the force of arms.*\* The communal feuds you see here are, in my opinion, partly due to the presence of the British. If the British were not here, we would still go through the fire no doubt, but that fire would purify us.\*\*

In the meanwhile the communal position had worsened in Noakhali; and workers began to feel that Gandhiji's presence was necessary either for the purpose of winding up the existing organization or transferring the entire responsibility of such work as was still being carried on upon permanent residents of the district. The Government of Bengal could not legitimately raise any objection against such an arrangement as they could with regard to workers

---

\* Italics, present author's.
\*\* *Harijan*, 18-5-1947, p. 156.

or organizations from other parts of Bengal.

The controversy referred to between the Bengal Government and workers of the Gandhi Camp in Noakhali continued as indicated in the previous chapter; and so finally Gandhiji decided to pay a brief visit to Calcutta in order to meet the Chief Minister personally and see what could be done in order to improve the present situation.

Accordingly, he left Delhi on the 8th of May; and even while in the train, he finished a very important letter to the British Viceroy, which was despatched by hand when the letter was completed. On a close perusal, it appears clear how desperately Gandhiji was trying to keep the British completely out of the proposed partition of the country.

The letter ran:

On the train to Patna,<br>8-5-1947

Dear Friend,

It strikes me that I should summarise what I said and wanted to say and left unfinished for want of time, at our last Sunday's meeting.

Whatever may be said to the contrary, it would be a blunder of first magnitude for the British to be party in any way whatsoever to the division of India. If it has to come, let it come after the British withdrawal, as a result of understanding between the parties or an armed conflict which according to Qaid-e-Azam Jinnah is taboo. Protection of minorities can be guaranteed by establishing a court of arbitration in the event of difference of opinion among contending parties.

2. Meanwhile the Interim Government should be composed either of Congressmen or those whose names the Congress chooses or of Muslim League men or those whom the League chooses. The dual control of today lacking team work and team spirit is harmful for the country. The parties exhaust themselves in the effort to retain their seats and to placate you. Want of team spirit demoralises the Government and imperils the integrity of the services so essential for good and efficient government.

3. Referendum at this stage in the Frontier (or any province for that matter) is a dangerous thing in itself. You

have to deal with the material that faces you. In any case nothing should or can be done over Dr. Khan Sahib's head as Premier. Note that this paragraph is relevant only if division is at all to be countenanced.

4. I feel sure that partition of the Punjab and Bengal is wrong in every case and a needless irritant for the League. This as well as all innovations can come after the British withdrawal not before, except always for mutual agreement. Whilst the British Power is functioning in India, it must be held principally responsible for the preservation of peace in the country. That machine seems to be cracking under the existing strain which is caused by the raising of various hopes that cannot or must not be fulfilled. These have no place during the remaining thirteen months. This period can be most profitably shortened if the minds of all were focussed on the sole task of withdrawal. You and you alone can do it to the exclusion of all other activity so far as the British occupation is concerned.

5. Your task as undisputed master of naval warfare, great as it was, was nothing compared to what you are called to do now. The single-mindedness and clarity that gave you success are much more required in this work.

6. If you are not to leave a legacy of chaos behind, you have to make your choice and leave the government of the whole of India including the States to one party. The Constituent Assembly has to provide for the governance even of that part of India which is not represented by the Muslim League or some States.

7. Non-partition of the Punjab and Bengal does not mean that the minorities in these Provinces are to be neglected. In both the Provinces they are large and powerful enough to arrest and demand attention. If the popular Governments cannot placate them the Governors should during the interregnum actively interfere.

8. The intransmissibility of paramountcy is a vicious doctrine if it means that they can become sovereign and a menace for Independent India. All the power wherever exercised by the British in India must automatically descend to its successor. Thus the people of the States become as much part of Independent India as the people of British

India. The present Princes are puppets created or tolerated for the upkeep and prestige of the British power. The unchecked powers exercised by them over their people is probably the worst blot on the British Crown. The Princes under the new regime can exercise only such powers as trustees can and as can be given to them by the Constituent Assembly. It follows that they cannot maintain private armies or arms factories. Such ability and statecraft as they possess must be at the disposal of the Republic and must be used for the good of their people and the people as a whole. I have merely stated what should be done with the States. It is not for me to show in this letter how this can be done.

9. Similarly difficult but not so baffling is the question of the Civil Service. Its members should be taught from now to accommodate themselves to the new regime. They may not be partisans taking sides. The slightest trace of communalism among them should be severely dealt with. The English element in it should know that they owe loyalty to the new regime rather than to the old and therefore to Great Britain. The habit of regarding themselves as rulers and therefore superiors must give place to the spirit of true service of the people.

II

10. I had a very pleasant two hours and three quarters with Qaid-e-Azam Jinnah on Tuesday last. We talked about the joint statement on non-violence. He was agreeably emphatic over his belief in non-violence. He has reiterated it in the Press statement which was drafted by him.

11. We did talk about Pakistan and partition. I told him that my opposition to Pakistan persisted as before and suggested that in view of his declaration of faith in non-violence he should try to convert his opponents by reasoning with them and not by show of force. He was, however, quite firm that the question of Pakistan was not open to discussion. Logically, for a believer in non-violence, nothing, not even the existence of God, could be outside its scope.

Rajkumari Amrit Kaur saw the first eight paragraphs,

the purport of which she was to give to Pandit Nehru with whom I was to send you this letter. But, I could not finish it in New Delhi. I finished it on the train.

I hope you and Her Excellency are enjoying your hard-earned rest.

Yours sincerely,<br>M. K. Gandhi.

To
    H. E. The Viceroy,
        Simla.

## XXI. ON A VISIT TO BENGAL'S CAPITAL

SOME of us met Gandhiji at Burdwan Station which is about sixty miles from Calcutta and acquainted him with conditions prevailing in Bengal. There was a consultation on the problem of rehabilitation in Noakhali. A number of questions had been kept ready to which Gandhiji dictated answers one by one in the train. A few of them are reproduced below:

*Q.* The Government are at present unable to supply requisite material for building purposes; should a non-official organization now take up this task?

*A.* In my opinion the task of rehabilitation is entirely Governments' work. If a private agency takes up any financial responsibility it would be a dangerous thing. For it would carry with it the implication that those who have been rehabilitated by private financial help would also be defended privately. I hold this to be impossible; and unwise, if not impossible.

It should be our endeavour to induce local Muslims to help the evacuees in rehabilitation when Government aid is inadequate. But if neither the former nor the Government prove helpful, no non-official organization should or can undertake the task for reasons given above.

*Q.* Many cases are being withdrawn by the police after enquiry as evidence is reported to be lacking; we have heard of more than 600 of such cases. Should these be reopened and a legal committee set up for the purpose? The Noakhali District Relief, Rehabilitation, Rescue Committee has a legal branch. But it is not active. Should Satish Babu try to take up this work with the help of the N.D.R.R.R.C.?

*A.* I think this we must not do on any account. The legal committee must work efficiently and effectively. It does not fall within our province. Our province is to teach the people to help themselves even up to the point of defence against Government or other oppression; that is the meaning of 'Do or Die.'

Q. Rice now sells at Rs. 25 a maund. The Government have stopped selling rice to riot-affected people at controlled rate. If we store rice and sell at controlled rate it will require a capital of 20 lacs of rupees. Should we undertake this work?

A. I think in dangerous areas such as Noakhali we must not supply rice through private agency. I would far rather that after a clear statement the people trek to safer parts and in doing so they get all the help necessary, financial or other.

It is strange but true that every difficulty that faces us in Noakhali is present in Bihar almost to the same extent as in Noakhali. Realization of this fact should make us think furiously and enable us to deal with the Noakhali problem clearly and bravely. We should on no account countenance any lethargy, falsehood, cowardliness or selfishness on the part of the refugees.

Sarat Chandra Bose saw Gandhiji after his arrival in Sodpur.

Shortly after his arrival, one of the first things which Gandhiji did was to correct a reply by Satish Babu to H. S. Suhrawardy's letters received some time ago. It is reproduced below:

'I have your two letters of the 27th and 28th April. I thank you for the instructions that you have issued.

'I certainly agree with you that volunteers should not circulate reports of incidents which are founded on panic. No such instance has come under my notice. As for *Dinalipi*, it is a circular letter designed to be circulated only among workers and friends who are kept informed of corporate activity. It rigorously eschews all but authentic reports. None of your officials has complained of any exaggeration.

'Nothing will please me better than to be able to say that there is such general help from the local Muslims as to dispel all fear and suspicion from the Hindu mind. I am sorry to say such is not as yet the case.

'You have asked me to contact Maulana Fazlul Karim

and Maulvi Mujibar Rahman. I shall try to contact them when they come back. Nobody wishes that innocent people should be victimized.

'Regarding complaints against volunteers I would suggest that every instance of misbehaviour should be exposed and dealt with under the law. As for those who are under the discipline of Kazirkhil, I can give the assurance that any specific complaint shall be dealt with immediately. We are here to serve, not to hinder the cause of peace.

'You have advised me to speak to the Muslims not as potential enemies but as friends. The Muslims to me are part of ourselves. I do not and cannot look upon them as potential enemies.

'You have in your letter to Gandhiji attributed to me the saying that "all the crime and lawlessness which Noakhali is witnessing today is directed against the Hindus". I do not think I ever made any such statement. I must have been misrepresented.'

On the 9th, Gandhiji said at the prayer meeting at Sodpur that he had not expected to come to Calcutta but when he had reports from friends about events in Calcutta, he thought that he should go to Calcutta and put in his work in pursuit of the same object that had taken him to Noakhali and then to Bihar.

They saw before them Gurudev's (Rabindranath Tagore) portrait with floral decorations. For 9th May was Gurudev's birthday. That was why they had two hymns from Gurudev's pen sung to them. Great men never died and it was up to them to keep them immortal by continuing the work they had commenced. The second was most apposite at the moment when Hindus and Muslims were fighting. The purport of the hymn was that God should take them from darkness unto light, from untruth unto truth and from misery unto bliss indefinable. This was the *mantra* with which he had armed Deenabandhu* Andrews and Pearson when he permitted them to proceed to South Africa. These two were among the best of Gurudev's numerous devotees throughout the world.

* A title lovingly given to the Rev. C. F. Andrews, which meant 'Friend of the lowly and oppressed'.

It was a good thing that Q. A. Jinnah's words uttered to the Pathan deputation that had waited on him were to the same tune. They should read those words for themselves. If all followed the advice, India would truly become a unique land of real peace. They knew that he was joint signatory to the document on non-violence. That at once imposed on him the duty of fasting unto death if either Hindus or Muslims descended to the level of savages or beasts. Let the Hindus of Bihar and Muslims of Noakhali remember the fact. He had earned the right to fast by the service which he had and was still rendering to the Mussulmans of India.

The British were surely going to quit India. If we had any difference between ourselves let us make it completely our own affair and not approach the British for a settlement, for the latter had no duty except to quit at the earliest possible moment.

*Sodpur, Saturday, 10-5-1947:*
There is considerable agitation in Bengal on the question of partition. Most people are of opinion that if there is to be a partition of India, Bengal should also be divided in order to save those portions of it where Hindus are in a majority.

A new proposal has recently been sponsored by some members of the Muslim League and Sarat Chandra Bose's name is also being associated with the scheme. This is a tripartite division of India into India, Pakistan and a United Sovereign Bengal. Sarat Babu had apparently spoken about this scheme to Gandhiji; and in order to discuss all sides of the question, he brought Abul Hashem, M.L.A., the Secretary of the Provincial Muslim League to Sodpur in the afternoon. Abul Hashem talked with Gandhiji for about an hour and a half, while Sarat Babu sat silent throughout the interview.

Hashem Sahib opened his case by stating that Bengalis were after all Bengalis whether Hindu or Muslim. They had a common language, a common culture and did not wish to be ruled by Pakistanis who lived a thousand miles away. Gandhiji said, 'But haven't we been so long ruled by people who live seven thousand miles away?'

'Yes,' said Hashem Sahib, 'but then that would mean that Pakistanis of the West would rule over us in Bengal.'

'But supposing they do not rule over you, and you wish to form a voluntary alliance with Pakistan because you have a common religion which both of you wish to propagate throughout the world, then where is the objection?'

'But, then, you are talking of Pan-Islamism.'

Gandhiji said, 'Yes I am. Perhaps you do not know how deep the Muslim feeling about it is. I had evidence of that even while I was a student in England many years ago. What is then your objection to a voluntary federation of different countries professing the same religion?'

Hashem Sahib did not reply.

Then Gandhiji asked me to bring a Bengali primer which he had been reading lately. There were two of them, one of which was by a Muslim author. When this was brought, Gandhiji proceeded to tell Hashem Sahib that, to all intents and purposes, he was trying to become a Bengali. He found hardly any difference between the language of a Bengali Hindu and a Bengali Muslim. Bengal was the only province in India where common Muslims did not understand Urdu. His intention in learning the Bengali language was to be able to read Gurudev's poems in the original, for from them he received the message of the Upanishads which lay at the root of the culture of the whole of India.

Hashem Sahib said that every Bengali looked upon Rabindranath with the highest veneration, and in this, Muslims were one with Hindus. That was the chief reason why Bengali Muslims did not want Bengal to be broken up into two.

Gandhiji then said quietly, 'It is the spirit of the Upanishads which binds Rabindranath to the whole of Indian culture. Does not Bengal derive her deepest culture from what is the priceless heirloom of all India? If that is so, and Bengal wishes to enter into voluntary association with the rest of India, what would you say about that?'

Hashem Sahib had no reply for this question either.

Gandhiji then said, 'You have not really made up your mind about Pakistan. Please think about it once more, and then we shall discuss the new proposal.'

During the evening prayer Gandhiji dealt with two

questions, one of which related to the burning problem of the day.

*Q.* Could partition of Bengal be avoided in view of the rising Hindu opinion in its favour?

*A.* Gandhiji recognized the force of that opinion. He was not in a position to pronounce an opinion. But he could say without fear of contradiction that if partition came about, the Muslim majority would be responsible for it and, what was more, the Muslim Government that was in power. If he were the Prime Minister of Bengal, he would plead with his Hindu brethren to forget the past. He would say to them that he was as much a Bengali as they were. Difference in religion could not part the two. Both spoke the same language, both had inherited the same culture. All that was Bengal was common to both, of which both should be equally proud.

If the Chief Minister could possibly take up this attitude, the speaker would undertake to go with him from place to place and reason with Hindu audiences. He made bold to say that there would not be a Hindu opponent left of the unity of Bengal, the unity for which Hindus and Muslims* had fought together so valiantly and undone the 'settled fact' of so powerful a Viceroy as Lord Curzon. If he were Janab Suhrawardy, he would invite the Hindus to partition his body before they thought of partitioning Bengal. If he had that sturdy love for Bengal and Bengalis, whether he was a Hindu or a Mussulman, that love would melt the stoniest Hindu heart. As it was, fear and suspicion had seized the Hindu mind. He could not forget Noakhali or even Calcutta, if all he heard was true, as it was equally true of the Muslim mind in Bihar. And he had not hesitated to tell the Hindus (of Bihar) that they should remove all suspicion and fear from the Muslim mind. He believed in the sovereign rule of the Law of Love which made no distinctions of race, colour, caste or creed and he was glad that he had in Q. A. Jinnah a powerful partner in the belief which was no secret from the world.

* This is not historically true —N.K.B

*Sodpur, Sunday, 11-5-1947:*

H. S. Suhrawardy paid a visit to Gandhiji at Sodpur. He is the chief sponsor of the United Sovereign Bengal scheme and he drew a rosy picture of the proposal before Gandhiji. After listening to his advocacy Gandhiji said that a new Bengal could not be born in utter disregard of the past. When the past was so full of wrongs, how could people believe in the sincerity of the new proposal unless past wrongs were set right? Suhrawardy Sahib broke into an eloquent defence of his Government. He said, it had been wholly impartial and equal justice had been meted out to all; otherwise how could it have the support of a large number of Hindus? Gandhiji expressed the opinion that this was no different from the argument of British imperialists.

A friend of mine, who had been one of the worst sufferers in Calcutta, so far as loss of property in the riots was concerned, had written a letter in which he described the utter incompetence of the Government and the veiled connivance of police officers in encouraging Muslim rioters. Gandhiji had read this letter earlier in the day and asked me now to hand it over to the Chief Minister. The latter went through it and said, 'Yes, it is a bad case. But I am sure you realize that this is an exception'.

Then with Gandhiji's permission, I placed before Suhrawardy Sahib another case of murder in which the Police had not taken up any enquiry even when seven days had passed, although the case had been given wide publicity in the Papers. It was the murder of Prof. Jadunath Sarkar's son, and a European missionary who had administered first aid to the victim had said to a friend of mine that the Police had not yet turned up to him for enquiry. Suhrawardy Sahib tried to bypass the charge against his Government by saying, 'Do you know, there are more than half a dozen versions of that event? One even accuses me of complicity in the murder'. Gandhiji had been silently listening to our conversation. He now broke in by saying, 'Yes, you are responsible not only for that murder but for every life lost in Bengal, whether Hindu or Muslim'.

Suhrawardy Sahib was perhaps taken aback, but he

## ON A VISIT TO BENGAL'S CAPITAL

immediately retorted by saying, 'No, it is you who are responsible for it, for you have denied justice to the Mussulmans'.

I have rarely seen Gandhiji lose his temper in public. For one moment he flared up and said, 'Don't talk rot!' But immediately he became restrained and calmed down.*

At the prayer meeting that evening there was a veiled reference to the proposals which were being discussed with Sarat Babu and H. S. Suhrawardy.

*Q.* You have advised us to work for an undivided Bengal. But can there be an undivided Bengal with a divided India?

*A.* The answer was that if what he had said was well understood it followed that nothing could happen without the joint wish of both Hindus and Muslims. If a third party was not to decide their fate it could be only decided by their joint will. If the distant event unfortunately did come to pass, the joint and free will of Hindu and Muslim Bengalis would decide which to join.

---

\* Readers may perhaps feel interested in learning what the actual situation in Bengal was in those days. The prevailing feeling was that, quite apart from the mutual killing of Hindus and Muslims, the Government had also unleashed forces for the preservation of 'law and order', which resulted occasionally in wanton brutality. In proof of this, one statement which was submitted to Gandhiji, is reproduced below. On local enquiry the statement was found to be correct.

'Statement of Narendranath Nag of 13/1/1, Beniatola Lane, Calcutta, dated 14-5-1947.

'On 29th April, '47 when I was returning from my evening walk (at about 6 p.m.), with my grand-daughter (3 years) in my lap, I was caught hold of by some armed policemen at the front of my door and was beaten severely and fell down unconscious.

'My daughter Padmabati Nag (19) who came to open the door, was chased by them (policemen), but she was able to close the 2nd door.

'The armed policemen then broke the said door and going upstairs fired at my daughter.

'She had a shot on her left thigh, she is now undergoing treatment at the Calcutta Medical College Hospital.' It remains to be said that the girl expired shortly after her father paid a visit to Gandhiji.

*Sodpur, Monday, 12-5-1947:*

Suhrawardy Sahib came in the evening in order to plead once more the case for a United Sovereign Bengal. He confessed that the chief obstacle was that no Hindu would listen to him today; he found it hard to prove the utter sincerity of his proposal.

Gandhiji suddenly made a sporting offer to him. He said, he would act as Suhrawardy's secretary, live under the same roof with him and see to it that the Hindus at least gave him a patient hearing. Was he prepared to accept the offer?

Suhrawardy Sahib said nothing and bade him good-bye. As I reached him up to his motor car, he muttered almost to himself, 'What a mad offer! I have to think ten times before I can fathom its implications'.

When he left, I reported the matter to Gandhiji. Gandhiji immediately took up his pen and on two old slips of paper wrote down the following:

I recognise the seriousness of the position in Bengal in the matter of partition. If you are absolutely sincere in your professions and would disabuse me of all the suspicion against you and if you would always retain Bengal for the Bengalis—Hindus and Mussulmans—in tact by non-violent means, I am quite willing to act as your honorary private secretary and live under your roof till Hindus and Muslims begin to live as brothers that they are.

Yours sincerely,<br>M. K. Gandhi.

I typed out the letter at once, and tried to contact Suhrawardy Sahib over the phone at his residence. But he did not return till very late at night. So I went to him early on the following morning in order to deliver the letter to him.

*Sodpur, Tuesday, 13-5-1947:*

A very important interview* took place between

---

* Not corrected by Gandhiji.

Syamaprasad Mookerjee and Gandhiji today. Syamaprasad Babu had heard that the scheme for United Sovereign Bengal had received Gandhiji's blessings, so he had come to ascertain the truth of the report. Gandhiji replied that he had not yet made up his mind about it but was trying to find out what the proposal really meant. Then he asked Syamaprasad Babu for his own opinion on the scheme.

Syamaprasad Babu began by saying that although Mr. Suhrawardy was apparently its author, it was really being sponsored by British commercial interests in Bengal. If Bengal were partitioned, it would create serious difficulties for the jute industry, for the mills would be in West Bengal and the raw materials in another State. Moreover, he said that the Viceroy, Lord Mountbatten, had personally asked him to give the proposal careful consideration.

Gandhiji said, 'So your objection is on account of its parentage! No, I want you to criticize the scheme on merits.'

Then Syamaprasad Babu proceeded to say that although Mr. Suhrawardy was now sponsoring the cause of a United Bengal, yet, once division had taken place, what was there to prevent this Bengal from seeking voluntary alliance with Pakistan? He could surely manipulate a decision of this kind by means of the majority of Muslim votes.

Gandhiji said, 'But has he not spoken of "mutual consent" between Hindus and Muslims in the formation of a separate Bengal?'

Syamaprasad Babu asked what difference that made so long as the majority of the Legislative Assembly were Muslims.

Gandhiji replied, 'But a decision by a simple numerical majority is not "mutual consent". I would interpret that term differently. It ought to mean that if a majority of Hindu members and a majority of Muslim members agree to form a separate sovereign State, then it comes into being by "mutual consent", not otherwise. That majority may be 51:49 or may be fixed at any other figure by mutual discussion before the agreement is entered into. And if Suhrawardy has to win the majority of the Hindu members of the Assembly over to his side, don't you see that the present communal situation in Bengal will be immediately changed for the better?'

Syamaprasad Babu said, 'But supposing Suhrawardy does succeed in winning over many Hindu members and a separate State is formed, then, one day, that State may federate itself with Pakistan if the decision is by majority of votes.'

Gandhiji said, 'No. Such a decision should also be by "mutual consent" as interpreted before separation from India.'

Syamaprasad Babu then asked what would happen if the majority of Hindu members wanted to federate with India and the majority of Muslim members with Pakistan.

Gandhiji said, 'Then there would be a partition of Bengal. But that partition will be brought about by mutual agreement of the people of Bengal and not by the British. It is a partition by the British which has to be prevented at any cost.'

Syamaprasad Babu then asked Gandhiji, 'But can you contemplate Bengal lying separated from the rest of India?'

Gandhiji replied with emotion, 'You ask me that question!'

Finally, Gandhiji said to Syamaprasad Babu that we should take Mr. Suhrawardy's new proposal at its face value, even if we may have no faith in him personally. Preservation of United Bengal in a United India should not be made the condition precedent in the present negotiation, that would defeat one's purpose. Having placed faith on the bona fide of Mr. Suhrawardy's proposal for a United Bengal, we should work out its logical implications. An admission that Bengali Hindus and Bengali Mussulmans were one would really be a severe blow against the two-nation theory of the League. If therefore Mr. Suhrawardy was prepared to accept the real meaning of the term 'mutual consent', then it would mean either the end of the League or of Mr. Suhrawardy.

Nearly a fortnight after Gandhiji returned to Patna, he wrote a letter to Sarat Chandra Bose on the same question, and later on another from Hardwar which bear reproduction in this connection. Photographic copies of both these letters were published in Sarat Babu's paper *The Nation* on the 11th of June 1949.

Patna, 24-5-1947

My dear Sarat,

I have your note. There is nothing in the draft stipulating that nothing will be done by mere majority. Every act of Government must carry with it the co-operation of at least two-thirds of the Hindu members in the Executive and the Legislature. There should be an admission that Bengal has common culture and common mother tongue—Bengali. Make sure that the Central Muslim League approves of the proposal notwithstanding reports to the contrary. If your presence is necessary in Delhi I shall telephone or telegraph. I propose to discuss the draft with the Working Committee.

Yours,
Bapu.

After the Mountbatten Plan had been accepted by the Congress and the League on the 3rd of June, of which the story is told in the following chapter, Gandhiji wrote again:

Hardwar, 21-6-1947

My dear Sarat,

I have a moment to myself here. I use it for writing two or three overdue letters. This is one to acknowledge yours of 14th instant.

The way to work for unity I have pointed out when the geographical is broken.

Hoping you are all well.

Love,
Bapu.

On a careful perusal of the evidence, it is clear how desperately Gandhiji was trying to deal a blow against the League's two-nation theory and thus against partition of the country into two. Responsible political opinion in Bengal had voted for partition of that province if India was going to be divided. The Congress and the League had been brought into an agreement on partition through the diplomatic intervention of Lord Mountbatten. And one of those who knew how things were shaping themselves in high diplomatic quarters therefore put the following question to Gandhiji at his prayer meeting on the 13th of May 1947:

*Q.* When everything at the top goes wrong, can the goodness of the people at the bottom assert itself against its mischievous influence?

*A.* If the people at the top went wrong, it was certainly open to and it was the duty of those at the bottom to remove the wrong top even as he would remove an umbrella, which appeared to be at the top but which was sustained by him.

Thus Pandit Nehru was at the top but in reality he was sustained by them. If he went wrong, those at the bottom could remove him without trouble.

Coming nearer home, if they found Suhrawardy Sahib to be unworthy, they at the bottom could certainly remove him not by physical force but by the ways he had the honour of putting before them.\* The argument that he was elected by Muslim voters was beside the point.

It all boiled down to the fact that if the people at the bottom were ignorant, they would be exploited. Such was the case with the English. When they realized their strength and the fact that the bottom sustained the top, it would be well with them. Therefore he would say that if the top was wrong, there was something radically wrong with the bottom.

Let them therefore dispel their ignorant helplessness.

At the prayer meeting, there was some disturbance from those who thought Gandhiji was in favour of the United Sovereign Bengal scheme and also those who did not want the Koran to be recited by him before a Hindu audience. To the former, Gandhiji said at the outset that the demonstrators need not be afraid of his doing anything which they did not like. He represented nobody but himself. Therefore he could only give advice which they were to

---

\* That is, by non-violent non-co-operation.—N.K.B.

accept or reject. Therefore if Bengal was divided or united it would be their act.

*Sodpur, Wednesday, 14-5-1947:*
A massive report was presented to Gandhiji by a number of journalists containing a detailed description of the riots which are even now going on in Calcutta, and of the failure of the Police and the Administration in this connection.

Gandhiji expressed a desire to the Government of Bengal that he would like to visit the affected parts of Calcutta. Necessary arrangements were immediately made and Gandhiji was driven through all the affected quarters in company with the acting Chief Minister, Mohammed Ali, and also important persons like Debendranath Mukherjee, the Secretary of the Bengal Provincial Hindu Mahasabha. The journey was over fifty miles; and when Gandhiji returned home he expressed the opinion to me that there was exaggeration in the description of damage in the Report. With regard to one particular quarter in which poor Hindus lived in huts, the Report said that the houses had been 'razed to the ground'. But Gandhiji had found that they were still standing, although the doors and windows had been broken, the earth and bamboo walls partly destroyed and the huts made completely uninhabitable. But, he said, it was wrong to describe the huts as having been 'razed to the ground'. One should never deviate from the truth even by a hair's breadth.

The prayer meeting was once more held at Sodpur. Gandhiji said at the outset that he was leaving for Patna and hoped to go to Delhi after a week and to return to Calcutta after his work in Delhi was finished. He passed with the acting Chief Minister two hours in visiting the scenes of recent disturbances. He could see that the destruction was small compared to the August disturbances and hoped that this was the last.

As he was taking his evening walk after prayer, Gandhiji called me aside and said that I had not yet answered his letter of the 13th of April 1947. He said, it was necessary to find out clearly who was mistaken, himself or me. One should not leave a question like that unattended to on the score of other important duties. It was no less important to know oneself more fully. Moreover, if I had any disrespect for him I would not be able to put in my full service at his disposal.

Gandhiji left Howrah in the evening, and I returned home from the station after having seen him off.

## XXII.  CRISIS IN NON-VIOLENCE

GANDHIJI was in Bihar from the 15th to the 24th of May 1947, after which he left again for Delhi. Even while he was at Sodpur in Bengal, his advice to the people of India was never to submit to the tyranny of Mr. Jinnah if the latter insisted upon his pound of flesh. 'Had India,' he asked, 'forgotten the technique of fearless civil disobedience which had been so successfully employed against the British power?'\* In Delhi again, he started clearly that 'if he had his way, there never would be Pakistan before peace and certainly not through British intervention.'\*\* Someone invited his opinion with regard to those nationalists who held that, unless the Muslim League agreed to the partition of Bengal and the Punjab, their grounds for the establishment of Pakistan became illogical and unjust. Gandhiji's reply was, 'If Pakistan is wrong, partition of Bengal and Punjab will not make it right. Two wrongs will not make one right.'\*\*\*

Riots of a very violent character had broken out in the Punjab, while they had become almost a chronic feature of the life of Calcutta. There was wanton bloodshed everywhere, and finally on the 3rd of June 1947, Jawaharlal Nehru announced that the Working Committee had come to a decision favourable to the division of India and that it recommended the Resolution for ratification by representative assemblies of the people.

Commenting upon the Viceroy's statement on the same occasion, Gandhiji remarked that 'to yield even an inch to force was wholly wrong. The Working Committee hold that they had to yield to the force of circumstances. The vast majority of Congressmen did not want unwilling partners. Their motto was non-violence and, therefore, no coercion. Hence, after weighing the pros and cons of the

---

\* *Harijan*, 1-6-1947, p. 173.
\*\* *Harijan*, 8-6-1947, p. 182.
\*\*\* *Harijan*, 1-6-1947, p. 172.

vital issues at stake they had reluctantly agreed to the secession from the Union that was being framed of those parts which had boycotted the Constituent Assembly.... Gandhiji could not blame the Viceroy for what had happened. It was the act of the Congress and the League. He (the Viceroy) had openly said that he wanted a United India but was powerless in the face of Congress acceptance, however reluctantly, of the Muslim position.

'He (Gandhiji) had done his best to get people to stand by the Cabinet Mission Statement of May 16th but had failed. But what was his duty and theirs in the face of the accepted fact? He was a servant of the Congress because he was a servant of the country and he could never be disloyal to them.... Referring to the newspaper report that Gandhiji had differed from the decision of the Working Committee and that the A.I.C.C. would raise its voice against it, Gandhiji said that the A.I.C.C. had appointed the Working Committee and they could not lightly discard its decision. The Working Committee might make a mistake. They could punish it by removing it. But they could not go back upon the decision already taken by it. As for the people, he would ask them to oppose the Congress only when

---

\* *Harijan,* 15-6-1947, p. 193.

It is significant, in this connection, to refer to the following report published in the *Harijan* of June 22, 1947, which clearly shows how Gandhiji was beginning to feel and express the idea that he was being left out by the entire country in his opposition to the vivisection of India. This only meant, from another point of view, that he did not at the moment feel confident of leading the country in the direction which he thought was politically the best.

The report ran: 'A correspondent wrote to Gandhiji that he, who had proclaimed that the vivisection of India would mean a vivisection of himself, had weakened. The writer had also invited him to lead the opposition to the proposed division. He could not plead guilty to the taunt. When he made the statement he was voicing public opinion. But when public opinion was against him, was he to coerce it? The writer had also argued that he had often held that there was to be no compromise with untruth or evil. The assertion was correct. He made bold to say that if only non-Muslim India was with him, he could show the way to undo the proposed partition. But he freely admitted that he had become or was rather considered a back number....

it tried to mislead the public deliberately. They knew his method of resistance. After all, he had preached rebellion against the mighty Sanatanist Hindu stronghold on the subject of untouchability and the result was quite good. He might differ from the Working Committee. But having stated the fact, he would recommend their decision for acceptance. He was of opinion that they could still mend the situation to a large extent.'*

The emergent meeting of the All-India Congress Committee was held in Delhi on the 14th and 15th of June 1947. There was strong opposition against the Resolution on the ground that it was a surrender to Mr. Jinnah's two-nation theory and so a denial of the very foundation of Indian nationalism. It was moreover no solution of the communal problem. Yet, the majority eventually decided in favour of the Resolution. It is interesting and instructive to study the reasons set forth in favour of the Resolution, and also the reason which led Gandhiji to reconcile himself to the position taken by the A.I.C.C. on the historic occasion.

In course of his speech on the 15th of June, Sardar Vallabhai Patel is reported to have said, 'Never in the history of the Congress before had the A.I.C.C. to take a decision on such an important issue. He fully appreciated the apprehensions of his brothers from Sind and the Punjab. Nobody liked the division of India and his heart was heavy.

'Some people have criticized the acceptance of Dominion Status during the interim period. They went so far as to say that the drama of independence was finished once for all. The present Viceroy was more dangerous than his predecessors who dangled before them the naked sword. He had tricked the Congress into submission by his persuasive powers. Gandhiji said that the correspondent had paid a high, though unintended, compliment to the Viceroy and at the same time belittled the intellectual capacity of the Congress Ministers. Why could not the writer see the obvious? The country, i.e., the vocal part of it was with them. They were no fools. They disliked dismemberment of India as much as any other. But they were the people's representatives in power. If the writer was in power, things might not have been different. In any case, it was not dignified to swear at the Viceroy if the leaders were ill-chosen or if the people were not true to the country. "As the king so the people" was less true than "As the people so the king"' (p. 202).

But there were stark realities of which they should take notice. The choice was whether there should be just one division or many divisions. The fight today was not against the British. They definitely had no desire to govern this country.

'The May 16th Plan, no doubt, gave them a United India. But there was a snag. The Plan could not be executed if one or other party withheld co-operation. The communal veto which was given to the League would have arrested our progress at every stage. The majority would have to stand back and look on and they would have been unable to do anything in the administration.

'But the position today was different. Now they had a chance. They could eradicate the plague of communalism, weightage etc. which existed in no other constitution of the world. The Congress must face facts. It could not give way to emotionalism and sentimentality. They must coolly assess the pros and cons and arrive at a deliberate decision. Sardar Patel sympathized with the minority in Sind. But mere sympathy without power was no good. They must build up strength.

'Sardar Patel denied that the Working Committee accepted the plan out of fear. They had never known fear. He deeply regretted the many massacres that had happened. In one family of thirty, there were only two survivors. Many were maimed or disabled for life. They had gone through all that. But he was afraid of one thing and that was that all their toils and hard work these many years should not go to waste or prove unfruitful. They worked for independence and they should see as large a part of this country as possible become free and strong. Here was a chance for India to attain her independence. Was she going to throw it away? They had now a great opportunity to develop over three-fourths of India. They had not much time to waste. Freedom was coming. Congressmen should work hard to make that freedom a living thing and make India strong. They must build up industries. They must build up the army, make it strong and efficient.'*

* *Indian Annual Register*, 1947, Vol. I, pp. 135-6 (adapted).

One of the most significant speeches delivered on the occasion was the concluding address of the President, Acharya Kripalani. He said, 'I have been with Gandhiji for the last thirty years. I joined him in Champaran. I have never swayed in my loyalty to him. It is not a personal but a political loyalty. Even when I have differed from him I have considered his political instinct to be more correct than my elaborately reasoned attitude. Today also I feel that he, with his supreme fearlessness, is correct and my stand is defective. Why then am I not with him? It is because I feel that he has as yet found no way of tackling the problem on a mass basis. When he taught us non-violent non-co-operation he showed us a definite method which we had at least mechanically followed. Today he is himself groping in the dark. He was in Noakhali. His efforts eased the situation. Now he is in Bihar. The situation is again eased. But this does not solve in any way the flare-up in the Punjab. He says he is solving the problem of Hindu-Muslim unity for the whole of India in Bihar. May be. But it is difficult to see how that is being done. There are no definite steps as in non-violent non-co-operation that lead to the desired goal.

'And then unfortunately for us today though he can enunciate policies they have to be in the main carried out by others and these others are not converted to his way of thinking.

'It is under these painful circumstances that I have supported the division of India.'\*

Another singular feature of the momentous A.I.C.C. session was the speech delivered by Gandhiji himself in support of the Resolution on the 14th of June 1947. Unfortunately, no official version of that speech is available and we have to depend upon the report as published in the Press. He said that 'his views on the Plan were well known.' Although 'the House had the right to accept or reject the Working Committee's decision, they must remember that the Working Committee as their representative had accepted the Plan and it was the duty of the A.I.C.C. to stand by

---

\* *Ibid.*, p. 125.

them.... If the A.I.C.C. felt so strongly on this point that this Plan would do injury to the country, then it could reject the Plan. The consequence of such a rejection would be the finding of a new set of leaders who would constitute not only the Congress Working Committee, but would also take charge of the government. If the opponents of the Resolution could find such a set of leaders it could then reject the Resolution if it so felt.... The members of the Working Committee were old and tried leaders who were responsible for all the achievements of the Congress hitherto and, in fact, they formed the backbone of the Congress and it would be unwise, if not impossible, to remove them at the present juncture.... The Congress was opposed to Pakistan and he was one of those who steadfastly opposed the division of India. Yet he had come before the A.I.C.C. to urge the acceptance of the Resolution. Sometimes certain decisions, however unpalatable they might be, had to be taken.'*

The result of Gandhiji's advocacy was that the opposition was considerably weakened, and eventually the Working Committee's Resolution was, as we have already said, ratified by a large majority.

It soon however began to grow increasingly clear that, in spite of his valiant effort to defend the Congress leadership and Democracy, Gandhiji's own views on the question of partition did not change even after the fateful meeting in Delhi. In a written message to the prayer gathering on the 15th of June itself, he said, 'One more question has been and is being asked. If you are so sure that India is going the wrong way, why do you associate with the wrong-doers? Why do you not plough your lonely furrow and have faith that if you are right, your erstwhile friends and followers will seek you out? I regard this as a fair question. I must not attempt to argue against it. All I can say is that my faith is as strong as ever. It is quite possible that my technique is faulty.'**

A few days later, he said again, 'The fact that there are two Indias instead of one was bad enough in itself. Both

---

\* *Hindusthan Standard*, 15-6-1947.
\*\* *Harijan*, 29-6-1947, p. 209.

had the same status. Qaid-e-Azam Jinnah and the Muslim League were entitled to claim full credit for bringing about a state of things which seemed to be impossible only as it were yesterday. They had undone the solemn declaration of the Cabinet Mission. They had succeeded in compelling consent from the Congress and the Sikhs to the division. The thing that was in itself bad did not become good because the parties concerned accepted it, no matter that the causes dictating were different in each case. It was hardly any comfort that the Qaid-e-Azam did not get all that he wanted. The difference was not at all in kind. He wanted a sovereign State. That he had in the fullest measure.'*

Another month after, while talking to some interviewers, he remarked, 'The leaders had agreed to partition as the last resort. They did not feel that they had made a mistake. Rather than let the whole country go to the dogs, they had agreed to partition, hoping to give the country a much-needed rest. He felt differently. He had said that he would rather let the whole country be reduced to ashes than yield an inch to violence.'** 'It is permissible to say that India had accepted partition at the point of the bayonet. This settled fact cannot be unsettled in the same way. The two can become one only when there is heart unity. The omens today seem to point to the contrary.'***

In one of his after-prayer speeches he said, 'Last evening I showed why the coming freedom seemed to create no enthusiasm. This evening I propose to show how we can, if we will, turn the calamity into a blessing. It will profit us nothing to brood over the past or to blame this party or that. Technically, freedom is yet to come a few days hence. In fact the parties have jointly accepted the situation and there is no turning back. Only the inscrutable Providence can undo what men have agreed to do.

'One easy and ready way is for the Congress and the League to come together and arrive at a mutual understanding without the intervention of the Viceroy. The League

---

\* *Harijan*, 13-7-1947, p. 235.
\*\* *Ibid.*, 27-7-1947, p. 253.
\*\*\* *Ibid.*, 10-8-1947, p. 272.

has to make the first move. I do not at all suggest the undoing of Pakistan. Let that be treated as an established fact beyond dispute or discussion. But they can sit together in a mud hut large enough to accommodate not more than ten representatives and undertake not to part till they have reached an agreement. I dare swear that if such an event occurs, it will be infinitely better than the Bill recognizing the independence of India cut up into two States enjoying equal status.

'Neither the Hindus nor the Muslims are happy over what is happening before their helpless selves. This is firsthand evidence unless the Hindus and Muslims who see me or correspond with me are deceiving me. But—it is a big *but*—I seem to be aiming at the impossible. Now that the British intervention has done the trick, how can the League be expected to come down to their adversaries and produce an agreed settlement as between brothers and friends?'*

It was with some amount of bitterness that he wrote again, 'Man had the supreme knack of deceiving himself. The Englishman was supremest among men. He was quitting because he had discovered that it was wrong on economic and political grounds to hold India in bondage. Herein he was quite sincere. It would not be denied, however, that sincerity was quite consistent with self-deception. He was self-deceived in that he believed that he could not leave India to possible anarchy if such was to be India's lot. He was quite content to leave India as a cockpit between two organized armies. Before quitting, he was setting the seal of approval on the policy of playing off one community against another.'**

Politically, therefore, it was evident that Gandhiji held the partition to be the final result of England's policy of Divide and Rule, as applied to the specific situation in India. From the strategical point of view, it meant a partial defeat for the Congress leadership, in so far as they were forced to apply a closure to the War of Independence, in the hope that they would gain the power and opportunity to exercise

---

\* *Harijan*, 20-7-1947, p. 241.
\*\* *Harijan*, 20-7-1947, p. 242.

the authority of the State in order to check any further progress of the communal canker. Obviously, India had developed too little staying power to take much punishment; although the total amount of punishment suffered by her in course of the riots was negligible in comparison with what takes place in a war. This attitude stood in sharp contrast to the calmness displayed by Gandhiji himself, who never lost sight of the nature of the coming freedom, and who refused to be hustled into a political settlement which fell far short of his conception of Swaraj.

As early as 1920, he had warned the nation in the following terms, 'Before we become a nation possessing an effective voice in the councils of nations, we must be prepared to contemplate with equanimity, not a thousand murders of innocent men and women, but many thousands before we attain a status in the world that shall not be surpassed by any nation.'* While advising the Working Committee in the end of 1946 to reject the Cabinet Mission's original proposal, he had envisaged the possibility of a satyagraha movement for the final and complete vindication of the national will. Referring to that, he said in February 1947, 'India's independence rested with the people and no outside power. Nor was there any question as to what India would do if the State Paper was withdrawn. India has been accustomed to life in the wilderness. Naturally, he could speak with confidence when the people had only non-violence in view as a steadfast policy without reservation. If they thought that they could drive away the English by the sword, they were vastly mistaken. They did not know the determination and courage of the English. They would not yield to the power of the sword. But they could not withstand the courage of non-violence which disdained to deal death against death. He knew no other power higher than non-violence. And if they were still without real independence, it was, he was sure, because the people had not developed sufficient non-violence.'*

An occasion similar to the present one had developed in 1940 when Gandhiji had differed from the leaders of the

* *Selections from Gandhi*, 1948, p. 121.
* *Harijan*, 2-3-1947, p. 45.

Congress on the score of non-violence. The Congress wanted to render help to the English people in the War under certain conditions. Gandhiji's contention was that this would not bring freedom to the masses of India, and therefore he advised the country to devote itself completely to the constructive programme instead, as a part of its 'real war effort.' But there was hardly any response. In one of his speeches on that occasion, he therefore said, 'It has been somewhat justly said that if I am a good general, I must not grumble about my men. For I must choose them from the material at my disposal. I plead guilty. But I have qualified my admission by the adverb 'somewhat', for I laid down the conditions from the very inception of the programme of non-violence. My terms were accepted. If from experience it is found that the terms cannot be worked, I must either be dismissed or I must retire. I retired but to no purpose. The bond between Congressmen and me seems to be unbreakable. They may quarrel with my conditions but they will not leave me or let me go. They know that however unskilled a servant I may be, I will neither desert them nor fail them in the hour of need. And so they try, though often grumblingly, to fulfil my conditions. I must then on the one hand adhere to my conditions so long as I have a living faith in them, and on the other take what I can get from Congressmen, expecting that if I am true, they will someday fulfil all my conditions and find themselves in the enjoyment of full independence such as has never before been seen on earth.'* On that particular occasion, however, Gandhiji had acted outside the Congress through the initiation of the Individual Civil Disobedience movement. On the present occasion, he refrained from asserting himself in a similar manner, although the risks for the entire country were infinitely greater than on the last occasion.

So, when Gandhiji was once more in Calcutta about two months after the meeting of the A.I.C.C., I had the temerity to ask him why he had refused to give the necessary lead to the country when he felt so strongly on the question of division. As far as I can remember, for there

---

* *Studies in Gandhism*, 1947, p. 314.

is no record to this effect in my diary, his answer was that if every time the Congress committed a mistake, he had to step in to set it right, then India would never learn the art of democracy. My feeling, however, was that Gandhiji no longer relied upon the Congress, in its present shape and form, to serve as his instrument of collective non-violence. Gandhiji suppressed himself more or less completely and left the organization free to follow its own course. About a month after the transference of power had taken place, he went so far as to prescribe for the Congress a course of action in accordance with the path which it has independently chosen for itself. In September 1947, when the tension between India and Pakistan became acute on the question of aggression in Kashmir, he said in one of his after-prayer speeches, that 'he had been an opponent of all warfare. But if there was no other way of securing justice from Pakistan, if Pakistan persistently refused to see its proved error and continued to minimize it, the Indian Union would have to go to war against it. War was no joke. No one wanted war. That way lay destruction. But he could never advise anyone to put up with injustice. If all the Hindus were annihilated for a just cause he would not mind it.

'As for himself, his way was different. He worshipped God, which was Truth and *Ahimsa*. There was a time when India listened to him. Today he was a back number. He was told that he had no place in the new order, where they wanted machines, navy, air force and what not. He could never be party to that. If they could have the courage to say that they would retain freedom with the help of the same force with which they had won it, he was their man. His physical incapacity and his depression would vanish in a moment.'*

But we are anticipating events. At the moment with which we are concerned, Gandhiji felt that he should no longer exercise his personal influence over the Congress. He had to strike out a new path for himself, adapt the non-violent technique to the new situation, and once more

* *Harijan*, 5-10-1947, p. 362.

make it possible for many men to act together in the vindication of their just demands. We remember how, even at Noakhali, he had said on the 9th of December 1946, that for the time being he had given up searching a non-violent remedy applicable to the masses, he was seeking a way for his own sake. To an interviewer who thanked him for his kind interest in Bengal, Gandhiji had promptly replied that it was no kindness; and if it was, then it was kindness to himself. 'My own doctrine was failing. I do not want to die a failure, but as a successful man. But it may be that I may die a failure' (5-12-1946). On another occasion, on the 26th of November 1946, he had said that a wise gardener tries to raise one seedling properly instead of sowing broadcast, and then he is enabled to discover the exact conditions under which the plant will thrive.

This was apparently the task to which Gandhiji wanted to devote himself now that the Congress had brought political freedom to the country. Even at Noakhali, a preliminary vision of the new way had apparently been opened to him. He had felt and said in February 1947 that a community which hoped to employ non-violence for purposes of self-defence must eschew such rights and privileges as could only be gained by means of violence. Private capital, social privileges of an exclusive character had to be put an end to before satyagraha could exercise an effective appeal upon one's opponent. Now that the Hindus had lost their all through the riots, he wanted them to seize the opportunity and turn the calamity into a blessing. He wanted them, by intelligent and determined effort, to set their lives in tune with the supreme moral law of bread labour. His appeal in Noakhali had however fallen upon ears which were in no mood to listen. But Gandhiji wished to try again. For he knew that without that preparation, without the fundamental social and economic revolution attained through non-violence, the chances of the substitution of force by satyagraha in the sphere of State operations was also remote.

Gandhiji thus determined to go into retirement in order to prepare the ground for a fresh advance in terms of satyagraha when the time was ripe for it. In one distant sense, this was comparable to the retreat of the British Army after the fall of France, when England retired to devote herself to preparation for the final advance when she was ready.

And thus it was that, shortly before the 15th of August 1947, the people of Bengal once more found Gandhiji in their own midst.

In the meanwhile, he had paid a brief visit to Kashmir and the riot-affected portions of the North-West Frontier Province in the end of July and the beginning of August 1947.

## XXIII. BENGAL CALLING AGAIN

ON receiving the news that Gandhiji was coming to Calcutta, I proceeded to Burdwan station on the evening of the 8th of August 1947. When the train steamed in about four in the morning of the 9th, I found Gandhiji still fast asleep while Manu, Sailen and others were already awake. Manu welcomed me warmly. Gandhiji woke up a few minutes after the train started again, and asked her what station had just been passed. Manu said it was Burdwan and that we were already in Bengal. Then she announced that I had come. Gandhiji said, 'So we are in Bengal and Nirmal has come! Naturally, he would.' Then I went into his compartment and paid him my respects.

The train reached Howrah shortly after eight and we drove straight to the Khadi Pratisthan at Sodpur.

As the partition of Bengal had already become a settled fact, a 'Shadow Ministry' under Prafulla Chandra Ghosh was already functioning along with the League Ministry from whom they were to take over charge on the 14th. H. S. Suhrawardy was still the Chief Minister officially.

Gandhiji passed a busy day. He was anxious to meet both Suhrawardy Sahib and Khwaja Nazimuddin, the former Premier of Bengal, for any instruction which they might wish to give him with regard to East Bengal. In the meanwhile, the British Governor sent him a personal invitation. So he left for Government House at 3-30 p.m. returning at 5-5 p.m. just five minutes after the scheduled time for prayer.

An officer of the Information Department of the Government of India came for some message from him which was to be published on the momentous 15th. But Gandhiji's reply was that 'he had run dry'; there was nothing he would like to say. Two more Government officials came again for the same purpose and said that if he did not give any message to the nation, it would not be good. Gandhiji replied again, 'There is no message at all. If it is bad, let it be so' (*Hai nahi koi message, hone do kharab*).

Riots in a bad form had once more broken out in Calcutta. This time, apparently, the initiative had come from the Hindus. The latter felt that the power of the League Ministry was now broken and the police could therefore no longer encourage the Muslim goondas by their incompetence. Under the new regime of the Congress, the time had therefore come for the Hindus to strike back. This was perhaps the reason why, on the present occasion, the targets of attack were certain slums, as in Miabagan or Paikpara, which had been known to harbour gangs of Muslim goondas in the previous phase of the riots. Usman Sahib, the former Mayor of Calcutta, came with another friend to plead with Gandhiji to save the Muslims of Calcutta before he went to Noakhali. All these left Gandhiji in a heavily burdened frame of mind.

So he devoted the whole of his address in the prayer meeting to the local situation. His destination he said was Noakhali but he had been listening the whole day long to the woes of Calcutta. Some Muslim friends and even some Hindus complained that the Hindus seemed to have gone mad. He was rightly asked before he went to Noakhali to tarry in Calcutta and pour a pot of water over the raging fire that was burning. He would love to give his life if thereby he could contribute towards the quenching of the mob fury. He would never be able to subscribe to the theory that the doings in Calcutta were the result of goondaism. He held that the crude open goondaism was a reflection of the subtle goondaism they were harbouring within. Hence it was the duty of the Government to hold themselves responsible for the acts of the goondas so-called. He hoped that Calcutta would not present the disgraceful spectacle of hot goondaism when they were entering upon full responsibility.

*Sodpur, Sunday, 10-8-1947:*
Usman Sahib came with a representative body of Muslims in order to request Gandhiji to postpone his departure. Gandhiji listened to their request and said that Usman Sahib was taking upon himself a very heavy responsibility. Gandhiji's intention was to be in Noakhali on the 15th; but if he could not go there and anything untoward

happened, there would be no alternative for him except to end his life by fasting.

It was indeed a heavy responsibility; but Muhammad Usman took upon himself, and on behalf of the Muslim League, the responsibility of sending workers to Noakhali who would try to maintain absolute peace in that district.

The Congress Ministers of the Government of Bengal interviewed Gandhiji at 3-30 p.m. One of the questions which they wanted to discuss was the manner in which the 15th should be celebrated. Gandhiji said, according to him, the advice could only be for fasting, prayer and a dedication to the spinning wheel. What else could they do when all around the country was burning, when people were dying from lack of food and clothing? *Sab dik jal rahe hain, bhukhon mar rahe hain, nange mar rahe hain.*

The question of the relation between Pakistan and India was also raised by one of the Ministers. Gandhiji said, 'Each State should perform its duty properly. If the conduct is straight, there is likelihood of reunion. But what he witnessed today was a preparation for hostility not for friendship.'

There was an enormous crowd to listen to Gandhiji during prayer time. Their acclamation was piercing. Gandhiji had to speak to them for a few minutes to establish complete quiet if they wanted the prayer and his speech. The audience responded splendidly and listened in perfect silence.

He said that though he was to go to Noakhali tomorrow (Monday), owing to the pressure from many Muslim friends who had seen him, he had decided to stay to see if he could contribute his share in the return of sanity in the premier city of India. The argument of the Muslim friends went home. He had at the same time held that if he did not go to Noakhali and any mishap took place, his life would become forfeit as he had said already about Bihar. He had seen the Ministers and **others too during** the day. He would see the places where destruction was said to have been wrought by Hindus. He had also learnt that there were parts of Calcutta which were inaccessible to Hindus, though many premises therein used to be occupied by them. Similar was the case with the Hindu localities. His head hung in shame to listen to this recital of man's barbarism. He would love to go to those places and see for himself how much truth there was in these recitals. He was told that there were not more than 23% Muslims in Calcutta. It was unthinkable that such a minority could coerce the majority without countenance from or incompetence of authority. Similarly it was unthinkable that in the midst of a Government which knew the art of government, the majority could for one moment be permitted to coerce the minority. He was also told that what the Muslim police and officials were alleged to be doing before, now that the Congress Ministry was in power, the Hindu police and officers were doing. They had become partial in the administration of justice.

If this wretched spirit of communalism had entered the police force, the prospect was black indeed. He hoped that the police would realize the dignity of their profession.

*Sodpur, Monday, 11-8-1947:*

Early in the morning, I started for Government House with a personal letter to the Governor which is reproduced below.

Sodpur, 11-8-1947

Dear Friend,

What you could not do a big Muslim deputation was able to do yesterday. And so, I am here at least till tomorrow. Man is invariably clay in the hands of the Great Potter.

All my good wishes with you and yours.

Yours sincerely,<br>M. K. Gandhi.

Later on in the day, a representative of the British Broadcasting Corporation came with a request for a short message from Gandhiji which would be broadcast all over the world on the 15th of August. But Gandhiji sent word through me that he had nothing to say. When the request was repeated with the additional remark that it would be broadcast in various languages, as the whole world would naturally expect to hear something from Mahatma Gandhi on the historic occasion of India's freedom, Gandhiji wrote back on a slip of paper which had already been used for conveying other messages to me:

'I must not yield to the temptation. They must forget that I know English.'

Gandhiji started on a tour round Calcutta at 2-12 p.m. in company with Prafulla Ghosh, Usman Sahib and others and came back at 4-17 p.m.

H. S. Suhrawardy came with Usman Sahib at 9-5 p.m. in the night and left at 11 p.m. The following is a summary of the conversation which took place between them as recorded in my diary of even date.

*Gandhiji*: Do you want to suggest, I should not leave on Wednesday and pass the whole of my time in bringing peace to Calcutta?

*Suhrawardy*: Yes.

*Gandhiji*: I stayed (for these two days in Calcutta) very much against my will. But Usman Sahib overpowered me. He made a successful appeal to my heart. He asked me to see things with my own eyes and do something to allay the present communal feelings. I would remain if you and I are prepared to live together. This is my second offer to you.* We shall have to work as long as every Hindu and Mussulman in Calcutta does not safely return to the place where he was before. We shall continue in our effort till our last breath.

I do not want you to come to a decision immediately. You should go back home and consult your daughter; for the implication of what I mean is that the old Suhrawardy will have to die and accept the garb of a mendicant (fakir).**

*Sodpur, Tuesday, 12-8-1947:*

Usman Sahib arrived at about one in the afternoon with Mr. Suhrawardy's message stating that the latter had agreed to Gandhiji's proposal.

---

\* The first, as the reader will perhaps remember, was made in May, 1947.

\*\* Suhrawardy Sahib is a widower with an only daughter.

Gandhiji wanted Usman Sahib and myself to fix a quarter for him in Calcutta; but I excused myself and Satish Babu's brother Kshitish Babu and his son Arun Dasgupta accompanied the ex-Mayor on an exploratory tour and finally fixed upon a vacant Muslim residence at 150 Beliaghata Main Road for the new enterprise.

Beliaghata is a predominantly Hindu area; but the outlet of this quarter across the canal is commanded by the predominantly Muslim slum of Miabagan. Miabagan had earned the unenviable reputation of harbouring a large number of goondas during the riots. So, a few days back, the young Hindus of Beliaghata had attacked this bustee with locally manufactured hand-grenades and a few sten guns which had been procured from soldiers at the end of the last war, and cleared it of all inhabitants whether good or bad. A short distance from Beliaghata there were Maniktala, Kankurgachi, Ultadanga and other places which had been almost wholly denuded of Hindus by the depredation of Muslim goondas. This was thus the place fixed upon by Usman Sahib and Kshitish Babu for Gandhi's residence. The building belonged to an aged Muslim lady and lay beside a match factory owned by a Muslim proprietor.

In the prayer meeting, Gandhiji said that the 15th instant was to be a landmark in India's history. It was the day when India would be declared free of the foreign yoke. It was to be an independent nation. He had said how the day was to be observed. But he was probably alone in the view. Already there was an announcement that the Muslims of Calcutta were to observe it as a day of mourning. He hoped it was not true. No man could be compelled to observe the day in a particular manner. It was to be a perfectly voluntary act. He would ask his Muslim countrymen not to mourn over the freedom. The present distemper was bound to go. What were the Hindus in Pakistan to do? They should salute the Pakistan flag, if it meant the freedom and equality of all in every respect, irrespective of caste, colour or creed.

He then came to another important subject. They knew that he prolonged his stay in Calcutta by two days at the instance of Muslim friends. Last night Shaheed Sahib* came

\* Shaheed is Mr. Suhrawardy's personal name.

to see him. He suggested that it would be contrary to his (Gandhiji's) practice to leave Calcutta while it was going through the horrors of communal strife. Shaheed Sahib suggested that Gandhiji should prolong his stay in the city and work until real peace was restored. Gandhiji replied that Suhrawardy Sahib and he should live under the same roof in the disturbed parts. It would be best to live unprotected by police or military. In brotherly fashion, they would approach the people, argue with them and tell them that now that partition had taken place by agreement, there was no longer any reason for them to continue the old fight. The decision of the Boundary Commission was going to be announced in a day or two, and it was in the fitness of things that all the parties should abide by the decision in a becoming manner. After all, the parties had appointed an arbitration tribunal. They were in honour bound to abide by the award whatever it was.

Gandhiji's proposal to Suhrawardy Sahib was of such an important nature that the latter could not afford to give a hasty reply. Gandhiji had therefore asked Shaheed Sahib to consult his aged father as well as his daughter before coming to a decision. During the afternoon, Usman Sahib, the ex-Mayor of Calcutta, had arrived with Shaheed Sahib's reply stating that the latter had accepted Gandhiji's proposal without reservation. It was now time therefore for the two friends to choose quarters in the midst of the worst-affected areas and see what could be done by joint effort.

Gandhiji said that he was warned that Shaheed Sahib was not to be relied upon. The same thing was said about him (Gandhiji). He was described as the worst enemy of Islam. He was supposed to be a consummate hypocrite. God alone knew men's hearts. He asserted that he spoke and acted as he believed. He had known Shaheed Sahib since the days of the Faridpur Conference to which the late Dashbandhu\* had taken him. Nobody had any right to prejudge anybody. He would trust as he expected to be trusted. Both would live under the same roof and have no secrets from one another. They would together see all visitors. People should have the courage to speak out the truth under

---

\* C. R. Das, the great nationalist leader.

all circumstances and in the presence of those against whom it had to be said.

He finally referred to what the common citizen could do in order to help the cause. They were to bless them in the mission on which they were embarking.

*Beliaghata, Calcutta, Wednesday, 13-8-1947:*

While still at Sodpur, at about one in the afternoon, Gandhiji said that the step he was taking was like a gamble and, for him, it was also his last throw. He would observe carefully how the plan worked. The plan was bound to succeed if there was no mental reservation on either side; but all depended on how Mr. Suhrawardy reacted. His final aim was to see not only that Hindus and Muslims returned to their own places and lived together as formerly, but mutual trust was also restored. Only then could he say that his object had been fully attained.

We left Sodpur at 2-30 p.m. in a car and reached the house which had been selected at Beliaghata at 3-5 a.m. A number of young men had gathered at the gate with black flags and some posters which said that Gandhiji should go back and rather settle in a quarter like Kankurgachi or Ultadanga from where Hindus had been driven away, instead of coming here to look after Muslim interests. After having seen Gandhiji settled in his room, I met the crowd and then went to the house of one important leader of the locality, where I tried to explain till after ten o'clock in the night what Gandhiji's purpose in coming here was. When I came back to Gandhiji's room at half past ten, I found that he had not yet gone to sleep. He expressed satisfaction at what he had done in the meanwhile. A number of demonstrators had approached him and he had argued with them for several hours. He felt glad that the demonstrators had not merely the courage to oppose him openly, but also to charge Mr. Suhrawardy to his face with all that they had to say against him. Such courage was good; it was indeed a contrast to what he had witnessed in the district of Noakhali hitherto.

And thus we settled down in our new quarters in the city of Calcutta.

## XXIV. BUILDING UP FREE INDIA

*Beliaghata, Thursday, 14-8-1947:*

Nirmal Chandra Chatterji, Major Bardhan and some other members of the Hindu Mahasabha had a long interview with Gandhiji on the East Bengal situation. Nirmal Babu's suggestion was that joint squads of volunteers belonging to the Congress, League and Hindu Mahasabha should tour the districts in order to restore confidence among the Hindus in East Bengal.

There was a packed audience during prayer time, which listened to Gandhiji without the slightest disturbance. He explained once more the reason for postponement of his visit to Noakhali and his intention of staying in the present place. Let them not think that the parts of Calcutta which were deserted by their Hindu inhabitants and were occupied by Muslims were being neglected. They were working for the peace of the whole of Calcutta and he invited his audience to believe with them that if Calcutta returned to sanity and real friendship, then Noakhali and the rest of India would be safe.

News began to reach our camp towards evening that a strange thing had started in different parts of Calcutta. For one whole year, ever since the beginning of the Muslim League's Direct Action on the 16th of August 1946, Hindus and Muslims had strictly avoided one another's company. Transference of population had taken place, so that Calcutta had virtually become divided into exclusively Hindu and Muslim zones. But news began to pour in now that the Hindus and Muslims were both coming out in the streets, embracing one another and the latter were even inviting their erstwhile enemies to visit their masjids. It reminded me personally of what I had read in Eric Maria Remarque's *All Quiet on the Western Front*, when on Christmas Eve, the common French and German soldiers came out of their trenches and forgot, even if it were for a brief moment, that they were to regard each other as enemies. I left in a jeep and passed through some of the most affected quarters and witnessed an upsurge of emotional enthusiasm which somehow rang untrue; for to my mind it was a reaction against the inhibitions of a war through which the citizens had been passing for one whole year.

Gandhiji wished to observe the demonstration himself and he was therefore driven in a closer car as he sat between two or three passengers, so that people might not recognize him and out of enthusiasm make it impossible for him to proceed.

*Beliaghata, Friday, 15-8-1947:*

Gandhiji had started a one-day fast in observance of the day of deliverance of India. The new Governor of this province, C. Rajagopalachari, paid him a respectful visit and congratulated him on the 'miracle which he had wrought.' But Gandhiji replied that he could not be satisfied until Hindus and Muslims felt safe in one another's company and returned to their own homes to live as before. Without that change of heart, there was likelihood of future deterioration in spite of the present enthusiasm.

At 2, there was an interview with some members of the Communist Party of India to whom Gandhiji said that political workers, whether Communist or Socialist, must forget today all differences and help to consolidate the freedom which had been attained. Should we allow it to break into pieces? The tragedy was that the strength with which the country had fought against the British was failing them when it came to the establishment of Hindu-Muslim unity.

With regard to the celebrations, Gandhiji said, 'I can't afford to take part in this rejoicing, which is a sorry affair.'

There was then a half-hour interview with some students of Beliaghata to whom he explained in detail why the fighting must stop now. We had two States now, each of which was to have both Hindu and Muslim citizens. If that were so, it meant an end of the two-nation theory. Students ought to think and think well. They should do no wrong. It was wrong to molest an Indian citizen merely because he professed a different religion. Students should do everything to build up a new State of India which would be everybody's pride. With regard to the demonstration of fraternization he said, 'I am not lifted off my feet by these demonstrations of joy.'

There was a great rush of visitors all through the day; and every time a large number gathered in the garden and the open lawns attached to the house, Gandhiji stepped up to the window of his room and stood with folded hands returning the salute of the multitude.

At the prayer meeting to which Gandhiji walked on foot, the rush was very great. And what could have been done in five minutes' time took twenty minutes to cover. Gandhiji referred to Lahore from where sorry tales of rioting had been reaching him every day and said that if the noble example of Calcutta were sincere, it would affect the Punjab and the rest of India. There was also a reference to Chittagong which was now in Pakistan but where floods had recently caused severe damages. Were the two portions of Bengal to treat one another as foreigners? Nature's floods were no respecter of persons or of political divisions between man and man. Hindus and Muslims were equally affected thereby.

On the 16th, Rev. John Kellas, Principal of the Scottish Church College, came to see Gandhiji with some members of his staff. The chief question discussed was the relation between education and religion. Gandhiji was emphatic in his opinion that the State being secular, it could never promote denominational education out of public funds. Incidentally he said that although India had discarded foreign power it had not discarded foreign influence. 'Although we have thrown overboard British political supremacy, we haven't done so with regard to the cultural one.'

With reference to the task lying before the country, he said that we must demolish the status which goondaism had acquired in course of the last one year and devote ourselves to the organization of the best in society.

One professor of science asked Gandhiji what scientists should do if Free India ordered them to produce atom bombs, for instance. Without a moment's hesitation he replied: 'Resist them unto death. Scientists to be worth the name should only do like that.'

On the following day, while speaking with an interviewer on the question of rehabilitation, Gandhiji casually remarked, 'Producing a set of murderers is one thing, to produce a set of constructive workers who will toil from day to day is another thing.'

On the 18th, a number of Congress workers came from Khulna. Khulna is a district with Hindu majority and the Congress workers had hoisted the tricolour flag to celebrate the 15th of August, because they believed it would naturally remain a part of India. But the Award of the Boundary Commission which was announced later, placed Khulna within Pakistan. And so the workers had come to ask Gandhiji what should be done in regard to the Union of India Flag which had been hoisted there. As it was his day of silence, he wrote out on a slip of paper, 'There can be no two opinions. The Union Flag *must* go, Pakistan must be hoisted without demur, with joy if possible. Award is award, good or bad.'

Although Calcutta had become quiet now, yet stray incidents continued against Muslims in the suburbs of the city. So Gandhiji paid a visit to Barrackpore on the 18th and to Kanchrapara on the 19th, where he met a large number of Hindu and Muslim citizens and argued with them why they should now wipe off all memories of the past and treat one another with complete equality.

At Kanchrapara there had been police firing in which several dozens of men had been killed or injured. On the 19th, after his return from a visit to that place, Gandhiji referred to the matter in his after-prayer speech in Beliaghata when he warned people against being unduly elated by the fraternization which they were witnessing. Behind it there were pointers like Barrackpore, Kanchrapara and other places he could mention. He would not let them plead excuse or extenuation. There was neither excuse nor extenuation for the majority in Pakistan or Hindustan.

And thus, day after day, in numerous interviews as well as in prayer meetings held in different parts of the city, Gandhiji told people how to behave and how to live so that they could become worthy of the new freedom which had come upon the land.

On the 30th of August, the Ruling Chief of Rangpur in Orissa paid a visit to Gandhiji in company with his mother. Rangpur had joined the Indian Union and the Raja Sahib was anxious to know if the Union would stand by the Princes after accession. Gandhiji's reply was that the Union would surely accord to the Princes 'full support in vindicating the liberty of their subjects.'

On the same evening, Randolph Churchill, son of Winston Churchill, paid a call in the evening. Mr. Suhrawardy was also present in the room at the time. One of the questions which Mr. Churchill asked was, what Gandhiji's ideas were with regard to the re-union of Pakistan and India. Gandhiji said that his views on partition were very well known, and he, even now, considered partition to be a 'sin.' But whether there would be re-union or not was not for him to decide. If the people of both States became so friendly that they voluntarily wished to be one, there would indeed be nothing like it.

To other visitors he had already expressed the opinion that we in India should immediately create a State which lived for the poor and meant real freedom for them. And then the goodness of that State would cross geographical boundaries and affect the life of the common people in the neighbouring States.*

Syamaprasad Mookerjee, who is now a member of the

---

* Indeed, it was reported by Amrit Kaur that to a French interviewer he had said in Delhi in May 1947 that, 'he felt that a socialistic state was bound to come into being in India. He himself naturally clung to the hope that future society in India would be built on non-violence. And only in that case would socialism become a permanent way of life'. (*Harijan*, 18-5-1947, p. 153.)

He also said on the 4th of July that 'he was sorry to have to confess that he saw no sign of the Kingdom of God being born out of the coming Dominion Status.... Be that as it may, it was open to both the new States as soon as they framed their constitutions to declare complete independence of the exclusive family of British Dominions and aim at a family of independent World States which necessarily ruled out all internal armies. He could not visualize a dog-in-the-manger policy for India whereby it would become a menace to world peace, another Japan or Germany celling itself falsely a democracy. Democracy and the military spirit he held to be a contradiction in

Cabinet, came on a visit at 3-55 p.m. and was with Gandhiji for twenty minutes. He acquainted the latter with recent developments in the Punjab, and also how the two Governments had come to an agreement on the transfer of population. The Union Government was however under the impression that the terms of the agreement were not being duly implemented by the Government of Pakistan.

News poured in almost every day that in comparison with the recent killings and arsons in the Punjab, the happenings of Bengal and Bihar paled into utter insignificance. Gandhiji was therefore urgently needed there in order to restore peace.

Professor Stuart Nelson, who had met Gandhiji in Srirampur, came on a call before leaving for his University in Washington. Professor Nelson asked him why it was that Indians who had more or less successfully gained independence through peaceful means were now unable to check the tide of civil war through the same means? Gandhiji replied that it had become clear to him that what he had mistaken for satyagraha was not more than passive resistance, which was a weapon of the weak.\* Indians harboured ill-will and anger against their erstwhile rulers, while they pretended to resist them non-violently. Their resistance was, therefore, inspired by violence and not by a respect for the better element in the English people, which they were trying to awaken by means of self-suffering.

Now that the latter were voluntarily quitting India, our

---

terms. A democrat relied upon the force not of arms his State could flaunt in the face of the world but on the moral force his State should put at the disposal of the world. If by India's effort such a world federation of free and independent States was brought into being, the hope of the Kingdom of God, otherwise called *Ramarajya*, might legitimately be entertained'. (*Harijan*, 13-7-1947, p. 235.)

\* Cf. 'The weak of heart could not claim to represent my non-violence at all. The proper term (for what India has been practising for the last thirty years) was passive resistance. Passive resistance was a preparation for the active resistance of arms.' (*Harijan*, 13-7-1947, p. 236.) 'Passive resistance, unlike non-violence, had no power to change men's hearts. The consequences they knew but too well. The Swaraj of their dream was far off.' (*Harijan*, 20-7-1947, p. **243.**)

apparent non-violence was going to pieces in a moment. The attitude of violence which we had secretly harboured, in spite of the restraint imposed by the Indian National Congress, now recoiled upon us and made us fly at each other's throat when the question of the distribution of power came up. If India could discover a way of sublimating the forces of violence and diverting them along constructive lines whereby differences of interest could be peacefully liquidated through satyagraha of one kind or another, then it would be a great day indeed.

Gandhiji then proceeded to say that it was indeed true that many English friends had warned him that the so-called non-violence of India was no more than the passivity of the weak, it was not the non-violence of the stout in heart who disdained to surrender their sense of human unity even in the midst of a conflict of interests but continued their effort to convert the opponent instead of coercing him into submission.

Gandhiji proceeded to say that it was indeed true that he had all along laboured under an illusion. But he was never sorry for it. He realized that if his vision had not been clouded by that illusion, India would never have reached the point which it had done today.

India was now free, and the reality was now clearly revealed to him. Now that the burden of subjection had been lifted, all the forces of evil had come to the surface. It was evidently a healthy sign. But what remained to be done was to marshall all the forces of good; so that we could build a great country which forsook the accustomed method of violence to settle human disputes, whether it was between two sections of the same people or between two States. He had yet faith that India would rise equal to the occasion and prove to the world that the birth of two new States would be, not a menace, but a blessing for the rest of mankind. It was the duty of Free India to perfect the instrument of non-violence in resolving collective conflicts if its freedom was going to be really worth while.

## XXV  THE FAST

THINGS had become normal in the city of Calcutta when there was a sudden turn for the worse on the 31st of August 1947. We were to leave for Noakhali on the following morning, and Mr. Suhrawardy who used to be with us at Beliaghata had left in the evening for his residence for gathering certain things which were needed on the journey.

It was about 10 p.m. when a large crowd of Hindus came to the house and after having entered the hall where most of us used to work during the day began to smash to pieces whatever they could lay their hands upon. The furniture, window-panes, crockery were all reduced to bits; and what the people demanded was the presence of Suhrawardy Sahib with whom, they said, they had an account to settle.

The Commissioner of Police, the Chief Minister Prafulla Chandra Ghosh came to the scene within a short time and persuaded the crowd to disperse without any further untoward incident.

The 1st of September began with ominous portents. News arrived that anti-Muslim riots had started in Central Calcutta. Some of the poorer people in Miabagan and other quarters of Beliaghata had already returned to their homes on the assurance of Gandhiji's presence in their midst. But on this day, as the news of fresh riots poured in, they felt nervous and one batch of them boarded a truck belonging to a Hindu merchant for being escorted to Rajabazar which is the nearest Muslim neighbourhood.

Gandhiji advised evacuation if we felt things were going to worsen. Just as the open truck with about thirty passengers sped past our camp and was passing by the side of a graveyard, hand grenades were hurled upon it from the roof of a building which lay within the gate of the graveyard and two young Muslims were instantly killed. As soon as we heard the report we rushed to the scene, and Gandhiji also followed suit in a few minutes' time. His face hardened, and shortly after we reached back home, he set himself down to complete a Press statement that he had been preparing in the meanwhile.

He had decided to enter upon a fast for the return of sanity among the people of Calcutta.

In the meanwhile, some young men of Beliaghata took me to the deserted bustee of Miabagan where a few old Muslim men and women, including a patient of tuberculosis, were still living. The young men said that although a small batch from among them had erred and hurled the fatal bomb on the refugee truck, yet they themselves would request Gandhiji to stop any further evacuation. It was a point of honour with them, after they had given their word a few days ago to Gandhiji, to protect the remaining Mussulmans from further harm. And for this purpose they might even have to use sten guns at night; only they would request Gandhiji to advise the Police not to arrest anybody in possession of unlicensed arms. I listened to them and then reported the whole matter to Gandhiji. Gandhiji gave a most unexpected reply. He asked me to tell the young men that 'he was with them. If Prafulla Babu, the Chief Minister, could not protect the minority with his government forces, and the young men decided to do so, they deserved his support.'*

C. Rajagopalachari, the Governor, came to see Gandhiji at 8-15 p.m. and argued with him till half past eleven against the decision to fast. Rajaji asked Gandhiji, was it because of his success during the 14th and the 15th of August that he had become so anxious to see peace restored in Calcutta through his fast? What would he have done if he had been away at Noakhali as planned already? He should allow the Government of the State some time to bring about peace.

---

* Long afterwards when I was reporting the incident to a Jewish friend from the Palestine University, Dr. Walter Zander, he said, he could understand this quite well. For Gandhiji was here not encouraging violence; he was trying to protect those who were against him from the hand of his own people. And if violence was condoned for this purpose, it was no more than cutting off one's own hand to prevent it from doing mischief. Whether Dr. Zander was right in his judgment or not, the incident does throw some light on Gandhiji's attitude towards violence and non-violence.

Gandhiji's reply was that his fast was not the result of any subtle pride in his own command over the people of Calcutta. The Government were surely to pursue their own course of action for the restoration of peace. But should he remain idle for even twenty-four hours and do nothing in the meanwhile? His obvious duty was to go to every citizen of Calcutta and argue with him until he was convinced that any attack upon the Muslim community, as such, was wrong. But as that was physically not possible, he had decided upon the other alternative of a fast. Then people's heart might be touched and perhaps his reason would appeal to them more readily.

The statement which Gandhiji had prepared was examined in great detail, and then released for the Press. In the statement, the last but one paragraph stated: 'I shall, as usual, permit myself to add salt and soda bicarb to the water I may wish to drink during the fast.' The original draft ran differently: 'to add salt and soda bicarb and sour limes to the water I may wish to drink during the fast.' When Rajaji read the words 'and sour limes', he asked, why it should be there if Gandhiji's intention was to fast unto death as an appeal to the heart of the people. Gandhiji immediately scored through the words, and later on, he said to me, 'You see, how my weakness did not escape Rajaji's keen eyes! Indeed, there was evidently a desire in my mind to survive the fast and a hope it would prove fruitful in its purpose. You are new with me, but Rajaji has known me for many years and the departure from truth did not escape him.'

The statement is now given below in full:

'I regret to have to report to you that last night some young men brought to the compound a bandaged man. He was reported to have been attacked by some Muslims. The Prime Minister had him examined and the report was that he had no marks of stabbing, which he was said to have received. The seriousness of the injury, however, is not the chief point. What I want to emphasize is that these young men tried to become judges and executioners.

'This was about 10 p.m. Calcutta time. They began to shout at the top of their voices. My sleep was disturbed but

I tried to lie quiet, not knowing what was happening. I heard the window-panes being smashed. I had lying on either side of me two very brave girls. They would not sleep but without my knowledge, for my eyes were closed, they went among the small crowd and tried to pacify them. Thank God, the crowd did not do any harm to them. The old Muslim lady in the house endearingly called Bi Amma and a young Muslim stood near my matting, I suppose, to protect me from harm.

'The noise continued to swell. Some had entered the central hall, and began to knock open the many doors. I felt that I must get up and face the angry crowd. I stood at the threshold of one of the doors. Friendly faces surrounded me and would not let me move forward. My vow of silence admitted of my breaking it on my occasions and I broke it and began to appeal to the angry young men to be quiet. I asked the Bengali grand-daughter-in-law to translate my few words into Bengali. All to no purpose. Their ears were closed against reason.

'I clasped my hands in the Hindu fashion. Nothing doing. More window-panes began to crack. The friendly ones in the crowd tried to pacify the crowd. There were police officers. Be it said to their credit that they did not try to exercise authority. They too clasped their hands in appeal. A lathi blow missed me and everybody round me. A brick aimed at me hurt a Muslim friend standing by. The two girls would not leave me and held on to me to the last. Meanwhile the Police Superintendent and his officers came in. They too did not use force. They appealed to me to retire. Then there was a chance of their stilling the young men. After a time the crowd melted.

'What happened outside the compound gate I do not know except that the police had to use tear gas to disperse the crowd. Meanwhile, Dr. P. C. Ghosh, Annada Babu and Dr. Nripen walked in and after some discussion left. Happily, Shaheed Sahib had gone home to prepare for to-morrow's proposed departure for Noakhali. In view of the above ugly incident, which no one could tell where it would lead to, I could not think of leaving Calcutta for Noakhali.

'What is the lesson of the incident? It is clear to me that

if India is to retain her dearly-won independence all men and women must completely forget lynch law. What was attempted was an indifferent imitation of it. If Muslims misbehaved, the complainants could, if they would not go to the ministers, certainly go to me or my friend, Shaheed Sahib. The same thing applied to Muslim complainants. There is no way of keeping the peace in Calcutta or elsewhere if the elementary rule of civilized society is not observed. Let them not think of the savagery of the Punjab or outside India. The recognition of the golden rule of never taking the law into one's own hands has no exception.

'My Secretary, Dev Prakash, in Patna, wires: "Public agitated Punjab happenings. Feel statement necessary impressing duty of public and the Press." Shri Dev Prakash is never unduly agitated. There must be some unguarded word by the Press. If that is so, at this time when we are sitting on a powder magazine, the Fourth Estate has to be extra-wise and reticent. Unscrupulousness will act as a lighted match. I hope every editor and reporter will realize his duty to the full.

'One thing I must mention. I have an urgent message calling me to the Punjab. I hear all kinds of rumours about recrudescence of trouble in Calcutta. I hope they are exaggerated, if not quite baseless. The citizens of Calcutta have to reassure me that there would be nothing wrong in Calcutta, and that peace, once restored, will not be broken.

'From the very first day of peace, that is August 14th last, I have been saying that the peace might only be a temporary lull. There was no miracle. Will the foreboding prove true and will Calcutta again lapse into the law of the jungle? Let us hope not, let us pray to the Almighty that He will touch our hearts and ward off the recurrence of insanity.

'Since the foregoing was written, i.e., about 4 o'clock, during silence, I have come to know fairly well the details of what has happened in various parts of the city. Some of the places which were safe yesterday have suddenly become unsafe. Several deaths have taken place. I saw two bodies of very poor Muslims. I saw also some wretched-looking Muslims being carried away to a place of safety. I quite see that last night's incidents so fully described above, pale into insignificance before this flare-up. Nothing that I may do in the way of going about in the open conflagration could possibly arrest it.

'I have told the friends who saw me in the evening what their duty is. What part am I to play in order to stop it? The Sikhs and the Hindus must not forget what East Punjab has done during these few days. Now the Muslims in the West Punjab have begun the mad career. It is said that the Sikhs and the Hindus are enraged over the Punjab happenings.

'I have adverted above to an urgent call for me to go to the Punjab. But now that the Calcutta bubble seems to have burst, with what face can I go to the Punjab? The weapon which has hitherto proved infallible for me is fasting. To put an appearance before an yelling crowd does not always work. It certainly did not last night. What my word in person cannot do, my fast may. It may touch all the warring elements in the Punjab if it does in Calcutta. I therefore, begin fasting from 8-15 to-night to end only if and when sanity returns to Calcutta. I shall, as usual permit myself to add salt and soda bicarb to the water I may wish to drink during the fast.

'If the people of Calcutta wish me to proceed to the Punjab and help the people there, they have to enable me to break the fast as early as may be.'

The fast continued for three days and when the necessary assurance came from important citizens that they were prepared to lay down their lives if necessary for the restoration of peace in Calcutta, the fast was broken. An account was prepared by me for the Press and subsequently revised by Gandhiji. It is also given below in full.

Gandhiji began his fast for allaying the communal frenzy and restoration of sanity in Calcutta at 8-15 p.m. on the 1st of September 1947, and broke it at 9-15 p.m. on the 4th instant with a glass of sweet lime juice which Mr. Suhrawardy served to him.

It is necessary to go into the history of the fast in order to prepare the background of the story as to how and under what circumstances it was finally broken.

## THE FAST

From the 14th of August till the 31st, peace reigned. That evening there was a demonstration against Gandhiji's peace mission. On the following morning communal frenzy in a very intense form, once more swept over several parts of the city. There were already indications in the morning that Gandhiji might fast; but the final decision was taken at eleven in the evening when, according to him, friends had failed to show any satisfactory reason why he should not take the contemplated step. The last sweet drink was taken at 7 p.m. He made the provisional decision at 8-15 p.m.

Anyway, the fast was taken and perhaps partly on account of it and partly also because the common citizen, who had tasted peace after one year's life in the trenches, did not want the recrudescence, the riots rapidly cooled down, so that on the 4th, the Government as well as the public were able to report to Gandhiji that not one incident had taken place during the last twenty-four hours. Party after party came to Gandhiji either with reports or with promises, and in spite of his weak state, he insisted on talking in his feeble voice to every batch of interviewers. Dr. Sunil Bose, the celebrated physician and brother of Netaji Subhas Bose, came to Gandhiji with a request that he must take plenty of rest and not talk at all. But Gandhiji told him he could not exclude relevant talk. Such necessary loss of energy was inevitable. He was certainly desirous of living, but not at the cost of work that duty demanded. 'I can't interrupt the work,' he said to Dr. Bose, 'which has made me fast and which makes me live. If my life ebbs away in the process, I would feel happy.'

This was at half past eleven in the morning. A few minutes later a batch of twenty-seven citizens belonging to Central Calcutta came to see him. During communal disturbance of last year, resistance groups had grown up here and there, and the present party represented such a group in Central Calcutta, which had become the focus of recrudescence on Monday. They had come to see Gandhiji with the promise that henceforth there would be no more incidents in their part of the city and he should, therefore, break his fast now, otherwise all of them would go on a sympathetic fast with him. Gandhiji argued long with

16

them, and what he said in substance was this. The present occasion was not one in which there was scope for a sympathetic fast. Hindus and Mussulmans had fought for one whole year, at the end of which the major parties had agreed to divide India into two States. Both had Hindu and Muslim subjects. It was now time for every one to create the sense of common citizenship, to rebuild the land, so that men might taste the fruits of freedom. To this end all should work. Gandhiji said that if the friends had come to him only for the sake of saving his life, it was not worth while.

Referring to the Poona Fast which ended with the desired amendment of the Communal Award, it was suggested by some that though the amendment was not to their desire, they had accepted it for the sake of saving his life. This was a wholly wrong approach. Such fasts were intended to stir men's conscience and remove mental sluggishness. Truth could not be sacrificed even for the sake of saving a life, however precious it might be. Gandhiji, therefore, warned the present company that they should create real Hindu-Muslim unity by educating the people into a sense of common citizenship of the State, where every single man enjoyed perfect equality of rights which flowed from duty performed. If they worked with this aim in view and succeeded after a few days' effort in making the Muslims in Calcutta feel safe where they now did not, it would be time for him to break the fast. Gandhiji was clearly of opinion that although his work was now confined to Calcutta, yet his one aim with respect to the Hindu-Muslim question was that the solution would be complete only when the minority, whether in the Indian Union or in Pakistan, felt perfectly safe even if they were in the minority of one. There would be no favoured and no depressed community anywhere. All should forget their religious affiliations. He was working in such a manner that the majority community in each State would go forward and create the necessary conditions of freedom.

Some one asked him: Was it possible that his fast would have any effect on the anti-social elements in society? Today, i.e., during the present recrudescence, it was this element which had gained the upper hand. Could their hearts be converted by Gandhiji's expiation? Gandhiji's answer was very clear and emphatic. He said that goondas were there because we had made them so. During one year of past anarchy, it was understandable how these elements in society had gained respectability. But the war between Pakistanis and those for Undivided India had now ended. It was time for peace-loving citizens to assert themselves and isolate goondaism. Non-violent non-co-operation was a universal remedy. Good was self-existent, evil was not. It was like a parasite living on and round good. It would die of itself when the support that good gave was withdrawn. The heart of the anti-social elements may or may not be changed; it would be enough if they were made to feel that the better elements of society were asserting themselves in the interest of peace.

To the interviewers from Central Calcutta, Gandhiji's advice, therefore, was that they should desist from a sympathetic fact, contact the oppressed in each quarter, assure them that they were safe, and rebuild life so that safety would be a permanent feature of the new State of India. He would personally have loved to move about from quarter to quarter in Calcutta in order to place his views before the various bodies, but his physical condition would not permit that. If others worked, how could he rest? He was bound to make his contribution. He felt that it should be in the shape of a fast.

The citizens of Central Calcutta were followed by others. There came a deputation from the Bar Association of Calcutta with the promise that its members would do all that lay within their power to restore peace. Citizens of Beliaghata, who had a few weeks back looked upon Gandhiji's peace mission with suspicion, had been electrified by the fast. They appreciated now the full significance of the mission and had, with all their energy, set about the task of rehabilitating the deserted Muslim bustees. Pressmen who had met the evacuees who had returned home testified to the sincerity and solicitude with which those who had driven them away a few weeks back now treated them. All this was good news for Gandhiji, but yet he did not reach the point when the fast could be broken.

Towards evening, N. C. Chatterji, President of the Hindu Mahasabha, Debendra Nath Mukherjee, its Secretary, Sirdar Niranjan Singh Talib, Sikh Editor of the *Desh Darpan*, G. Gilani of the Muslim League, Abdur Rashid Chowdhury and Mohibur Rahaman of the Pakistan Seamen's Union came accompanied by some other friends to report on the quiet and with their request to Gandhiji to end his fast. Rajaji, the Governor of West Bengal, Acharya Kripalani, P. C. Ghosh and H. S. Suhrawardy were also there. They had a long discussion with Gandhiji which left him rather worn out. Gandhiji heard what they had to say and did most of the talking. This is what he said:

He said that ever since the 14th of August, although he had relished the fraternization between the Hindus and Mussulmans, yet he looked on the ebullition of emotion with caution and reserve. If the feeling was due entirely to friendship new found, to the sense of brotherhood through common citizenship newly attained, there would be more signs of it, e.g., in intensified efforts for rehabilitation. That sign was lacking. The recrudescence had then come. Therefore, Gandhiji felt, he must fast. God had at least given him the capacity to work and die for common peace. If there were anti-social elements in society, where a rowdy or a goonda plundered or killed a man, whether Hindu or Muslim, his fast might not affect him. He knew his limitations. He fasted for the restoration of communal harmony. The sanity that had been in evidence for the last twenty-four hours was not enough for him. If the present company were going to assure him that it was a sincere affair and was likely to be permanent, he would expect them to give him something in writing. It must state that supposing Hindu-Muslim riots broke out once more in Calcutta they assured him that they would lay down their lives in the attempt to quell the riots. If they agreed, that would be enough. They must so work from the next day that real peace and common citizenship were created as a feature of Calcutta life, no matter what happened elsewhere. Communal peace should be their prime occupation. Their other occupations or avocations must henceforth occupy a second place.

There was another matter, but that was a condition which automatically attached itself to the situation. In Bihar, as in Noakhali, so also in Calcutta, he wanted to tell the friends who were making themselves responsible for the termination of his fast, that if communal frenzy broke out in Calcutta again, Gandhiji might have to go on an irrevocable fast. The present fast was meant to activize the better, peace-loving and wise elements in society, to secure them from mental sluggishness and make goodness active.

Realizing their responsibility, the friends retired to another room. Free and frank discussions took place between them. Suspicions were freely expressed, fears that the signatories might not rise to the height demanded of them were discussed in an atmosphere of frankness, and finally came the decision to sign the document with all its implications.

Gandhiji felt glad. He took the signatories at their word; prayed that God might give them the courage and strength to implement their promise in daily life from the following morning; and with that prayer on his lips, he broke his fast last night. A heavy responsibility now lies upon the people of Bengal who have to implement the promise made sacred in Gandhiji's presence. May we have the requisite wisdom, strength and perseverence to see it through.

Before breaking the fast, Gandhiji dictated a note which is reproduced below:

'Before breaking his fast and after prayer which he always has when he breaks his fast, Gandhiji said a few words to the signatories of the document, which induced the breaking of the three days' fast, and their friends and co-workers.

'Gandhiji said, he wanted to break the fast as soon as he legitimately could in view of the work that awaited him in the Punjab. But the deciding motive was not so much the written document that they were good enough to give him, but the confidence that he reposed in them and their constituents, that they would prove as good as their word and continue to regard it as their special business to see that communal peace in Calcutta was never broken. For, he liked them to think that observance of peace in Noakhali, in the Punjab or other parts of India would depend upon Calcutta. He would like them to realize the importance of their position. He knew that our final refuge was God, who was the Maker of our destiny. But he used human instruments for His purpose, if such a mundane word could be attributed to Divinity. Therefore he was breaking his fast in His name and let his friends become instruments in the Maker's hands to fulfil the purpose upon which they had set their hearts.'

In the meanwhile Calcutta witnessed some of the noblest deaths that have ever taken place in the city. Sachin Mitra, Smritish Banerji and some more volunteers had gone forth among the Muslim elements in the city in order to ask them not to retaliate even if the Hindus had opened the attack; and both of them had laid down their lives at the hand of misguided Muslim ruffians, without any trace of bitterness. Sachin's case was particularly tragic. He was accompanied by a peace-loving band of Muslims whom he had first collected round him before proceeding to the storm centre in Zachariah Street. These friends had tried their utmost to protect Sachin and two more Congress volunteers who had accompanied him. But they had failed, and all of them had been brought back to the hospital after severe injuries. Sachin expired on the 3rd of September without a shadow of regret in his mind.

There was an immensely crowded meeting at the Maidan on the 6th of September 1947, which was organized by the Corporation of Calcutta.

In course of the speech, Gandhiji referred to the martyrdom of Sachin Mitra and Smritish Banerjee. He was not sorry. Such innocent deaths were necessary to keep the two communities together.

Then referring to his fast, he said that by breaking it only after one day's absence of strife, on the strength of the pressure of friends drawn from all communities in Calcutta and outside, he threw the burden on them of preservation of peace at the cost of their lives. Let them not be guilty of having, though unwillingly, brought about his death by the abrupt end of the fast. What all wanted was not peace imposed by the Government forces but by themselves. If unfortunately it was broken, there would be no alternative but a fast unto death. He could not, like a child, play with them and each time say, he was going to break his fast if they resumed sanity. He made that solemn declaration for Bihar, then for Noakhali and now for Calcutta. As his life was made, he had no other alternative. If God willed that he should still do some service, He would bless all with wisdom to do the right thing in the matter. Consider the consequence of Calcutta remaining sane. It must mean the automatic sanity of all Bengal, East and West. It meant also Bihar and consequently the Punjab where God was sending him, and if the Punjab came to its senses, the rest of India was bound to follow. So may God help them all.

*Calcutta, Sunday, 7-9-1947:*

Gandhiji had his last prayer speech in the compound of his residence before a crowded audience. He congratulated them upon their exemplary silence. He congratulated also the Santi Sena (Soldiers of Peace) upon their useful service during the past critical days. But they heavier work of sustaining the peace commenced now. They were expected to die to a man—men and women—in the attempt to keep the glorious peace. The soldiering and discipline required by a man whose weapon was only love was infinitely greater than that imposed by the sword from without. The other was evoked from within. The sword which imposed peace forcibly, deepened the division between the two. In this mission, those who died were the heroes not the survivors.

After the prayer meeting had been over, the last act was a visit to the Leprosy Hospital at Gobra. Addressing the patients and the staff he said that he considered it wrong that leprosy should carry more stigma than any other infectious disease. Real stigma, in his opinion, attached to moral ailments rather than physical ones. The drunkards, the gamblers and those who suffered from such ailments of society deserved far more abhorrence than a disease like leprosy. The members of the asylum had no occasion whatsoever to feel dejected. The fact that moral lepers were worse than physical ones was surely a matter of some consolation to them. The real consolation lay in their reliance on God.

This however did not mean that society did not owe a great duty to lepers in its midst who, after all, were the outward symbol of society's many blemishes which, being general, were not noticed. He thought that the abhorrence which was shown towards lepers was superstition born of ignorance. This he had learnt during his visits to most of the leper asylums of India.

Arrangements had been made by the present Chief Minister, Prafulla Chandra Ghosh, to take Gandhiji by car to a station outside Calcutta from where he was to board the train for Delhi. Some were to accompany him to Delhi, others were to return from the railway station after seeing him off. I was somehow forgotten by the managers, and this was indeed good for me. So, in a moment of quiet shortly before he left his residence in Beliaghata, I stepped into his room in order to bid him good-bye. He asked me if I was not coming; and when I told him that I had apparently been forgotten and would prefer to salute him not in a crowd but rather alone, he allowed me to touch his feet for blessings.

And thus I departed, destined never to meet him again.

## XXVI. MARTYRDOM

It was the 30th of January 1948, and shortly after five o'clock in the evening. I live close by one of the newspaper offices in Calcutta; and as I was cycling past the garage of the Paper, one of the employees suddenly accosted me and asked me if I had heard the news, Gandhiji had been shot at. I sped along in my bicycle, and tried to shake off the news from my mind; perhaps it was not true, perhaps it was like the attempt of about a fortnight ago when a childish refugee had hurled a bomb on the prayer ground in Delhi. But the news gripped my mind and I turned back home. Within a few minutes' time, the radio announced that Gandhiji was no more.

The first thought which came to my mind was, who could the assailant be? If it were a Mussulman, it would mean that a mad fury would sweep over India and lead to a bloodshed whose magnitude it was frightful to contemplate. And what then? But then there was no reason why it should be a Mussulman. Could it be a refugee from the Punjab, some suffering but ignorant Sikh who could not bear Gandhiji's daily pleading for sanity, for forgiveness and for the administration of equal justice to all? It might be so. The radio said nothing. It was only when Pandit Jawaharlal Nehru made the announcement that the hand which had laid Gandhiji low was of a Hindu that I almost heaved a sigh of relief. After all, it would not plunge the whole country into the horrors of communal butchery once more! Perhaps Gandhiji's martyrdom would abate the communal frenzy if it could do nothing else.

For four months and a half, ever since Gandhiji had left Calcutta for a visit to West Pakistan, he had every day carried on his prayer meetings with clock-like regularity. The whole country had been forced into partition through communal bloodshed, and whatever might be said to the contrary, the western portion of Pakistan had, at least, succeeded in resolving the minority problem by a wholesale migration of the Sikhs brought about through butchery and barbarism. The Sikhs had struck back in the East Punjab with equal vehemence. All these could not easily be forgotten; and, moreover, the sufferings of the refugees had not yet been allayed by any well-planned and sympathetic action in the other provinces of India. The process of rehabilitation was proving slow, the suffering of the refugees was like an open sore which festered and nearly paralysed the Government of India notwithstanding its most earnest efforts for rehabilitation.

Under these circumstances, Gandhiji's daily sermon on equality of treatment to all Indian citizens fell on ears upon which his claim began to slacken. It began to be talked about that if there was an ardent Mussulman anywhere in India, it was Mahatma Gandhi. He had no word to say about the Hindu sufferers, all he wanted Indians to do was that they should be just even to those who had brought untold suffering and ruination upon millions of innocent people.

Towards the month of January, Gandhiji's prayer meetings or the speeches which he delivered, gradually failed to evoke the same enthusiasm as formerly. His voice seemed to have lost its magic equality. Personally, he had also begun to feel alone more than ever. In the prayer speeches, he made references now and then to the Government of India, how it no longer swore by the spinning wheel or khadi which had so long been the livery of our freedom, but had begun to follow the footsteps of the industrialized nations of the West who themselves did not know where they were going. Sometimes he asked himself, had India Free no longer any need of him as it had when it was in bondage?

The attendance in the prayer meetings dwindled appreciably. For a class of people it had become a sort of routine duty to join the prayers every day with their wives and children. In the meanwhile, Gandhiji's solicitude for suffering Muslims began to increase appreciably. This was taken as a sign of appeasement or favouritism, and people allowed themselves to forget that he never demanded anything for anybody, whether Muslim or otherwise, which pure justice did not allow. Nationalist Muslims of India or friendly Englishmen were known to have constantly brought case after case of Muslim suffering before him for adequate action; but this alone could not be held responsible for his special concern for such sufferers. His nature itself was such that he always stood by the side of the weaker party. And now that his own men, the Hindus, were in power and occasionally were turning aggressor, he felt it was his double duty to stand by the victims, double because so long the Muslims had treated him as Enemy Number One. He was actually behaving like a chivalrous knight who puts up a brave fight in order to protect a fallen enemy even if it were at the risk of his own life. The misunderstanding however continued and ultimately culminated in his assassination at the hand of one who thought he was serving the cause of Hinduism thereby.

Whatever else the assassination might have done, it at once transformed the value of Gandhi's life by converting him into a martyr. Without knowing why, people all over India felt instinctively that, whatever his political opinions may have been, whether one agreed with him or not, it was undoubtedly wrong to have killed him. And the whole country was swept by an upsurge of sorrow, the like of which has hardly been witnessed in the history of our times. One of the strangest phenomena which struck me very forcibly was the news that more than a dozen men died in course of the next few weeks because they failed to bear separation from Gandhi. Not that any of them were personally known or attached to Gandhi, not that their bodies were in all cases full of health, but some chord in their lives snapped when they heard that Gandhi was no more, and they also laid down their bodies in eternal sleep out of love for one without whose presence the earth had become too poor a place for them to live in.

The funeral in Delhi was held in great estate; but the very thought of the seething multitudes repelled me, and all that I could do at the fateful moment when the precious body was placed upon the sacred pyre was to reach the River Ganges in company with some friends in our own town and sprinkle a few drops of its holy water on our head, as is the custom when we salute a sacred river.

For indeed, Gandhi's life had been like the Ganges in

its influence upon the life of India. The land had become parched and dry and full of the dust of ages. Gandhi had given abundantly, he had swept the whole of Indian humanity in an emotional flood when he led the battle in the political or the social battle-field; and every movement of his had not only permeated the country with its life-giving sap but had also left it enriched by a layer of silt on which a new-born creative endeavour was bound to blossom forth if only the gardener knew how to turn it to good account.

And the river of life which Gandhi represented had its origin in the heights of the Indian Himalayas. For, in spite of the fact that he had been nourished by clouds, many of which had come wafting from distant foreign oceans, yet, after the raindrops had touched the living soil of his Indian life, they had been transformed and become completely Indian in form as well as in content.

Gandhi was an intense believer in individualism. According to him, a good society consisted of good individuals, and any social change was bound to begin with the transformation of the individual. The measure of reform achieved in the outward, objective, social sphere was no more than a measure and proof of the total and collective individual, internal transformation achieved. In this he represented one of the characteristic trends of Indian thought in which primacy is given to the individual. And that is the reason why, whenever he felt alone, when his soul was engulfed on all sides by a prevailing darkness, he fought against it the supreme battle on the lonesome field of individual enterprise. Fasting of one Satyagrahi of the purest kind was, according to him, enough to bring about the downfall of an empire or its benign transformation.

Gandhi's lonely effort to replace emotional unbalance by sanity, to melt the sword in order to build the plough in India went unheeled in the last days of his life. But that martyrdom which brought his life to a finale which is comparable to the Greek tragedies, acted as the touchstone which gave a new meaning and new significance to the words which had so long sounded commonplace or strange in our heedless ears.

Perhaps the time has not yet come for India to listen to the voice of sanity which Gandhi preached; perhaps after the success of large-scale mechanical endeavours which cover the earth with giant factories, we shall hesitate long before we can restore the individual to the primacy with which Gandhi's life and even more his death endowed it. Yet India is blessed because she gave birth to one who became Gandhi and perhaps blessed again that, by dealing him the blow of death, we endowed his life with an added radiance which shall enrich the heritage of humankind in all ages to come.

# APPENDIX A

*Confidential official report about the condition of Noakhali in May 1947*

Office of the Commissioner,
Chittagong Division.

*Top Secret*

To
    P. D. Martyn, C.I.E., O.B.E., I.C.S.,
        Additional Secretary to the Government of Bengal,
           Home (Political) Department, Calcutta.

Memorandum No. 457/C,
           Dated, Chittagong, the 13th May 1947.

Subject: *Noakhali Situation.*

Reference your Memo No. 647-PS, dated the 23rd April 1947. I spent the 27th to the 30th of April in Noakhali and visited Ramganj, Begamganj and Lakshmipur Thanas. I met leading Muslims and Hindus of all classes including office-bearers of the League, politicians, merchants, agriculturists, school-masters, doctors, relief workers, volunteers and Presidents and Members of Union Boards and interviewed them individually except in cases where they specially asked me to be heard in groups. Before leaving, I received a deputation of Hindus of all political persuasions and another deputation of Muslims including a non-Leaguer. I also had talks with the District Magistrate, the Superintendent of Police and the Sub-divisional Officers of Sadar and Feni. I now give my report.

*Analysis of Situation*

2. *Present Condition*:—The situation in Noakhali District is complex and has many facets, political, communal, economic and psychological. To the casual observer, the District seems normal enough. Most of the fields are green with *aus* paddy and jute, and the remainder are being ploughed. The bazaars and *hats* are functioning normally and both Hindus and Muslims may be seen moving about freely and without any apparent apprehension. Under the surface, however, there is definitely tension, and among

Hindus, a sense of insecurity. In many areas in the interior, away from the more populous centres, this tension manifests itself in the form of abuse and petty harassment of the Hindu minority. The harassment is, of course, magnified by the Hindus, and belittled or denied by the Muslims. In fact, everywhere one is met by lies and counter-lies and it is not easy to get at the truth.

3. *The Hindus*:—The number of Hindus in the District according to the last census is 4 lacs while the number of Muslims is 18 lakhs. The ratio of Muslims to Hindus is therefore nearly $4\frac{1}{2}:1$. The Hindus, especially *bhadralog* class, had a bad shaking during the October disturbances, and have not yet recovered their morale. They are apprehensive and suspicious. They do not want to leave the District because, for most of them, that would mean sacrificing their all, and though many of them are kept in a state of fear by open threats and petty persecution and molestation at the hands of the Muslims, they will not report these cases to the Thanas or the local officers for fear that if it became known that they had done so, worse things would befall them. Sometimes, however, they do report them to the local political relief workers (usually in exaggerated form), but if official enquiries are then made, they will more often than not deny that the incidents they reported ever occurred or that they brought them to notice. In many cases of this kind, it is well known that the incidents actually took place and there are Muslims who know of them and will admit it. All that the Hindus succeed in doing by adopting this attitude of secret report and subsequent denial of the facts is to impeach their own credit. But such is the state of their demoralisation. The credit of the Hindus has also suffered because, in some cases, members of their community named in the F.I.R.'s* Muslims who were not present in the scene of disturbances or who had actually gone out of their way to protect Hindus. This naturally caused much resentment among Muslims.

4. *The Muslims*:—The Muslims of the District may be divided into three district categories. Firstly, there are those

* First Information Report lodged in the Police Station.—N.K.B.

who generally abhor the communal war of nerves that is now in progress and want to live in peace with their Hindu neighbours as they used to do in the past. Many of this class have Hindu friends, and gave shelter to, and even protected Hindus during the disturbances at considerable risk to themselves. They would do the same again, and they provide a definite influence for good. Unfortunately, their number is not large. The majority of Muslims fall in the second category. This class, while strongly pro-Muslim (League?), and anxious to oust the Hindus from their present position in the District, does not favour violence as a means to attain that end. It sees no objection, however, to petty persecution of the Hindus, and if the persecution is somewhat extreme, it is ready to turn a blind eye to the fact, when not to do so might lead to unpleasantness or even unpopularity. This section will give lip service to communal harmony and peace, and will often be outwardly friendly to Hindus. It will not however take any part in preventing disturbances or protecting the Hindus and may, even under the influence of rumour and the excitement of the hour, take part in disturbances and encourage others to do so. Many members of Union Boards belong to this class. The third category is the most dangerous. To this class belong those Muslims who, for reasons of religious zeal, economic jealousy or personal enmity, hate the Hindu and want to see him wiped out. This class would not ordinarily be powerful, but circumstances have combined to make it so today and it has the advantage of having attracted to its side the goonda element of the District, which sees in disturbances the prospect of the easy acquisition of wealth and power. Many persons who fall in this category are able, if violent, speakers and can work up a mob into a state of frenzied anger. To this class belong Abul Kasem and Ali Akbar, the two most important absconders.

5. *The Goonda Problem*:—In the last paragraph mention has been made of goondas. There has been a large addition to the number of bad characters in recent years. The reason of this is probably largely economic. In 1911, the area of the District was computed 1,644 sq. miles and the population 11,74,728, giving a density of 694 persons per square mile.

# APPENDIX

Today the area of the District is 1,658 sq. miles and the population 22,17,402, giving a density of 1,338 persons per square mile. The pressure on land must therefore be well-nigh intolerable, and the inevitable result has been that the weaklings have gone to the wall and taken to crime. All parties were agreed that the number of goondas had increased enormously since the war, and a further accession of strength has been lent to this class by the gradual return of disgruntled ex-servicemen in the last eighteen months; over 56,000 men of this District joined the services during the war. They became accustomed to a standard of living much above that of their village compeers and are disillusioned and discontented now that they have returned and find that they cannot maintain that standard. What more natural than that many of them should take the easy path of crime, especially when the present disturbed conditions afford such little chance of detection. These goondas are no respecters of persons when their need is sufficiently pressing and many Muslims are uneasy at their growing strength and increasing depredations. Not a few said plainly that if their activities remained unchecked, ganster rule would soon be the order of the day. Their fears are justified. It is more than possible that the present phase of communal warfare will be followed by one of goonda domination in which goondas of both communities will combine to enrich themselves at the expense of the public generally.

6. *Crime*:—The growth of the goonda element has naturally led to an increase of crime in the District. The extent of this increase can be best shown by the number of reported cases during the first three months of 1946 and the first three months of 1947.

| *Offences* | | *1946* | *1947* |
|---|---|---|---|
| Dacoity | .. | 5 | 26 |
| Arson | .. | 6 | 43 |
| Robbery | .. | 5 | 12 |
| Murder | .. | 4 | 6 |
| Burglary | .. | 436 | 456 |
| Theft | .. | 176 | 220 |

Arson of course has always been a common offence to this District. According to the District Gazetteer, it was prevalent as far back as 1911, but it has never been as widespread as it is today.

Both local Muslims and the Police have been at pains to explain that in the increase of crime which has taken place this year, the Muslims have been sufferers equally with the Hindus, and that the increase has no communal colour. This is palpably untrue. Although the Hindus are outnumbered in the District by $4\frac{1}{2}:1$, the crime took place for the most part in Hindu houses. In the case of arson, the number of houses affected in the last eight weeks alone was 3 Hindu to 1 Muslim. In other words, allowing for the disproportion in population, the true ratio of Hindu and Muslim victims was $13\frac{1}{2}:1$. Similarly in the case of dacoity, the ratio of houses affected works out to 9 Hindus to 1 Muslim. It is true, of course, that many of the Hindus are better off than the Muslims, and economically it is therefore often more profitable to rob a Hindu house than a Muslim one, but there is little room for doubt that most of the arson committed was for communal reason, and that in many of the other cases, Hindu houses were selected in preference to Muslim ones because the owners were Hindus and because for that reason, the offence would be regarded as venial. The brunt of the crime wave has fallen on them because they are Hindus and if further argument is needed to support their contention it will be found in the fact that during the last eight weeks there have been no less than five cases involving desecration of Hindu holy places.

7. *Hindu persecution*:—Apart from being the main victim of the crime wave, the Hindus are being persecuted in many more subtle ways. The extent and intensity of this persecution varies, of course, from area to area, and in some areas, it is entirely absent. The persecution does not take the form of economic boycott (though this is still advocated by the more extreme Muslim leaders), because the cultivating class cannot afford to allow any land to go untilled or to lose the returns which the cultivation of that land would bring them. What is happening is that a section of Muslims is taking advantage of the demoralised condition

of the Hindus to insult, threaten and cow them down into a state of resigned submission, after which they fatten on their property and treat them as an inferior race. It is quite usual for Hindus while moving about to be addressed as *malaun* or *kafir*. Sometimes they are searched by parties of Muslims and deprived of anything the latter fancy. Cases have occurred of Hindus returning to their houses with their daily bazaar and having their purchases snatched away; the removal of cocoanuts and betelnuts from the gardens of Hindu homesteads is a common occurrence, corrugated iron sheets and timber are often taken from Hindu houses with the frightened consent of the inmates; cattle belonging to Hindu households have developed a habit of freeing themselves from their tethers and disappearing, the paddy plants of Hindus have been uprooted and thrown away. If an aggrieved Hindu reports these occurrences to the Thana, his sufferings are increased, and there have been cases in which such reports had led to the burning of the victims' huts; efforts are being made to have Hindu-owned cinema houses closed, and although the vast majority of weavers in the District are Hindus (Naths), the demands are being made that 50% of the loom licences should go to Muslims. There is a move to rid the bazaars of Hindu merchants and one of the larger Hindu merchants told me that he and many others has been receiving threatening letters. Long established Hindu shopkeepers are being ousted from the markets to make way for Muslims. Hindus who have rebuilt their houses (including even women) have been told that they will not be allowed to live in them and that it will be better for them to leave the District. There is reason to believe that complainants in cases arising out of the disturbances are being threatened by Muslims and compelled to agree to their cases being compromised. Much of this persecution is comparatively petty, but it is lawlessness nonetheless and it shows that the virus which was injected into the District before the October disturbances has not yet been eradicated. The danger now is that the war of nerves which is in progress may lead to more trouble if positive steps are not taken to bring it to an end. In some areas, even an indiscreet speech by an All-India leader, or a persistent rumour of Muslims being persecuted, might at present be sufficient to start fresh rioting.

This happened in Feni, but is mentioned as being indicative of the state of Muslim feeling.

8. *Rehabilitation*:—Considering the unsettled state of the affected Thanas, the progress of rehabilitation has not been unsatisfactory. According to the figures furnished to me by the District Relief Officer, 7,710 families have received house-building grants, and of this number 2,774 families have been provided with building materials by Government. As against these figures, 3,496 families have rebuilt their homes, 1,519 with materials supplied by the Government and 1,977 with partially burnt materials or materials obtained from other sources. The District Magistrate states that there is still a number of families who have received building materials from the Government and who will be using them as they feel sufficiently secure.

Owing presumably to the shortness of building materials, less than 50% of those who have received house-building grants have been provided with building materials by Government. Such materials can only be obtained from the local market at fantastic prices, and there is no doubt that if adequate supplies were made available by Government, the process of rehabilitation would be accelerated. Stories have been put about that Hindu families which have been provided with house-building materials by Government have sold the materials in the black market. Such cases may have occurred, and that risk must be taken. In point of fact, I am assured that the number of such cases is negligible. Similarly an allegation that is frequently made by Muslims in Noakhali, is that Hindus have been burning their own houses in order to implicate Muslims and to secure house-building grants. Such allegations must be heavily discounted. The morale of the Hindus is too low for them to dare risk the consequence of such an action, it is most unlikely that grants made would be sufficient to cover the extent of the damage.

An interesting point is that of 22,066 artisans affected by the disturbances, 17,853 families have received rehabilitation grants and 13,602 families have now resumed their occupations. Most of these artisan families are weavers (cf. para 7), 4,121 agricultural families were affected by the disturbances and of these 3,275 have returned to their holdings and resettled.

9. *Volunteers*:—The number of volunteers in the district does not appear to be large and very few are doing anything of value in the matter of relief and rehabilitation. There is a feeling among influential Muslims that most of these volunteers (including members of the Gandhi Camp) are not only making no attempt to bring the two communities together, but are acting in such a way as to keep open the breach that has existed between them since last October. There is much truth in this. The members of the Gandhi Camp and certainly other volunteers seem to be much more interested in cataloguing the woes of the Hindus than in attempting to bring those woes to an end by meeting and discussing matters with the leading Muslims of the locality concerned and generally trying to bring about a reconciliation. There is in fact no contact between those volunteers and the Muslims and there is a wall of suspicion between them. Most of the time of the Gandhi Camp is spent in receiving reports, some directly and some indirectly, from aggrieved Hindus which, without any form of check or verification, they either pass on to Government or publish in the Press. This in itself is irritating to the local people and serves no useful purpose except that, in the absence of information from the Police, it may give the District Magistrate a line of enquiry. The publication of the 'Shanti Mission Dinalipi', a cyclostyled news sheet, is particularly harmful as this paper publishes the most trifling incidents and gives them a communal colour which may or may not be correct. There is no doubt that the Gandhi Camp members and other volunteers are encouraging the Hindus in their district of the administration and their desire to avoid going to the Police or to the local authorities for the redress of their grievances.

10. *The Riot Cases*:—One thing which, more than anything other, had served to increase the demoralisation of the Hindus and the turbulence and aggressiveness of the

Muslims is the way in which the cases arising out of the October disturbances have been handled. The figures below give at a glance the position of these cases as on the 15th April:

1. Cases started on regular *ejahar* (deposition) .. 1,529
2. Number of persons involved .. .. 13,539*
3. Number of persons arrested .. .. 1,074
4. Number of accused still at large .. 566
5. Number of persons discharged for want of evidence .. .. .. 397
6. Number of persons released on bail .. 627
7. Number of persons detained in custody .. 50
8. Number of charge sheets submitted .. 164
9. Number of final reports submitted .. 862

The points which stand out from these figures are, (1) that out of 1,529 cases no less than 862 have remitted in final reports, and that only 164 in charge sheets; (2) that no less than 566 accused are still at large, including several of the most dangerous ring-leaders, and (3) that out of 677 arrested accused only 50 are now in custody. In the nature of things, a large number of cases must end in final reports and the high proportion of such cases would have eased apprehension to the Hindus and anxiety to the civil administration, had all the ring-leaders and those known to have committed murder been arrested, and had it been that the cases against these persons would be rigorously prosecuted. This is not the case, and the Hindus now feel that the Police are not serious in their attempts to track down the culprits and bring them to book, while the Muslims, who were told that they would be immune from prosecution, are confident that retribution will not overtake them. The two leading absconders—Abul Kasem and Ali Akbar—are still known to be visiting the District and even holding meetings. In fact, these men are now giving it that they made a mistake in the last disturbances by not killing all the Hindus and that they will not make the same mistake next time. The fact that they are still at large and are able to make these

---

* This figure is inflated as many persons have been mentioned in more than one *ejahar*.

statements is demoralising the Hindus in one way and the Muslims in another, and though the bulk of the Muslim population, either through fear or sympathy, will not give any information about their movements, there is no doubt that both these men could have been arrested weeks ago. The lack of confidence engendered by these aspects of the situation has been increased by laxity on the part of the magistracy in releasing persons on bail owing to political pressure, and the failure of the Police to keep a tag on those released on bail and press for the cancellation of the bail bonds of those believed to be interfering with witnesses. Only three bail bonds have been cancelled up to the end of 30th of April. To anyone in touch with the situation in the District such a figure is preposterous. If any degree of confidence is to be restored it is of paramount importance that these matters should be set right.

11. *The Police*:—A sign of weakness in the Police Administration is the fact that the Police are not receiving information of what is going on in the interior of the District, and they appear to be making no attempt to obtain such information. The District Intelligence Branch is either paralysed or intentionally dormant, and the lack of information is so remarkable that one cannot but suspect that when information does come within the grasp of the Police, they shut their eyes to it. This virtual suppression of information is embarrassing to the District Magistrate, as it means that he must use his Relief and other officers to keep him informed of the situation, and even have recourse to the garbled information supplied by the Gandhi Camp. The reason for this state of affairs is not clear, that incidents involving interference with Hindus should be suppressed and suppression lends colour to the frequently stated opinion of the Superintendent of Police that conditions in the District are satisfactory. It was complacency of this kind which led to the holocaust in October last, and which may yet result in a repetition of that disaster.

# APPENDIX B

## CONGRESS POSITION

### By M. K. Gandhi

INDIAN National Congress which is the oldest national political organization and which has after many battles fought her non-violent way to freedom cannot be allowed to die. It can only die with the nation. A living organism ever grows or it dies. The Congress has won political freedom, but it has yet to win economic freedom, social and moral freedom. These freedoms are harder than the political, if only because they are constructive, less exciting and not spectacular. All-embracing constructive work evokes the energy of all the units of the millions.

The Congress has got the preliminary and necessary part of her freedom. The hardest has yet to come. In its difficult ascent to democracy, it has inevitably created rotten boroughs leading to corruption and creation of institutions, popular and democratic only in name. How to get out of the weedy and unwieldy growth?

The Congress *must* do away with its special register of members, at no time exceeding one crore, not even then easily identifiable. It had an unknown register of millions who could never be wanted. Its register should now be co-extensive with all the men and women on the voters' rolls in the country. The Congress business should be to see that no faked name gets in and no legitimate name is left out. On its own register it will have a body of servants of the nation who would be workers doing the work allotted to them from time to time.

Unfortunately for the country they will be drawn chiefly for the time being from the city dwellers, most of whom would be required to work for and in the villages of India. The ranks must be filled in increasing numbers from villagers.

These servants will be expected to operate upon and serve the voters registered according to law, in their own surroundings. Many persons and parties will woo them. The very best will win. Thus and in no other way can the Congress regain its fast ebbing unique position in the country. But yesterday the Congress was unwittingly the servant of the Nation, it was *khudai khidmatgar*—God's servant. Let it now proclaim to itself and the world that it is only God's servant—nothing more, nothing less. If it engages in the ungainly skirmish for power, it will find one fine morning that it is no more. Thank God, it is now no longer in sole possession of the field.

I have only opened the distant scene. If I have the time and health, I hope to discuss in these columns what the servants of the Nation can *do* to raise themselves in the estimation of their masters, the whole of the adult population, male and female. New Delhi, 27-1-'48.

## APPENDIX C

### LAST WILL AND TESTAMENT
(of Mahatma Gandhi)

THOUGH split into two, India having attained political independence through means devised by the Indian National Congress, the Congress in its present shape and form, i.e., as propaganda vehicle and parliamentary machine, has outlived its use. It has still to attain social, moral and economic independence in terms of its seven hundred thousand villages as distinguished from its cities and towns. The struggle for the ascendancy of civil over military power is bound to take place in India's progress towards its democratic goal. It must be kept out of unhealthy competition with political parties and communal bodies. For these and other similar reasons the A.I.C.C. resolves to disband the existing Congress organization and flower into a Lok Sevak Sangh under the following rules with power to alter them as occasion may demand.

Every Panchayat of five adult men or women being villagers or village-minded shall form a unit. Two such contiguous Panchayats shall form a working party under a leader elected from among themselves.

When there are one hundred such Panchayats, the fifty first grade leaders shall elect from among themselves a second grade leader and so on, the first grade leaders meanwhile working under the second grade leader and so on. Parallel groups of two hundred Panchayats shall continue to be formed till they cover the whole of India, each succeeding group of Panchayats electing second grade leaders after the manner of the first. All second grade leaders shall serve jointly for the whole of India and severally for their respective areas. The second grade leaders may elect, whenever they deem necessary, from among themselves a chief who will, during pleasure, regulate and command all the groups.

(As the final formation of provinces or districts is still in a state of flux, no attempt has been made to divide this group of servants into Provincial and District Councils and jurisdiction over the whole of India has been vested in the group or groups that may have been formed at any given time. It should be noted that this body of servants derive their authority or power from service ungrudgingly and wisely done to their master, the whole of India.)

1. Every worker shall be a habitual wearer of Khadi made from self-spun yarn or certified by the A.I.S.A. and must be a teetotaller. If a Hindu, he must have abjured untouchability in any shape or form in his own person or in his family and must be a believer in the ideal of intercommunal unity, equal respect and regard for all religions and equality of opportunity and status for all irrespective of race, creed or sex.

2. He shall come in personal contact with every villager within his jurisdiction.

3. He shall enrol and train workers from amongst the villagers and keep a register of all these.

4. He shall keep a record of his work from day to day.

5. He shall organize the villages so as to make them self-contained and self-supporting through their agriculture and handicrafts.

6. He shall educate the village folk in sanitation and hygiene and take all measures for prevention of ill health and disease among them.

7. He shall organize the education of the village folk from birth to death along the lines of *Nayee Talim*, in accordance with the policy laid down by the Hindustani Talimi Sangh.

8. He shall see that those whose names are missing on the statutory voters' roll are duly entered therein.

9. He shall encourage those who have not yet acquired them legal qualification, to acquire it for getting the right of franchise.

10. For the above purposes and others to be added from time to time, he shall train and fit himself in accordance with the rules laid down by the Sangh for the due performance of duty.

The Sangh shall affiliate the following autonomous bodies:

1. A.I.S.A.
2. A.I.V.I.A.
3. Hindustani Talimi Sangh
4. Harijan Sevak Sangh
5. Goseva Sangh

### FINANCE

The Sangh shall raise finances for the fulfilment of its mission from among the villagers and others, special care being laid on collection of poor man's pice.

New Delhi, 29-1-'48.
                                                 M.K.G.

# INDEX

Anand, Swami, 149, 150, 151
Appeasement policy, 89
Azad, Abul Kalam, 4

Banerji, Smritish, 246
B.B.C., 223
Bose, Sarat Chandra, 59, 96, 193, 195, 202, 203
Bhattacharya, Chapalakanta, 59, 61
Brahmacharya, 1, 134 ff, 149 ff, Ch. XVIII
Burrows, Sir Frederick, 32, 220, 223

Chakraverty, Amiya, 83
Chakraverty, Anukul, 53, 55
Chatterji, N. C., 84, 228, 244
Chatterji, Sailen, 57, 63, 80
Chaudhuri, Manoranjan, 52, 53
Christ, Jesus, 101
Churchill, Randolph, 232
Communist Party of India, 65, 140, 229
Congress, 3, 4, 6, 28, 67, 82, 90, 99, 112, 122, 140, 207
Constituent Assembly, 82, 83, 112

Dasgupta, Satish Chandra, 30, 39, 42, 44, 181
Defence through non-violence, 94, 125, 126
Democracy, Gandhi on, 55, 59, 62, 183

Evacuation from East Bengal, 129
Evacuees, Advice to, 122

Freud, 154, 158

Gandhi, Abha, 49, 88
Gandhi, Kanu, 32
Gandhi, Manu, 98, 100, 101, 103, 120, 138, 162 176
Gandhi Seva Sangh, 14
Ghosh, Prafulla Chandra, 81
Ghosh, Surendramohan, 67, 99

Hashem, Abul, 195

Jinnah, M. A. or Q.A., 28, 65, 180, 186
Kellas, Rev. John, 230
Khan, Abdul Ghaffar, 8, 9, 145
Kripalani, 15, 81, 89, 111, 211
Krishnadas, 80, 95

Mashruwala, Kishorlal, 15, 48, 116, 134, 136, 137, 138
Mitra, Sachin, 246
Mookerjee, Syamaprasad, 201, 232
Mountbatten, Lord, 3, 179, 188 ff
Mukherjee, Debendranath, 84, 205
Muslim League, 28, 29, 35, 60, 85, 103, 106, 122, 185

Naidu, Sarojini, 120, 121
Nayyar, Sushila, 32, 34, 39, 41, 55, 57, 66, 68, 94, 96, 99, 101, 103, 104, 118
Naoroji, Khurshed, 17 ff
Nathji, Kedar, 149, 150, 151
Navajivan Trust, 136
Nehru, Jawaharlal, 35, 37, 62, 86, 103, 105, 111, 179
Nelson, Prof. Stuart, 81, 223

Pakistan, 142, 145, 184 ff, Ch. XXII. See also Partition

Parasuram, 45, 55, 66, 99, 100, 103, 111, 114 ff
Parikh, Narahari, 48, 116, 136
Partition, 91, 186, 187, 197 ff. See also Pakistan
Patel, Vallabhbhai, 4, 35, 209

Rajagopalachari, C., 229, 236
Rajendra Prasad, 48
Ramakrishna, 2, 177
Rolland, Romain, 21

Ruskin, 86

*Selections from Gandhi*, 19, 20, 97
*Stern Reckoning*, 29
*Studies in Gandhism*, 11, 20
Suhrawardy, H. S., 31, 33, 81, 87, 130, 183, 188, 193, 198, 224, 240

Tolstoy, 86

Usman, Md., 221 ff